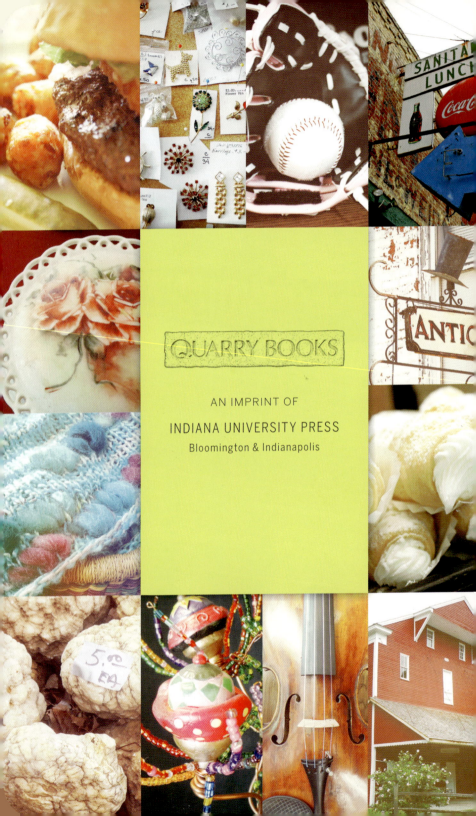

QUARRY BOOKS

AN IMPRINT OF

INDIANA UNIVERSITY PRESS

Bloomington & Indianapolis

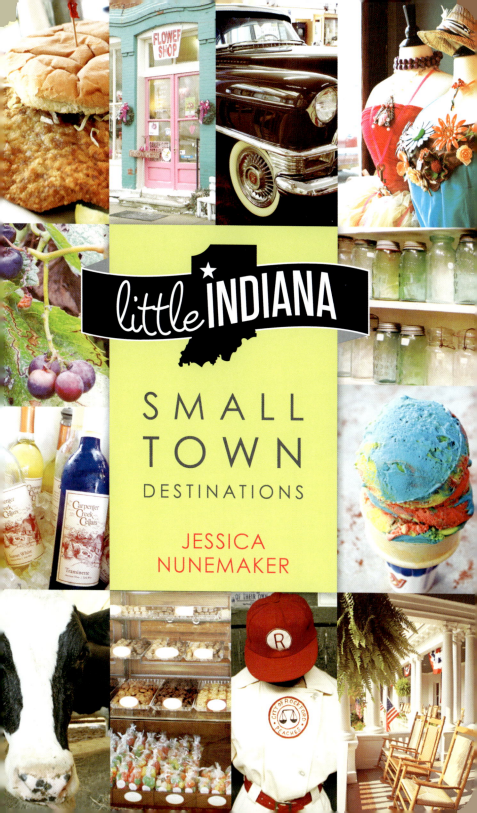

little INDIANA

SMALL TOWN DESTINATIONS

JESSICA NUNEMAKER

This book is a publication of

Quarry Books
an imprint of

INDIANA UNIVERSITY PRESS
Office of Scholarly Publishing
Herman B Wells Library 350
1320 East 10th Street
Bloomington, Indiana 47405 USA

iupress.indiana.edu

The paper used in this publication meets the minimum requirements of the American National Standard for Information Sciences—Permanence of Paper for Printed Library Materials, ANSI Z39.48–1992.

Manufactured in China

Library of Congress Cataloging-in-Publication Data

Nunemaker, Jessica.
Little Indiana : small town destinations / Jessica Nunemaker.
pages cm
Includes index.
ISBN 978-0-253-02061-1 (pbk. : alk. paper) — ISBN 978-0-253-02070-3 (ebook) 1. Indiana—Guidebooks. 2. Cities and towns—Indiana—Guidebooks. 3. Indiana—Description and travel. 4. Indiana—History, Local. I. Title.
F524.3.N86 2016
977.2—dc23
2015034021

1 2 3 4 5   21 20 19 18 17 16

For Jeremiah, Joey, and Jack.
Here's to hours more car time,
my awesome parking ability,
made up songs,
Baby's Butter,
and a whole lot of laughs!

For my Dad,
Richard Holobowski,
the original little Indiana.

Contents

CENTRAL INDIANA

SOUTHERN INDIANA

Preface

It began with sirens. Our first December in our small town had so far been a typical Indiana winter: bleak. We were just getting ready to sit down for dinner when sirens started wailing. They sounded so close. My husband decided that he would hurry out and see what he could do to help because they droned on and on. He rushed out the door and burst almost right back in, yelling, "Get your coats on! You aren't going to believe this, but there's a Christmas parade down the street!"

Christmas lights twinkled in storefronts. Color-guard flags rippled in time to the marching band music. Teens driving red or green tractors threw out candy, while bundled-up folks followed alongside floats passing out candy canes. Even Santa was there. All this holiday cheer was happening a mere block and a half from our home—and we had no idea. That got me thinking. If we didn't know about the parade, and we lived right in town, then how many other people didn't know?

After walking through a crumbling opera house where James Whitcomb Riley once took to the stage, somewhere I had never even heard about yet I lived less than an hour away from, I knew I had a good thing going. After a few trips, I began to see a recurring theme: every small town had something. Whether it was a winery, chocolate shop, pioneer cemetery, or other attraction, these little communities had all the appeal of the big-city stops but without the high prices, traffic, or anonymity. Customers weren't just people to hurry out the door but opportunities to socially connect and pass along the latest town news. It's the kind of places where one dollar can still (amazingly) buy a cup of coffee, kids ride their bikes down Main Street, and folks sit on their front-porch swing most evenings.

It took more than a year to fine-tune the idea. The website went live in 2009, eleven days before the birth of our second son. After visiting so many towns, after speaking with so many people, and reading e-mail after e-mail from online readers or television viewers asking for help planning trips, a book seemed the next natural step. The majority of travel guides focus on cities, or when they actually include small towns, it's the same small towns and same recognizable landmarks used in every other print publication. *Little Indiana* is different. I have traveled to each and every one of these destinations. Knowing, as I do, that some of you are trying to follow along in my travels, a handy checklist (with contact information) is included to make your travels that much easier. There is no scheduled itinerary. Part of the fun of small-town traveling is discovering the unexpected and incorporating it into your day. During our travels, some of our happiest memories were made because we ditched our schedule and embraced the accidental. Always remember to call ahead, carry some cash, and learn to go with the small-town flow.

Events, festivals, and the everyday: there are so many incredible things inside these towns. Please do not consider an omission a lack of interest. As a one-woman show (with family in tow), I have tried to seek out a healthy range of towns that are fifteen thousand people or fewer but have certainly not visited all three thousand of them . . . at least not yet. They are a reflection of what we have seen and done. Do not take it as a final answer but as the base of a small town, the starting point. My "must travel" list is brimming with plenty more I'd like to tackle.

Although I originally saw *Little Indiana* as a sort of small-town travel guide, I learned that it has an audience reaching far more than travelers. Hoosiers, displaced Hoosiers, and even soldiers serving overseas have turned to the website to connect with home, to remember childhoods, to savor a memory, and to make new ones.

Little Indiana captures these small towns for a moment in time. Everything that a town is—the restaurants, museums, and bridges—is captured, cherished, and preserved right here. I hope this book will inspire you to venture off the interstate, explore your own backyard, see what is out there, and fall in love with Indiana all over again.

Acknowledgments

Since 2009 Little Indiana has been exploring. That kind of travel is made so much easier with the help of folks who know their stuff. From reader e-mails to social media connections and random chats on the street, thank you for sharing your small-town story with me.

With years of traveling Indiana behind me, there are a multitude of people more than deserving of a little recognition, like all of the small business owners who opened their doors to me and my camera, especially in the early days before the site had any readers. Thank you to the crew, hosts, and fabulous producer, Sarah Curtiss, of *The Weekly Special* for providing Little Indiana with another outlet to spread the shop-small message. Thanks to Laura Baich, electronic marketing manager at Indiana University Press, for setting things in motion, and Sarah Jacobi, my sponsoring editor, and Michelle Sybert for taking on this project. I apologize now for the barrage of questions to come.

These pieces of Indiana history are common knowledge . . . in the towns where it happened. Years of visiting town museums have provided plenty of fodder (when I could read my handwriting), and the historians behind the museums in this book are so incredibly capable. I am especially grateful to Jayne Beers of the Clay Township Historical Society Museum, Jerry Cole of Historic Farmland, Susan Cottingham of the Osgood Museum, Brandi Hess at the Perry County Museum, Roselyn McKittrick at the Milan 1954 Hoosiers Museum, and Mark Allen Smith, the Delphi/Carroll County historian who wears many hats. You've instilled a love of history in our children in addition to showcasing your town's past so wonderfully.

Tourism is a tough job, particularly when there's a family of four involved. Special thanks are in order for the organized and informed tourism pros I have worked with over the years. Although this is an incomplete list, the following folks' travel assistance went a long way toward becoming the book in your hands: Kim Blumenstock of Harrison County Convention and Visitors Bureau, Melissa Brockman at Spencer County Visitors Bureau, Kate Burkhardt at Hamilton County Tourism, Josh Duke with Hendricks County, Christine Flohr at Visit Wabash, Scottie Harvey at Randolph County CVB, Jackie Hughes at Elkhart County CVB, Cori Humes of Marshall County Tourism, Ken Kosky of Indiana Dunes, Jenny Lear (unofficially) of Fortville, Melanie Maxwell of Visit Greensburg, Beverly Minto (now retired) from Perry County CVB, Ann Mulligan at Visit Madison, Emily Perkins (formerly) of the Wabash County Museum, Nancy Sartain of Visit Richmond, and Katherine Taul of Ripley County. They have been wonderful resources throughout the years of Little Indiana. Their patience, knowledge, and friendship are appreciated.

This is for the town of my childhood, DeMotte, and the town of my present, Rensselaer. If it weren't for the festive annual Rensselaer Christmas parade, I may never have come up with the idea.

Thanks to Cathy Hitchings for being there, always. Words can't express my gratitude for everything you have done for us. You are family. For the guy that inspired me to want to write: Uncle Grumpy, who understands.

Deepest love and heartfelt thanks for our children, Jack and Joey. I'm sorry your name isn't on every page like you wanted, Jack. Joey, I loved your endless stream of title suggestions and your idea for a family variety show. We'll work on that. There's nothing better than your invention of the mom mailbox and the frequent pictures or notes from you both cheering me on.

Last but not least, for my husband, Jeremiah, my favorite sounding board (usually when he's trying to sleep). To think it all stems from you being on board with this whole small-town travel thing all those years ago (I appreciate the steady supply of ice cream). You've been trained well, Patch. Little Indiana would be Little Canada without you (I've got to work on my map-reading skills).

Northern Indiana

HISTORIC BREMEN DEPOT

Bremen Train Depot, Bremen.

1

Bremen

Bremen, otherwise known as the Mint City, was once the leading international supplier of mint oil. Used in gum, toothpaste, and even perfume (among other products), Bremen mint traveled the world. Although mint producer Sprig 'O Mint is no longer, and the property is now the site of a golf course, one other mint manufacturer remains. Operating since 1908 under the name of M. Brown & Sons, it has since merged with Lebermuth, Inc. The family is still involved.

With such impressive historical credentials, and an 1882 water tower, it may be surprising to note that Bremen isn't exactly a huge town, holding just under five thousand residents now—but it sure is bustling. The downtown strip carries a variety of shops and a few restaurants. But to really see Bremen jumping, schedule a visit during the week of July 4 during the annual Firemen's Festival. Join twenty thousand others for festival fun like carnival rides, crafts, food, parade, and even fireworks. It's a huge deal in the area.

Remember that this is Amish country, so drive with care. Respect the Amish decision to abstain from photographs. Though the area is not as populated with Old Order Amish as other parts of the state, horse and buggy still make frequent appearances. It's always a bit jarring to hear the sound of a horse clip-clopping along as an Amish buggy rolls right through the town.

☼ play

Bremen Historical Museum is loving its decked-out space with room to expand—and visitors do too. Vintage images from its mint farming days, the old recognizable landmarks, and town heroes are remembered here.

The Loft Art Studio, Bremen.

Relive the glory days of the railroad at the Bremen Train Depot. Set to mimic the old-fashioned depot, there's all manner of railroading items collected together, including tickets, forwarding cars, and a train-order hoop. The symbols used by hobos are an interesting exhibit.

Anyone with kids will want to look for the castles. Jane's Park, named for a mother who died of cancer shortly after childbirth, is a fantastic park. Multiple levels provide loads of places to play for kids of all ages. Surrounded by flowers, grilling areas, and even picnic seating, it's a popular family destination.

eat

Netter's Restaurant, named in honor of a daughter who passed away, serves fantastic homemade food. Pick the fried mushrooms appetizer. If they aren't famous yet, they soon will be. The handmade pork tenderloin is always a great dinner choice. Everything is freshly made to order. The oldest of the six kids may be out and about helping out, too, as it's a true family business.

shop

No hobby is too big or too small to be found at Bremen Hobbies and Art. From RC cars and planes to kites of all kinds, rockets, trains, cake-decorating supplies, and even puzzles, there's absolutely something for any hobbyist. If they don't have it, it doesn't exist.

It's not every day that a loft over a garage could be considered inspiring, but the Loft Art Studio certainly is. This knitter's destination is absolutely charming. Huge windows let the light shine, so knitters can easily find what they need. Such beautifully arranged yarns and textiles are a pleasure to browse. Workshops and meet-ups are frequent, making it not only a retail establishment but a community gathering place.

2

Brookston

Named for James Brooks, the president of the Monon Railroad, it is only fitting that Brookston was also located on the line of the old Monon rail, originally known as the New Albany and Salem Railroad. With a small downtown and a handful of shops, there's enough here for a little detour, especially when September rolls around. That's when this town of fewer than two thousand people swells to more than twenty thousand.

Mark the calendar for the third Saturday in September, when the Brookston Apple Popcorn Festival begins. Four local business women brainstormed this unique way to celebrate Brookston's agricultural heritage back in 1978. Kicking off with a town-wide yard sale and firehouse pancake breakfast, the lively downtown festival blocks off streets for the more than two hundred craft booths, an art exhibit, a cake walk, live music, and unique contests like the Men's Leg Contest. This older event is also one of the funniest. Contenders for best legs cover their faces and most of their bodies with a blanket, the same one used almost every year, to hide their identity. Then they lift up their pant legs to show off their gams for prizes and the coveted Dottie Smith Memorial Golden Leg trophy. There's also a bubble gum–blowing contest, a Big Wheel race, a hula-hoop contest, a pizza-eating contest, nail driving, and Frisbee dogs. That's just the short list.

🍴 eat

Klein Brot Haus or Klein Brothers Bakery is the local gathering place. With cases and shelves of homemade products, it's an obvious choice. The not-so-obvious choice is what to order. At this café and bakery, the options seem almost endless. On the sweeter side, the chocolate croissant, iced sugar cookie, pineapple bar,

Two Cookin' Sisters, Brookston.

Chocolate croissant from Klein Brot Haus in Brookston.

and turnovers are good picks. Locals dig the savory soups and sandwiches, especially when they are prepared with the home-made challah or rye breads.

🛍 shop

Since 1972 Twinrocker Handmade Paper has supplied innovative handmade paper to fine-book printers and binders. Differing shapes and sizes offer a unique paper for any need. A remarkable shop, it carries items from invitations and stationery to decorative and watercolor papers.

Big Sister Salsa was unveiled at the Brookston Apple Popcorn Festival back in 2001. After such high praise, Two Cookin' Sisters opened up shop. Combining their skills, these two sisters were able to cover most of the bases. Even Mom helps out with the canning of jellies, jams, relishes, pickles, mustard, chutney, and fruit butters that's done on site. Carrying an unbeatable selection of Indiana-made food items and even products like glassware, toss pillows, and linens, this is one fun shopping trip.

3

Chesterton

Beautiful baked goods from Tonya's Patisserie in Chesterton.

Situated between lake and wood, with a bustling downtown to keep things interesting, Chesterton is a popular place for city dwellers' summer homes and a convenient weekend getaway for everyone else.

The area was first settled in 1822 by French Canadian fur trader Joseph Bailey and his family, who quickly set up shop with a trading post. A decade later one family began farming, followed by the Thomas family, the founders of Chesterton, and other pioneers trundled in. Originally called Coffee Creek, named for the flowing stream nearby, it was settled in 1834 by the Thomas family. It's said that the creek got its name due to a man losing a bag of coffee in the high waters. The nickname stuck.

Back when the town was young, when the population numbered in the three hundreds, there were nineteen saloons. Locals were ready for a change of identity. After the Civil War it was renamed Calumet. The years passed and the railroad rolled through, successfully evolving Calumet from an agricultural community to a bustling rail center. Unfortunately, the name Calumet was discovered to be an exact match for another town on the railroad line, so the name was swapped yet again, this time for the last time.

European Market, Chesterton.

Riley's Railhouse Bed and Breakfast in Chesterton is set inside an old train depot.

The town grew, and word spread of the splendid new community. The annual Wizard of Oz Fest helped make Chesterton known throughout the region. Though the festival only recently ended after a thirty-five-year run, there are plenty of other reasons to make the trip to Chesterton. Downtown roads are closed off for European Market, an enormous farmers market that is like no other. It's open Saturdays from the beginning of May to the end of October. Browse booth after booth of artisan-quality foods, handcrafted items, woodworking, and so much more. Combine that with the ongoing Bandstand Concert and Family Film summer series at Thomas Centennial Park, the fire department's annual street dance each August, and the Hooked on Art Festival in September, and see why the family fun never ends. Of course, that's not including the vast Indiana Dunes ecosystem of which Chesterton happens to be a part. Beach access, festivals, events, shopping, and dining—this small town certainly has it all.

🛏 stay

Riley's Railhouse Bed and Breakfast was made for the train enthusiast. After years of collecting antique train–related items, the Riley family threw themselves into the large-scale renovations required after their purchase of the 1914 New York Central Freight Station—and finally had a place to highlight their collection. From replacing the slate roof to cleaning the brick, it was all restored. In fact, the seventy-five slate tiles in salvageable condition were used to create the fantastic counter downstairs. Trains do go chug, chug, chugging past the bed-and-breakfast fifty times a day, so choose the interior room for a quieter experience. Light sleepers should take note of the jar of earplugs conveniently situated by the bedside. The room upstairs contains a sweet little balcony and neat interior view of the elegant main living area below where the two contented resident dogs are most likely sleeping.

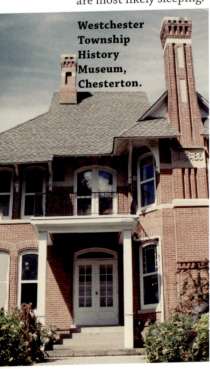

Westchester Township History Museum, Chesterton.

☀ play

First a family home, then a vacation home, then the office for the local school, the Brown Mansion is now the Westchester Township History Museum. It holds the history of Chesterton, Porter, Burns Harbor, and Dune Acres. Beginning with glacial times, it covers the range of area history through photos, artifacts, and interesting exhibits. Wander the rooms of the spacious 1885 Victorian home before heading to the lower-level museum. Genealogy researchers will appreciate the Leslie and Mary Pratt Local History Research Center also located inside.

Cool off with a visit to Dog Days Ice Cream Parlor. Made locally from fresh ingredients, this isn't a typical ice cream parlor. In fact, traditional ice cream isn't even on the menu. Here at Dog Days, find Italian favorites such as homemade gelato and sorbet. The flavors change weekly to keep things interesting, but some previous offerings include campfire combo, chocolate razzmatazz, and caramel pistachio gelato. It's all good. Pop by on a chilly day and warm up with homemade hot chocolate or apple cider made from Northwest Indiana apples.

Lucrezia Café, Chesterton.

Enjoy the seasonal shady patio at Lucrezia Café or dine indoors. Share the fresh and nontraditional ingredients on the antipasto platter. Personal picks include the mouthwatering chicken vesuvio, a disjointed chicken panfried with garlic, rosemary, and roasted potatoes, or the lamb shank paired with roasted potatoes, onions, and lovely braised red cabbage.

Expect unique sides, imaginative burgers, as well as changing specials at Octave Grill, in business since 2010. Six ounces of Tallgrass beef are worked into cleverly crafted hamburgers. Browse the tall chalkboard wall menu for memorable options like Chanute (grilled cremini mushrooms and bacon topped with habanero havarti and blue cheese) or Hot Pants (habanero havarti, homemade giardiniera, bacon, beer-battered onion rings, tabasco aioli, greens, and a tomato). There aren't typical appetizers, either. Fries get an update with a generous coating of buffalo sauce and blue cheese. Tater tots become adult friendly when made with sweet potatoes and paired with whole-grain honey mustard. Microbrews and cocktails are available.

Peggy Sue's Diner is a family-friendly, bustling breakfast option. Grab a seat at the counter and step back in time to the 1950s. Regulars lean toward the chicken-fried steak or the biscuits and gravy. Sneak in before prime breakfast hours to avoid the rush.

Can the exterior of Popolano's Italian Restaurant be any more inviting? Dine al fresco and gaze at the loveliness of this home turned restaurant. Some evenings boast live music. Known for a refreshing sangria, fresh bread, and scratch-made soups, it's a neighborhood gathering place inside and out. A signature dish, the tequila lime pizza gets rave reviews. The pizza's homemade garlic ranch sauce boasts a hint of jalapeño and lime. Topped with avocados, cilantro, mozzarella, shrimp, and tomatoes, it's definitely different.

Octave Grill, Chesterton.

Local foods, farm-fresh eggs, and gluten-free sandwich offerings make Red Cup Café a community-conscious sandwich shop. Add in the hip decor, vinyl music, and the variety of coffees, and the cool factor just bumped up another notch. Hint: go for one of the grilled sandwiches. Check the big board before leaving for local events.

With several big-city executive chef positions behind her, soft-spoken owner Tonya Deiotte returned to small-town life to open Tonya's Patisserie, a breakfast and lunch hot spot. People rave about the fresh menu with gluten-free and vegetarian alternatives, but desserts are the real star to snack lovers. Pastries, cakes, cupcakes, cheesecake—there's so much here. Look for the lemon curd and blueberry pastry or the hazelnut-filled pastries for a place to begin.

 shop

Take the scenic route. Buy or rent a bicycle at Chesterton Bicycle Station. It's come a long way since its start out of a garage in 1983. Expanding to a physical location in 1991, the shop was built by the owner's own two hands with a slew of help. Now this local bike shop is packed with bikes and other wheeled items like skateboards and even unicycles.

Stylish clothing, sharp accessories, and shoes? That's all in a day's shopping at Ella's Bella, a sweet downtown boutique. Specializing in women's clothing (and everything that goes with it), there's even a smidgen of home decor tucked in. It's classy yet comfortable.

Holly Jackson Art Studio and Gallery will revive any ho-hum wall. Taking inspiration from the everyday, and the nearby Indiana Dunes, her contemporary work is vivid. Paintings of landscapes as well as abstracts, still life, florals, and message art cover the walls or rest on surfaces in this funky gallery. Check out the studio and view this artist at work.

Flowing lovely blouses and stylish jewelry are just a small part of Indian Summer Boutique. Specializing in women's clothing, they don't carry just any brand. Picking and choosing the best of the best characterizes the quality found inside this attractive shop. Clothes shopping just became fun again.

The lovely green Victorian home has been the site of Katie's Antiques for what must be decades, considering the amount of antiques that are crammed into the first floor. It's a tight squeeze to get into sections of this shop, so for those shoppers who really love the thrill of the hunt, Katie's is an excellent fit. An appraiser is on site. Don't forget to browse the two outbuildings for more finds and possibly even sale items.

New books and even rare books have a place at O'Gara and Wilson Antiquarian Booksellers. Originally located in Hyde Park in 1882, the first shop exchanged hands before the purchase by Joseph O'Gara. Current owner Doug Wilson began as a scout and

O'Gara and Wilson Antiquarian Booksellers, Chesterton.

NORTHERN INDIANA

became a key part of the shop. Relocating the Chicago bookshop back to where a branch once thrived in the 1990s, he and his wife have created a clearly labeled, well-organized, and inviting space. Don't miss the super section of Indiana books.

Close to downtown, Russ and Barb's Antiques takes up a decent portion of their house. Dishware seekers, vintage brooch lovers, and art collectors will want to tour this one. Every surface is so full of items that it doesn't seem as though any more can fit—which is partly why the shop expanded to include the basement. With beaucoup boxes more in storage, be sure to ask for help when hunting for specific items.

Who wouldn't love a wall of records? That's just part of the hunting fun at Yesterday's Treasures Antique Mall. With more than twenty thousand square feet of booth space and more than seventy-five vendors, there's so much here. Upcycled pieces, vintage toys and games, books, loads of furniture, and even 1940s diner-style seating from Johnson's Drug Store in Nappanee are just a fraction of the oh-so-unique selection.

NOTABLES

Bill Collins (1882–1961) was a Major League Baseball outfielder. Chesterton born, he played for teams such as the Boston Doves/Rustlers (1910–1911), Chicago Cubs (1911), Brooklyn Dodgers (1913), and Buffalo Buffeds (1914). He was the first to hit for the natural cycle, a baseball term for collecting hits in order.

But it's not all about sports. Well-known Civil War and nineteenth-century historian Avery Craven made his home here, too. Though Craven passed away in 1980, the Organization of American Historians still yearly bestows the author of an exceptional Civil War–related book with an award in his name.

Pro basketball has a place here, too. Bob Dille (1917–1998) graduated from Chesterton's high school and was a professional basketball player and later a coach.

Currently living in New York with his wife and five children, stand-up comedian Jim Gaffigan (b. 1966) is originally from Chesterton.

Chesterton resident, former steelworker, and Major League Baseball left fielder and hitter Ron Kittle (b. 1958) was named the 1983 American League rookie of the year. His career began and ended with the Chicago White Sox.

Oklahoma City Thunder basketball player Mitch McGary (b. 1992) hailed from the town.

Mickey Morandini (b. 1966) played on the 1988 U.S. Summer Olympics baseball crew before playing for a range of Major League Baseball teams. After retiring from baseball, he and his family moved to Chesterton, and he began coaching at an area high school. He has since become a manager of a Philadelphia team.

Eddie Wineland may be an Ultimate Fighting Championship fighter, and in the top-ten official UFC Bantamweight rankings, but he still lives in Chesterton—and is a full-time firefighter to boot.

4

Converse

What small town was home to L. G. Murphy, business owner and manufacturer of world-class fishing rods including one used by Zane Grey, Denver Nuggets basketball player Monte Towe, and Ray Creviston, 1914 one-mile motorcycle-speed record holder? Tiny, quiet Converse, Indiana.

Two blocks make up the downtown, yet Converse somehow manages to have one atypical range of shops. Once known as Xenia, Converse was also the site of a twenty-year natural gas boom that began in the late 1800s. At that long-ago point, it had more than twenty passenger trains pass through each day. It has had its share of hardships, but its strength lies in its sense of community, such as can be witnessed at the annual holiday kickoff.

Residents turned out in droves to attend the Christmas event. Singing carols down the main street, they gathered for the tree lighting. Local businesses held open houses with later hours, special treats, and holiday cheer. It was good, clean family fun.

☀ play

If the Eastern Woodcarvers Association has a sign out front advertising an event that's open to the community, be sure to attend.

Eastern Woodcarvers Association, Converse.

From beginners to pros, this is where wood-carving enthusiasts gather. There's woodworking machinery on the inside and even a library of related books. These men, women, and even teens bring out amazing pieces for the contests.

There's a strong chance that anyone searching for Oak Hill Winery will drive right by. No one expects it to be downtown. Know what to look for, such as the 1894 carriage house converted into a winery at the west end of town. Making its wines naturally using old-fashioned methods, Oak Hill Winery prides itself on its unique offerings. Bottles are labeled with images from Charles Dickens novels, sporting clever names that highlight area landmarks and towns. Try before buying in the warm and cozy room.

Supremely clean, Big Dipper is 1950s fun but with a twist: there are ice cream and food inside. Walk the red and white tile floor to the front diner-style counter. There are a full menu and daily specials, including a pork tenderloin sandwich that's rumored to be wonderful. Classic treats use hard-packed ice cream and include favorites like old-fashioned sodas, malts, and thick shakes.

Galvanized metal and exposed brick walls, shiny buckets as light fixtures, and a chalkboard wall all add up to make Jefferson Street Barbecue one hip and happening barbecue joint. Wines, beers, and mixed drinks are available. The pulled pork is excellent. Pair it with a cup of award-winning white chicken chili for a memorable meal. The meats are smoked daily. Quantities are limited, so arrive early for the best selection.

shop

In a home that's fairly oozing with history, it's only fitting that Antiques, Collectibles, and Gifts set up shop. When the building was a boardinghouse back in the day, one young man and his pal would occasionally visit and take the lady of the house out shopping in the town. After one such afternoon trip, the man apologized for cutting his visit short. He shared that he

Jefferson Street
Barbecue, Converse.

had business to settle and took off. Imagine her surprise when she saw a picture in the newspaper of her guest soon after and discovered that he was none other than John Dillinger. The business that had called him away was robbing banks. Lovers of crystal, vintage jewelry, and primitive items will be pleased as punch with the eighteenth- and nineteenth-century selection. More modern-leaning antique shoppers will find a host of recognizable twentieth-century brands arranged among the rooms.

This small business began in a kitchen, rapidly expanding to become Cahoots Soap Company. With its offerings all natural, vegan friendly, and in biodegradable, recyclable packaging, this soap shop is environmentally conscious and whimsical. The shop is so strikingly decorated that it seems more fitting to a city boutique than a small town of barely twelve hundred people. Stripes of color or patterns run through these appealing bars of soap. It is not, however, all soap. Bath bombs, body scrubs, and other good-for-you products are available as well.

Home decor abounds in Itty Bitty Acres, a cute and well-arranged family business. Plaques, candles, lighting, bags, wallpaper borders, curtains, and bedding are just a few items to sift through. It is the go- to place for fairy garden or mini garden supplies. Enjoy the new children's boutique addition.

NOTABLES

The 1914 one-mile speed record holder for motorcycle racing was Converse resident Ray Creviston. In fact, his motorcycle racing career began in 1912 at the Converse Fairgrounds' half-mile track. After traveling the world racing on his Indian motorcycle, Creviston eventually returned to Converse, purchased a farm, and, as local legend tells it, never drove above thirty miles per hour.

Combining his love of woodworking with his lumber and building-supply shop, devoted angler L. G. Murphy set out to create a hickory fishing rod capable of snagging blue-fin tuna. Prolific author and avid fisher Zane Grey used a fishing rod crafted by the Converse resident to catch a record-setting tuna.

Cocreator of the "alley-oop," a basketball move created in a time when dunking was prohibited, National Basketball Association pro Monte Towe (b. 1953) grew up in Converse. He led the Oak Hill High School team, which defeated big rival the Marion Giants, sparking Towe's pro career. He played for the Denver Nuggets (1977–1979) and served as coach for a variety of teams over the years.

5

DeMotte

New, mostly Dutch, arrivals to the swampy, marshy land quickly set to draining the area for farmland. First called Little Village, the foundling settlement decided to come up with an official name. With so many members of the town having served in the Civil War, they decided to pay tribute to Valparaiso resident Colonel Mark L. DeMotte, an attorney who had served under Major General Robert H. Milroy from nearby Rensselaer during the Civil War. The post office originally labeled DeMotte as De Motte in 1882, although early documents show use of the name as early as 1868. The post office ditched the space in 1893, and DeMotte has retained its spelling ever since.

DeMotte Depot History Museum, DeMotte.

Tragedy struck in 1936. With a volunteer fire department only recently formed and a new fire truck not yet delivered, the bucket brigade couldn't control the flames that quickly consumed the lumberyard. One trash fire, an unexpected strong wind, and the business section of DeMotte was left a smoldering pile of ash, leaving $150,000 worth of damage in its wake, only half of which was covered by insurance. But in true small business fashion, life went on. The owners found places to set up shop, and life continued. Visitors to DeMotte today will find mom-and-pop shops along the main drag, Halleck Street.

To really get a good look at DeMotte, aim for an August visit. Back in 1975, a group of librarians wanted a way to raise money and to get local artists and crafting folks involved. The first Touch of Dutch Festival began, an event meant to embrace the strong Dutch heritage while showcasing local craftspersons. Over the years, it has expanded and increased in size until it took over space behind the DeMotte Elementary School and overflowed into Freedom Park, across the street. Moved to a larger area, this centrally located festival is now held at Spencer Park. There's a parade (with candy), loads of booth space for vendors of all kinds, and food. Stop by the DeMotte Depot History Museum for a look at its past.

Bub's BBQ, owned by 2015 pork spokesman R. J. Howard, is smoked-meat heaven. Beginning at four in the morning, meat is slowly smoked all day long to make it unbelievably tender. All the sides are homemade. Bub's personal favorite is the barbecue brisket—and it's excellent. Pair it with bourbon fried apples, dill potato salad, or homemade potato chips. Get in early. When it's gone, it's gone.

Craving a cup of coffee or a cup of tea? There's a lot to choose from at Jim's Café. Dishing up breakfast, lunch, and dinner, it's a busy place. For lunchtime visits, get the reuben sandwich with onion rings. The velvet coffee (in any flavor, though raspberry is extra special) is one excellent drink.

A golf course restaurant may not be a typical small-town find, but the excellent atmosphere, gorgeous outdoor seating, and well-placed big-screen televisions of Sandy Pines Sports Grill make it the perfect place to relax after a game of golf or a day spent exploring. Kids (and adults) enjoy snacking on the popcorn brought out before meals. Said to be the best burger in Jasper County, it is excellent, though the restaurant's own recipe Italian beef sandwich is equally fantastic.

shop

It might sound like a flower shop, and it is, but far more than fresh flowers graces Another Season Floral. Handpicked gift items and home decor combine in a shop that's pure beauty from head to toe. The shop also creates gift baskets with themes of fruit or chocolate.

Movie Madness has been in business for more than fifteen years. The store offers the largest selection of movie and video game rentals of a locally owned video store in the state, but the sale items put it way over

Fairchild House, DeMotte.

the top. Excellent deals are to be had on brand-new movies and used games.

Want a real bargain? For more than a hundred years, the Sell-It-Again Shop and DeMotte Mercantile has been there. Now offering new items in addition to its massive consignment collection (featuring more than four thousand consignors), this enormous building and basement is so much fun. Owner Nathan is supremely helpful.

NOTABLES

Fairchild House, built in 1922 by Charity May Fairchild, is one of the only architectural residential wonders in the town. Find it across the street from the DeMotte Public Library.

Born in DeMotte, Charles A. Halleck (1900–1986) was a Republican leader of the U.S. House of Representatives. He was portrayed in the 1974 made-for-TV movie *The Missiles of October* by Arthur Franz, winning its technical director an Emmy.

6

Denver

There's no better time to begin a town than when a railroad is going to pass right through it. That's how Denver got its start in the late 1800s. With no real downtown area but plenty of fields and woods, it's hard to believe that Denver was once a bustling small town—and even a college town at that.

Denver College was formed in 1876. But after changing hands a few times to different professors, no one was able to make a real go of it. The college was abandoned, and the property was then used for the public school. It has been a quiet town ever since.

☀ play

One of the oldest family-owned orchards in Indiana, Doud Orchards is worth a visit for many reasons. Five generations once worked at this family farm. Boasting more than nine thousand apple trees and over 150 varieties, this orchard even possesses experimental apple trees from Purdue University and the Midwest Apple Improvement team. Inside the barn lie fresh honey, fruit preserves, and a slew of other items—including a one-room schoolhouse. Back in the 1980s, the previous owner built the barn around the old Port Royal School. Neat bits of history, the live-bee exhibit, and the antique apple varieties put Doud Orchards in a class all its own.

Doud Orchards, Denver.

7

Francesville

Platted by New Albany and Salem Railroad president James Brooks in 1853, Francesville had humble beginnings. In a sweet display of fatherly love, Francesville was named for Brooks's beloved daughter, Frances. Fewer than one thousand people call this small town home. As they like to say, it's "the small town with a big heart." Nowhere can its heart be displayed more clearly than at the Francesville Fall Festival.

Not a product of residents looking to liven things up a bit, the Francesville Fall Festival began to solve a problem: the town was in need of a new fire station. The estimates showed it wasn't going to be cheap, so residents came up with a plan. Forming a nonprofit in 1961, they started receiving donations and pledges to pay for the firehouse. By the autumn of 1963, work could begin—without using a dime of taxpayer money.

Folks showed up with shovels and tractors. Farm trucks picked up load after load of Indiana limestone from southern Indiana. It

Banana split at the Patio Drive-In, Francesville.

took three years, but after the station's completion, everyone decided it needed a special commemorative event. Well, the Francesville Fall Festival just kind of stuck around after that. Look for it in September.

Gene Speicher Pottery, Francesville.

¶¶ eat

Five Loaves Bakery and Café focuses on fresh food. But the gorgeous wood display case is where the real magic happens. Mouthwatering baked goods are on display. This small-town bakery even prepares its own chocolates. Find (and enjoy) the typical varieties of chocolates such as creams and truffles. Frosted sugar cookies, sugar cream pie, cinnamon rolls, and strawberry smoothies are favorite picks.

"Ice cream makes you smile," as they say at the Patio Drive-In, although quick burgers, hot dogs, and other kid-friendly food items are also on the menu. At this seasonal ice cream shop, choose from hard-pack, soft-serve, and frozen yogurt treats, as locals have done since 1954. Try the peanut butter sundae and see the vintage school memorabilia (and photo of the original Patio) before having a seat—inside or out.

🛍 shop

Gene Speicher Pottery is a studio of lovely things, yes, but they are all useful, lovely things. He encourages his clients to think outside the box and to use his hand-thrown pottery in imaginative ways. Mugs, vases, plates, and bowls are a sampling of the different functional wares set up inside.

8

Furnessville

Furnessville was never officially platted. In fact, it was originally known as Murray's Side Track, then Morgan's Side Track, until the appointed postmaster, Edwin L. Furness, arrived in 1861. The name was then changed to Furnessville in his honor.

Although it has never had more than a smattering of homes, with the occasional business, its close proximity to the Indiana Dunes makes it an easy detour.

☀ play

Across the street from Schoolhouse Shops and Antiques lies the Furnessville Cemetery. Sources reveal that the cemetery does not appear on Westchester Township plat maps until 1921, although many headstones are far older than that. Several notables are here, including William Brincka and Basil Cross, who now have both a park and an art gallery in Michigan City named in their memory in honor of their long-term community arts involvement.

🛍 shop

It's hard to believe that the charming schoolhouse turned plethora of shops was once in danger of having its bell tower torn down and used as a chicken coop. Fortunately, it was saved from that sad fate to become Schoolhouse Shops and Antiques. Built in 1886, the two-roomed Porter County Schoolhouse, made of local bricks, educated area children up until the 1920s. Since the 1940s (and a few renovations), the once simple building boasts about a dozen rooms of antiques, gifts, apparel, toys, and items for the home. With the building broken up into separate shops, a florist (Lake Effect Florals), a kitchen store and café with outdoor patio seating (the Magic Pantry), Tree House Toy Room, and classy Dunes Clothiers make this a one-stop shop for so many reasons.

Schoolhouse Shops and Antiques, Furnessville.

9

Kniman

If there was ever a tiny town, it would be Kniman. Little more than a couple of buildings clustered together in a quiet downtown, with country homes farther out, there is still a reason to add it into the itinerary—particularly during the holiday season.

Tune in to the radio station suggested on the sign outside the Armstrong home for a big heaping helping of Christmas cheer. At this home, the twinkling lights are coordinated to keep the beat of the song. Just down the road lies another home all decked out in its merry best—and with loads of animated items, ranging from dancing poinsettias to carousels to Santa in a loader. Santa is even available at select times, passing out free candy canes to visiting children.

Kniman Tap, Kniman.

🍴 eat

Bars aren't typically a destination . . . unless they possess what many folks consider *the* best pizza in all of Jasper County. Kniman Tap doesn't offer up a menu with specialty toppings. But what they do, they do so well. Get it cheese, sausage, or supreme. The crust is excellent, the cheese is bubbly, and the taste is certainly memorable. Carry it out for parties that include those not yet aged twenty-one.

10

Kouts

A nother name changer. First deemed "Kouts Station" by the combination of its junction between two railroad lines in 1867 and the name of its founder, Barnhardt Kouts, sometimes referred to as Bernhardt Kautz, it was shortened to "Kout" in 1882 and then Kouts in 1890. Perhaps the most interesting piece of Kouts history lies along the Kankakee River. Fantastic hunting outside of town lured in big hunters. Hunting lodges, like Collier Lodge, sprang up to provide service to avid (and often wealthy) hunters in the 1800s. Collier Lodge sits on what was once the bank for the "old channel" of the Kankakee River before its straightening. A source of archaeological excavation and history, it has long been in need of terrific repair. Thus, the Aukiki River Festival was born.

Aukiki River Festival, Kouts.

Celebrated the same weekend as the long-running, ever-popular Porkfest, the Aukiki River Festival, named for the Native American pronunciation of the river, is fund-raiser and history reenactment all rolled into one. Its purpose is to raise the needed funding to save the Collier Lodge and to reinstall the one-lane steel-truss bridge that spanned a section of river southeast of town starting in the 1920s. The unique twist of this festival is that it doesn't focus on one specific time frame but is instead a showcase of life along the river through the years with encampments pertaining to the French and Indian War, Native Americans, fur trappers and traders, French voyageurs, and the Civil War. Representing 350 years of history, there's period food, music, and booths with neat themes. Tinsmiths and dyers, black-smiths and toy makers, all are busy at their craft. Admire the camps, the clothing, and the artifacts with a few kid-friendly elements thrown in.

☼ play

Farmer Isaac Dunn knew a deal when he saw one. Leftover met-al from the gigantic (and first) Ferris wheel was up for grabs. Thirty-three-year-old George W. G. Ferris was tasked with creating something for the Chicago's 1893 World's Colombian Exposition, something that would rival the Eiffel Tower, a big draw for the Paris exhibition of 1889. He planned the first Ferris wheel, a massive structure that lifted thirty-six wood-paneled gondola cars 250 feet into the air, with sixty seats in each gon-dola. At fifty cents a ticket, it was almost affordable. But after interest waned in the fair, Isaac Dunn purchased the scrap steel for his bridge that some believe was part of the original Ferris wheel. Others maintain that it wasn't a Ferris wheel but salvaged roof trusses from the Indiana House. Dunn's Bridge's 2003 resto-ration garnered a state award for engineering excellence, though the mystery remains.

🍴 eat

"Have you had a hot piece lately?" The Country Folks Pizza motto may generate a snicker or two, and while it doesn't look like it holds some of the world's best pizza, it is sure to surprise. For more than twenty years, this family pizza joint has kept folks coming back for more. Try the twenty-inch pepper-jack and swiss beef pizza. Based on their signature sandwich creation that received rave reviews from anyone who tried it, they decid-ed to capture those flavors in a pizza. What a pizza it is! Loaded with two pounds of roast beef, the equivalent of four foot-long roast beef sandwiches' worth, it is a monster. Pass the time by

Dunn's Bridge, Kouts.

admiring the walls full of colorful drawings and thank-you notes from area children and residents.

Overall-clad farmers amble over to George's Koffee Kup and heartily recommend the potato soup. Fancy tin ceilings and a chatty wait staff make visits fun. Sit at the counter for the real local experience. Try the reuben sandwich, a cup of homemade soup (or chili), or the gyro melt.

Piggies 'n Cream now occupies the old Kouts train depot. Almost everything served is local, farm raised, and homemade. There is a full menu that includes homemade pizza, sandwiches, and wraps. But dessert, oh the dessert! Even the ice cream is homemade. Be daring—try the gigantic chocolate chip cookie ice cream sandwich.

11

La Fontaine

Metocinyah's Village was once an influential one. Chief Metocinyah (which means "the Living") was the son of Ozandia and the father of Meshingomesia (born here in 1782, ending up the last Miami tribal chief in Indiana). In 1747 the British convinced Chief Metocinyah to join their side and be under their protection. In reality, it was probably the offer of cheaper trade that sealed that deal. Destroyed by John Campbell's troops (against orders) in 1812, the peaceful tribe never recovered. The area became dotted with the log cabins of settlers. Many Miami were later removed to a reservation around the mid-1840s. By 1845 the town was platted and called Ashland, for politician Henry Clay's Kentucky home, where ash trees thickly grew. The 1848 post office switched the name to La Fontaine to avoid a duplicate of the name found in Henry County. La Fontaine honored Chief François La Fontaine, the elected leader of the Miami Native Americans in 1841.

☀ play

Indiana's largest Native American cemetery, the Miami Indian Cemetery, and a chunk of the last reservation in Indiana lie way out in the country. Wander to the middle of the cemetery to see the old Miami Indian Village School, in use from 1860 to 1898. Locked and shuttered, it is hard to say what, if anything, lies inside. Though there are many unmarked graves at the cemetery (it's impossible to know exactly where they lie), there are also a few dozen marked with tombstones just beyond the school. These bear the names of Native Americans, including the family of Chief Metocinyah and Meshingomesia, the peaceful Native American chiefs who led two of the destroyed villages. Unless

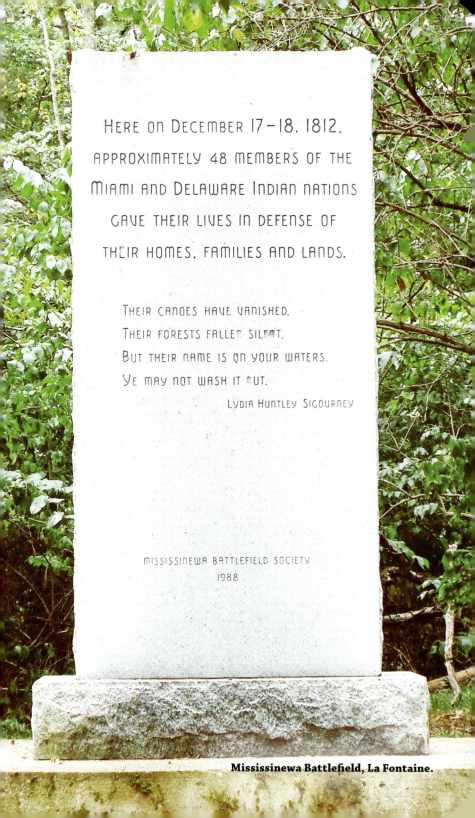

HERE ON DECEMBER 17–18, 1812,
APPROXIMATELY 48 MEMBERS OF THE
MIAMI AND DELAWARE INDIAN NATIONS
GAVE THEIR LIVES IN DEFENSE OF
THEIR HOMES, FAMILIES AND LANDS.

THEIR CANOES HAVE VANISHED.
THEIR FORESTS FALLEN SILENT.
BUT THEIR NAME IS ON YOUR WATERS.
YE MAY NOT WASH IT OUT.
LYDIA HUNTLEY SIGOURNEY

MISSISSINEWA BATTLEFIELD SOCIETY
1988

Mississinewa Battlefield, La Fontaine.

a Native American converted to Christianity, he or she used an unmarked grave. Whether the gravestones are due to Christian conversions or forced upon uncomplaining corpses too remains a mystery. A gently sloping hill and a strand of trees make it a lovely final resting place.

Follow the signs to the Mississinewa Battlefield. Hostile actions between Native Americans and the settlers were increasing. Joining forces with the British, the Native Americans' new alliance put the United States' hold on the Northwest Territory in jeopardy. The Forts of Mackinac, Dearborn, and Detroit were already lost, and quickly. In September 1812, William Henry Harrison believed that the Native American villages along the Mississinewa River (the Native American word for "falling waters") were strategic locales for further settler attacks. Lieutenant Colonel John B. Campbell and his six hundred troops on horseback left central Ohio to begin their eighty-mile trek with one mission: destroy the villages. Almost a month later, on December 17, 1812, they reached their destination and, in a sneak attack, killed eight Miami, took forty-two members of the Delaware tribe as prisoners (a tribe Campbell was actually ordered to avoid, as they were friendly), and then smashed three more vacated villages before setting up camp back at the remnants of the first village. Prior to sunrise the next morning, three hundred Miami and Delaware besieged the sleeping soldiers. With the attack lasting only one hour, twelve soldiers and perhaps forty-five Indians were dead, leaving forty-eight wounded. One of the captives revealed that a large group of men, led by Tecumseh, was on the way. Campbell decided to take the prisoners, mostly women and children, back to Fort Greene Ville. The return trip to Ohio was harsh, resulting in severe frostbite and an unexpected act of mercy: soldiers dismounted so the women and children could ride through the foot-tall snow drifts. The graves of the soldiers are located here, just off the road.

12

Lowell

Though no longer boasting more than fifty antique shops as it did back in the 1970s, there's still a healthy, thriving collection of vintage retailers along the main drag—and beyond. The entire downtown is on the National Historic Register. Long a hub of industry, it was even the site of a hold-up by the John Dillinger gang.

May 23, 1933, began like any other. Folks ambled along the streets of town, running errands and chatting together. Four gloved gunmen entered Lowell National Bank just after it opened at 316 East Commercial Avenue, ordering the employees to the floor, while they scooped up five thousand dollars in cash. It was said that the robbers weren't in a hurry but appeared to be old hands and familiar with the task at hand. One resident, D. C. "Doc" Driscoll, was apparently talking with a friend right outside but was too close to the man on guard and soon ordered in. On the way out of town, gang members waved at the town marshal as they fled. Working away from the bank as the marshal was, he didn't know what had happened and, in small-town fashion, waved back.

Just as friendly today, see this community really shine during the Labor Day parade. This town of fewer than ten thousand people has the oldest Labor Day parade in the state. Pulling out all the stops, it has also got to be one of the biggest. Arrive early to snag a spot in the front. Be prepared for a huge lineup of floats and plenty of candy. Kids will need a bag to hold it all.

🛏 stay

Thyme for Bed is one of a handful of monolithic homes in Indiana and certainly the only bed-and-breakfast. Able to withstand

Thyme for Bed, Lowell.

winds of up to three hundred miles an hour, it's a safe, snug, yet surprisingly spacious home. Add to that an ample yard, gardens, a balcony with cushy swings, and gorgeous firefly-lit country views, and it easily maintains its unofficial status as one of the more unique lodging options available.

☀ play

Irish immigrants, the Buckley family set up their Lowell farm in 1849. It grew from 79 acres, expanding over the generations, and morphed into a colossal 520-acre farm. Today, wander living-history farm Buckley Homestead. See life as it was in the early nineteenth and twentieth centuries. Buildings include a carriage house, the Main House Museum furnished with several original Buckley family possessions, the replica one-room schoolhouse, and more. Although the park is open year-round, the buildings are seasonally accessible, so look for special events scattered throughout the year.

Freedom Park is a magnificent playground. Meander around the duck pond on a paved walking path. Colorful, exciting playground equipment occupies a sizable area underneath aged shade trees. Truly, it's a delightful space for all ages. For those frequently traveling through Lowell, become a member and give Fido room to roam at Freedom Bark Park, a fenced-in portion of Freedom Park. *Dog Fancy* designated it America's Best Dog Park of 2009. More than twenty-seven hundred hours of volunteer time were needed to create the environmentally friendly dog park—and it didn't use a single cent of taxpayer money. Secure key entry keeps dogs safe.

Serving authentic Greek food in a casual setting since 1989, Athens Grill has several dishes that are family recipes passed down through the generations. There is a scrumptious menu of Greek favorites, but you'll find American style too—some with a tasty Greek twist. Chock-full of green olives, feta cheese, and mushrooms, the Athens double burger is an excellent possibility, as is the traditional gyro. Children will love the shish kebab. Because the restaurant's interior is small, dining in may occasionally prove tricky, so make alternate plans to take your food to nearby Evergreen Park.

Thin-crust fans will adore the Lowell Pizza House. Known for its ultra-thin and crispy crust, the restaurant's Chi-Town pizza will make it famous. Piled with Canadian bacon, pepperoni, sausage, mushroom, and onion, it's a lip-smacking pizza that's different from the usual offerings. Rumor has it that the Italian beef sandwich is equally amazing. Roomy enough for a crowd, the restaurant is by the tracks.

McVey's Restaurant is the place to head for an after-dinner drink. With a full-service martini bar, the restaurant's martini menu features more than twenty varieties. It is not something typically found in a small town and a welcome surprise. Both the melon martini and the orange-strawberry-banana martini are noteworthy choices.

Buckley Homestead, Lowell.

Athens Grill, Lowell.

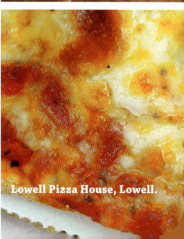

Lowell Pizza House, Lowell.

No matter if it is a sizable group or a dinner date for two, Mi Ranchito Mexican restaurant is anything but cramped. Tacos rancheros, steak fajitas, and chimichanga Acapulco are local favorites. Pair your meal with an adult beverage or follow it up with fried ice cream.

 shop

Aunt Nae's, formerly You Shouldn't Have, is one spacious shop. Gift baskets and gift balloons may be the shop's specialty, but anyone in search of that special something will most likely find it right here. For birthdays, weddings, thank you, or just because, Aunt Nae's is brimming with gifts.

Dragonfly Antiques and Accessories is nearing the decade mark. Full of furniture, pottery, glassware, vintage prints, and all kinds of home decor, it all began with an interest in collecting bee-sting crocks. Desks, armoires, tables, and chairs are in no short supply. Fine old-fashioned cards and postcards are near the front of the shop, as are baskets of vintage art.

Looking for country home decor? Focus on Earle's Home and Garden. Candles, potpourri, wall art, plates, toss pillows, furniture, and even collectibles prove there's no shortage of country style. Listen for a bubbling focal point at the back of the shop: a soothing oasis complete with koi fish.

Grandmothers' linens drape across tables, while long-ago favorite playthings perch on shelves at Felicia's Antiques, in business since 1997. The art here is particularly brilliant. Look for it closer to the back of the shop.

Four generations have handled watch and jewelry repair at Sickinger's Jewelry. Beginning in 1928, this downtown business has been in the same location for more than eighty years. From diamonds to birthstones, it's glittering inside this pleasant family-owned store.

Even those with only a passing interest in miniature trains will delight in Spike's Railhead retail and repair. A downtown destination for years, the shop carries all the major train name brands. Trains zip along the hefty, detailed train table. Shelves and boxes hold a variety of model trains, tracks, and accessories either new or gently used. There are excellent starter trains and holiday kits for any age. Bonus: the coffeepot is always on.

Folks have traveled off the beaten path and down tree-lined roads to visit Spring Run Farm since 1989. Possessing an admirable assortment of both vintage and home decor items, including bedding and linens, it's an excellent way to revamp any room! Special events and the Fall Harvest Festival featuring ham and bean soup (tips go to charities) are popular with the locals.

More than four thousand square feet are waiting to be explored inside Tish's Antiques. A second-generation shop, it all started with a few pieces of Depression glass back in 1975. Getting hooked on collecting, the family soon acquired a rental space until 1979, when the purchase of the present location was made available. Even the building is an antique. In what was once a harness shop, a Studebaker car dealer, and even an auto-parts store at different points in its long history, it is now a massive shop specializing in high-quality antique furniture. Expect a range of period styles.

NOTABLES

The graduating class of Lowell High School in 1897 was a lonely one: it contained only one grad.

By the time Mary Emma "Woodruff" Allison (1917–2010), school librarian, passed away in her Lowell home in 2010, this cocreator of the 1950 program UNICEF, the United Nations Children's Fund, had raised $160 million.

Lowell-born Jo Anne Worley (b. 1937) has tackled both stage and screen. The 1955 graduate of Lowell High School was voted school comedienne—and has kept audiences laughing ever since. Doing everything from appearing on talk shows to voicing Disney movies, and even a video game, she possesses quite the résumé.

13

Monon

Monon Connection
Museum, Monon.

Another small town platted by New Albany and Salem Railroad president James Brooks, Monon was laid out in 1853 under the name of New Bradford. With the Big Monon and Little Monon Rivers nearby, the town's name eventually changed to Monon. Later, the main routes of the train connected here—and it, too, became known as the Monon.

Yearning for small-town community? Find it at the annual Monon Food Fest. Featuring an excellent car show, parade, live music, craft booths, and then some, this event takes place the first Saturday in June. The entire town shows up for this one.

☼ play

All aboard for the largest detailed train museum in the world. The Monon Connection Museum carries one man's personal collection of items from the railroads' heyday, with signage or equipment representing one hundred different railroads. Notice that there are two red wooden cabooses, a new acquisition from the Kentucky Railroad Museum, and a rare one at that. Some of the last pieces of their kind, browse dining-car china patterns and place settings, a life-size re-creation of the old Illinois

Depot, and more than six thousand pieces including loads of lanterns, milestone pins, and memorabilia. It's an eye-opening look at a time when railroads were king in just one five thousand–square-foot portion of the museum. Serious train buffs will want to call ahead and find out when Harold Harvey serves as tour guide.

Papa Angelo's Café, Monon.

¶¶ eat

Every two weeks, one young man heads to Papa Angelo's Café for a jalapeño pizza. For everyone else wanting something a bit less zippy, the single-portion flat-bread pizza is delicious. They make their own sauce, so get a little extra on a stromboli sandwich or the white meatball sub. Bring along quarters to pass the time playing classic arcade games.

Reme's Monon Family Restaurant may be known for its pizza, but its Mexican food menu is where it is at. Authentic and fresh, the jumbo burrito dinner is one of the standout items on this full menu. Not just for breakfast, ask for the homemade potatoes as a side with their tasty pork tenderloin sandwich.

Kids and train lovers love the Whistle Stop Restaurant. Attached to the Monon Connection Museum (mentioned above), toy train cars actually zip and zoom overhead. Kid meals come with a scoop of ice cream. Grown-ups, however, will want to save room for homemade pie.

Reme's Monon Family Restaurant, Monon.

NOTABLES

Barton Rees Pogue (1891–1965), poet and author of five books, was born in Monon. Pogue did three thousand poetry readings and traveled through twenty states.

14

Monticello

With two lakes, Lake Shafer and Lake Freeman, plus large amusement-park Indiana Beach, it's no wonder that Monticello is a vacation destination. But throw in fishing, cross-country skiing, snowmobiling, and ice skating, and there's plenty to do year-round.

French explorer René-Robert La Salle originally traveled the area in 1650, back when it was a Potawatomi village. After a treaty relocated the tribe in 1834, settlers took over. Monticello was named for the home of Thomas Jefferson that same year. By 1838 any remaining Native Americans were forcibly removed by the government while Monticello took root—right where the Potawatomi village once was.

☀ play

Originally the Monticello Carnegie Public Library, there isn't a more fitting space than this appealing building. From the White County Genealogy Society on the main floor to exhibits featuring items from the area, the White County Historical Museum knows all the answers.

Whyte Horse Winery, Monticello.

It began with a horse. Larry and Connie Pampel saw a piece of property they couldn't resist. Downhearted, they learned it had already received a full-price offer. They made a backup offer anyway. The next day the couple received a phone call from the owner, asking if they would take Molly, the white horse on the property, as well. It marked the beginning of Whyte Horse Winery.

07 MERLOT

7-22-08 Racked #29 to #11
added 2.5 gal

Whyte Horse Winery,
Monticello.

Named for the horse, the county, and the style of wine that the couple prefers (Old World), the winery has been racking up the awards. Savor sips of memorable wines in the 1886 farmhouse, complete with cheeses and gift shop. Stroll down the path for gorgeous vineyard views and a distinctive gazebo.

¶¶ eat

Super-soft breadsticks warm from the oven hint at the tasty things to come out of Abe's Pizza. The pizza crust is wonderful: thick and chewy. Since the restaurant's move into a new space a few years ago, parking is certainly easier. Cold weather brings soul-warming homemade soups. It's a bit unusual for a pizza parlor, but it works.

Kinser's Bakery, Monticello.

John's Bakery and Cafe serves breakfast and lunch. Biscuits and gravy are popular here. But the donuts are what is really unique. Coconut crunch and maple with peanuts are a tiny sample of the fun flavors available inside. An assortment of homemade soups and freshly baked bread is always on the menu.

Locals have gathered at Kinser's Bakery for more than thirty years. The biscuits and gravy and excellent selection of fresh-baked donuts probably have something to do with it. The cake donuts are certainly worth a try. For a super-sized treat, look for the Texas donut, a donut so big it dwarfs the rest. The pocket pastries are excellent when warmed: flaky, soft, and delicious.

Wander the pathways through all of the green spaces of Garden Station, a block-long garden shop. Make a plant purchase? They will even pot it! So much more than just plants and flowers, the shop offers garden-themed decor, pottery, and a slew of concrete items, from pet memorials to fairies. The vintage gas pump out front is a nice accent.

Family members took Juanita's love of books and turned it into a business. Fixing her garage to become the Used Book Store Exchange, a haven for gently used books, it was a way they felt would help take her mind off her grandson's battle with cancer. Her goal is simple: make enough money each month to keep the power on. So far, so good. Friendly and chatty, she created a comfy, cozy bookshop in her own backyard. Find popular authors as well as obscure items too. Buy, sell, or trade!

NOTABLES

"Monticello" is the title and subject of a song in the musical *Edges* by Pasek and Paul.

Look for the unique "state of the art" stone barn (N 40°42′56.30″, W 86°45′44.32″) built by millionaire A. A. McKain (responsible for producing the towering soldiers monument in Winchester) in the early 1900s. Setting up house in Indianapolis, he had managers tend to his large mostly dairy Monticello farm.

Daren Jay "D. J." Ashba (b. 1972) is one of the lead guitarists in Guns 'n Roses and Sixx:A.M.

15

Morocco

The town started in 1851, but no one knows exactly where it got its name. Local lore points to a traveler's red Moroccan boots. They must have made an impact to become the name of a town. As the oldest town in Newton County, it is also really small. The population barely tops one thousand.

☀ play

Native plants and animal species flourish and roam in this seventy-eight-hundred-acre restoration project. Efroymson Restoration at Kankakee Sands features six hundred native plant species and more than one hundred rare or endangered species that have been restored to more than sixty-five hundred acres. But this is only one piece of the restoration puzzle. Throw in Conrad Savanna Nature Preserve, Beaver Lake Nature Preserve, Willow Slough Fish and Wildlife Area, and the Nature Conservancy's Conrad Station Savanna Preserve, and there's more than twenty thousand acres of Indiana slowly returning to their native roots. Efroymson Restoration features three completely different trails. If there's only room for one, the longer Conrad Station Savanna Trail is fantastic. Walk along the 1.8-mile path through black oak sand savanna and even through the ghost town of Conrad. Informational placards dot the trail in a few places to point out a few need-to-know pieces of info (as well as the town of Conrad's history).

Three generations of the Lucas family were raised in the Scott-Lucas House. When Virginia Ann (Lucas) Scott passed away in 1998, her will revealed that the home was left to the town. She intended for the home to serve as a museum in order to showcase her antique collection and her jewelry. The Scott-Lucas House

Efroymson Restoration at Kankakee, Morocco.

is the only building in Morocco that appears on the National Register of Historic Places. Built in 1912, it is a solid Craftsman home. Watch for when it will finally open to the public.

NOTABLES

On February 13, 1886, eleven males were arrested and fined for serenading Alonzo Bridgeman when he was married. Although it wasn't the best start to a marriage, the couple had ten children over the course of their union. The home, most likely constructed soon after the Civil War, still stands on Beaver Street and is one of the oldest in town.

Sam Rice (1890–1974), Major League Baseball Hall of Famer, pitcher, and right fielder, was born in Morocco. The town baseball fields are named in his honor.

16

Nappanee

Amish Acres Farm and Heritage Resort Round Barn Theater, Nappanee.

In 1874 Nappanee managed to snag a B&O Railroad line. The nearby town of Locke, disheartened but determined, decided to relocate the three buildings that composed their town the two and a half miles to Nappanee. Moved by sled, those buildings are surprisingly still alive and well today.

The clip-clop of horse and buggy isn't unusual in Nappanee. They possess a population of Old Order Amish that hovers somewhere around thirty-five hundred people. Roam the back roads and discover an array of country shops selling furniture, food, and quilts. But remember: take no photos of the Amish people.

Smell that pie baking? It's hard to miss at seven feet wide and weighing six hundred pounds. After it cools, the mammoth pastry is cut up and dished out as part of the Nappanee Apple Fest, a three-and-a-half-day event held the third week of September. An apple-peeling contest, pie-eating contest, goldfish race, tractor pull, car show, and talent show are only a few of the many scheduled events. That's not to forget the airplane flyover or the two stages for live acts.

🛏 stay

There's no resisting the front porch of the Homespun Country Inn Bed and Breakfast. Actually, there are a lot of nice things to note about this 1902 clapboard home. Wilma Terwillinger's Room displays an image of the original occupant who, in 1921, was married in front of the living room fireplace. Listen to

Amish buggies tromp by and dine by candlelight in the dining room. It's the kind of place where it's easy to unwind.

Gables and turrets adorn 1887 Queen Anne Victorian Guest House Bed and Breakfast. The eleven-foot dining room table still features a servant buzzer on the underside. Local artisans long ago crafted the stunning stained-glass windows. Upstairs, the Coppes Suite features quite a bathtub. Sixty-five gallons of water are required to fill the original claw-foot tub. It's a history-filled offering near the downtown.

☀ play

For live performances, the Amish Acres Farm and Heritage Resort Round Barn Theater is an unusual attraction. It was only a few short decades ago that one hundred Amish carpenters were hired to take the old 1911 round barn apart. Every piece was numbered, moved, and relocated before it was reassembled in its current location. Just like the name implies, the Round Barn Theater is, in fact, a round theater. It makes for an intimate show.

Three generations of Amish once lived and worked at the 1873 home and barn that make up the Amish Acres Home and Farm Tour. Learn about the Amish lifestyle in the late 1800s. Visit the summer kitchen and drying room and check out the seasonal demonstrations. Hear what Amish thought about the "newfangled" ideas back in the day. Educating and insightful but with enough for children to find interesting (the live animals roaming the yard certainly help), it is a family-friendly destination.

A welcome center would normally be a recommended suggestion, not so much a destination, if it weren't for the lengthy display of Nappanee history inside the Nappanee Welcome Center. Bypass the brochures and maps for exhibits of the *Air Force One* pilot from Nappanee, famed cartoonist Bill Holman of *Smokey Stover* fame, a few of the "Dutch kitchenettes" (mentioned below), and Hartman House, a residence turned attraction that is actually built into the museum, depicting life in the olden days. Loads of military items and even the old jail are found here, too.

🍴 eat

Arrive with empty bellies. Amish Acres Threshers Dinner is a table-buckling kind of feast. Served family style, it is meant to mimic the type of meal that an Old Order Amish family would have enjoyed at a host farm during the threshing season. The Amish ham and beans, fried chicken, and beef and noodles are a few favorites. Finish something and need more? Just ask for a refill. Too stuffed? Be sure to ask for a to-go container for the generous slice of homemade pie.

Savor Belgian-style chocolates that are hand-dipped and handmade at Veni's Sweet Shop, a Niles, Michigan, destination since 1901—and now in Nappanee. Preservative and additive free, these chocolates will perk up any palate. Enjoy nuts, candy, floats, hot chocolate, jelly beans, and licorice. Do try the orange crème chocolates.

🛍 shop

Once a furniture factory that began in the late 1800s that received national acclaim for the "Dutch kitchenette" (a type of kitchen cabinet), Coppes Commons is now one hundred thousand square feet of shops. Offerings range from books to tech as well as an ice cream parlor, bakery, and coffee shop. Handsome Hoosier cabinets, furniture, and other related odds and ends are a fitting complement to the building's past.

NOTABLES

Nappanee is often said to be the only city in the United States containing each letter in its name twice—but this is also wrong. It has plenty of company with the likes of Soso, Mississippi; Emmett, Idaho; Hannah, North Dakota; and Lolo, Montana.

Piloting *Air Force One* has let Nappanee-born Todd Beer fly Presidents Bill Clinton, George Bush, and the funeral casket of Ronald Reagan. He's flown foreign dignitaries, athletes, vice presidents, and celebrities in the seven years he spent as the pilot of *Air Force One*. He piloted George Bush's flight on September 11, 2001.

Comic creators Merrill Blosser (1892–1983) of *Freckles and His Friends,* Bill Holman (1903–1987) of *Smokey Stover,*

Veni's Sweet Shop, Nappanee.

and Fred Neher (1903–2001) of *Life's Like That* are all from Nappanee.

Born in Nappanee, David Crane (b. 1953) went on to design the award-winning video game *Pitfall*. More than four million copies of the game were sold in the 1980s. As the cofounder of Activision, and later cofounder of Absolute Entertainment, he was responsible for churning out many well-known titles.

Vance George (b. 1933), conductor of the San Francisco Symphony Chorus for more than twenty years, led the group to a four-time Grammy win.

A graduate of Nappanee high school, Rob Rensberger (1921–2007) was a professional basketball player for the Chicago Stags, though he had an active role in only three games.

17

North Judson

Fingerhut Bakery, North Judson.

Arose by any other name . . . yes, North Judson has also had an identity crisis of sorts. Once called Brantwood, the name later changed to North Judson, partly due to the first postmaster, Adrian Judson, and partly to keep it separate from a town with a similar name, Judson, Indiana.

Father's Day weekend is huge in North Judson. Resurrecting the annual Mint Festival has proven successful; it is enormous. The downtown is blocked off in places to make way for events like a pie-eating contest, water ball, and frog jumping. Carnival games, a library book sale, craft vendors, and food booths add to the excitement.

play

Saturdays at the Hoosier Valley Railroad Museum are reserved for anyone wanting a taste of old-fashioned travel. Sit inside a caboose, an open train trailer, or in coach (the air-conditioned option) as a vintage diesel-powered train chugs along a scenic route. There are steam and diesel trains on display, too.

eat

For more than sixty years, Fingerhut Bakery has been supplying the area with sweet treats. Admire the wood display cases while drooling over the contents inside. The chocolate delight cake, a signature creation featuring a layer of chocolate cake, a layer of yellow cake, and a layer of chocolate cake enveloped in chocolate frosting, is a must. For a smaller on-the-road sort of snack, turn to the cheerful display of butter cookies or the super-size cream horns.

Route 10 Bar and Grill is a comfortable place. It's the kind of restaurant where people know each other and will just as likely talk to any newcomers near their table as well. Amish teens even made an appearance. Get the burger or the hefty Saturday-night prime rib.

Known for its Italian beef, the Wooden Nickel Restaurant and Bar certainly has reason to boast. Now that is a sandwich. Still, the reuben sandwich is no slouch, either. See why it is the local favorite.

Fingerhut Bakery, North Judson.

🛍 shop

Pioneer Florist and Country Store has been in business since 1947. Fresh flowers and plants are abundant in this old grocery store turned floral and gift shop. Look for the neat cabinets located along the back wall, a throwback to its grocery store times.

NOTABLES

David Haugh (b. 1968), raised in North Judson, has been a journalist for the *Chicago Tribune* since 2003. He is the newspaper's seventeenth *In the Wake of the News* sports columnist.

North Judson–born Honorable Henry F. Schricker (1883–1966) graduated from the North Judson high school. In addition to practicing law, he had an impressive résumé behind him: he bought and edited the local paper, served as fire chief and bank cashier, was elected to the state senate, and became the first man to be the twice-elected governor of Indiana.

18

Anytime is a good time to visit North Liberty, but to really take part in some local traditions, hit the July 4 parade. It's not just for the candy; this one also includes water. Whether the parade watchers are armed with squirt guns or buckets or the firefighters on their trucks are using their hoses, everyone seems to have buckets or balloons, so prepare to get wet.

That evening, join the rest of the town for the annual fireworks show. Watch the rather impressive show from the elementary school. Although the event is free, locals sell all things that "glow," from bracelets to sticks, and kids just can't resist them.

🚌 stay

Once on the verge of demolition, this decaying home spent two years undergoing massive restoration, transforming into the cozy, light-filled space it is today. The Bluebird House Bed and Breakfast is so cheery. Rent a room and enjoy the whole place. The dining room, the kitchen, the front porch, even the backyard are all so inviting that picking one spot to relax is almost impossible.

☼ play

Fishing, boating, and swimming are easy when there's a large 327-acre lake. There's room for everyone without feeling cramped. Well-maintained bike trails, hiking, and even a dog beach mean the entire family can have a blast at Potato Creek State Park.

🍴 eat

Always a fun time, the Yum Yum Shoppe is an ice cream parlor and café. Serving pizza and sandwiches, those looking for the perfect ending will love the hand-dipped ice cream. Creative sundaes like the Durty [*sic*] Turtle, a yummy blend of butter pecan ice cream, caramel, and chocolate, and the S'mores Sundae, hot fudge, crunched-up cones, marshmallow, and chocolate ice cream, make any day instantly brighter. Moonlight Dips, a one-night-a-year themed event, features amusing activities and a late closing time.

Bluebird House Bed and Breakfast, North Liberty.

 shop

Focusing on gifts for the family and items for the home, Dogwood Designs is simply charming. This is one small business owner with a knack for knowing just what to place where to make it shine. Jewelry, seasonal decor, candles, and even some Indiana-made products are a sampling of lovely items that dot the shelves.

NOTABLES

Actor Jay Beyers grew up in North Liberty. Beyers is best known as the voice of the Damned in the Electronic Arts video game *Dante's Inferno* (2010) and for his roles in direct-to-video films such as *Mega Shark versus Giant Octopus* (2009) and *Moby Dick* (2010).

19

Peru

Miami County Museum, Peru.

Seven major circuses once called Peru "home" each winter. Though the golden days of the circus are gone, the big top isn't over just yet. The International Circus Hall of Fame performs each summer. Local kids get involved in July during Circus Week. The town puts on one amazing parade.

There's obviously unique history in this small town. View the home of songwriter Cole Porter, learn about the Wabash and Erie Canal, and hear the tear-jerking story of Frances Slocum, a child captured by the Delaware tribe and not found until sixty years later.

☼ play

The Miami County Museum is housed in the long-ago Senger Dry Goods Store. Look carefully up by the landing on the way to the second floor to see the track where purchase orders were once sent zipping below. With the town's distinction of holding the longest-running circus parade and the home of wintering circuses, the museum is definitely into all things big top. Denim trousers that belonged to a massive man, circus wagons, props, elephant harnesses and hooks, and costumes make up a sizable portion of the museum. Famed musician Cole Porter was born in Peru, so expect plenty of memorabilia. They even hold Porter's specially made sofa to accommodate his legs as well as his classy restored 1955 Fleetwood Cadillac—and even a Grammy. Native American artifacts from both the local Miami tribe and other

Miami County Museum, Peru.

East End Double Dip, Peru.

nearby woodland tribes are on display. Browse military history relics, pioneer items, and a whole second floor with storefronts that mimic a long-ago town. Step out and mosey down the street to the Museum Ulery Annex, the new home for the objects collection.

The Frances Slocum Trail runs along the top of the Seven Pillars. Eroded by wind and water for centuries, the limestone rock formation is a series of short caves that have served as a meeting space and even a trading post for the Miami Native Americans in years long past.

¶¶ eat

Rainbow outdoor umbrellas and a giant turtle make East End Double Dip, a seasonally open ice cream parlor, stand out. As a neighborhood joint, locals turn to the pizza or stromboli sandwiches for quick dinners. The turtle sundae, upside-down banana-split hurricane, Beagle (a peanut butter lover's new favorite thing), or the strawberry shortcake are a few top picks. Kids might want to request a clown cone.

McClure's Orchard, Peru.

The Siding, Peru.

McClure's Orchard features a barn, the Apple Dumpling Restaurant, and a winery. The beautiful grounds are a far cry from the neglected, shabby state the orchard was in when purchased by the McClures more than fifteen years ago. Only one apple tree was growing in the entire sixty-acre orchard. Family run, the orchard now produces wines, hard ciders, and fresh fruit. Selections include Grandpa's Bourbon Barrel Aged, Country Cottage, Fireball, and Jalapeño Hard Cider. There's a flavor here for everyone. Connected to the gift shop and wine-tasting room lies home-cooked food at the Apple Dumpling. Save room for the dessert of the same name.

Though the decor is slightly faded, the food inside the Siding is still incredible. Weekend evenings are buffet night. Prime rib, shrimp, and a beautiful dessert bar full of homemade treats are baked fresh that morning by a lady who has been crafting them for years. With the restaurant named for a railroad term, the attached train cars are sometimes open and available for seating. If not, ask to peek inside. No one beats their service.

Southside Scoops is yet another ice cream parlor. There are some really fun flavors and unexpected varieties. All the traditional ice cream treats like sundaes and banana splits are available. Look to the board for the special ice cream flavor—and get it.

🛍 **shop**

Explore three floors of antiques, gifts, and home decor inside Annie's Attic. Jewelry, wall art, baby gifts, seasonal decor, photo frames, candles, and purses . . . there's a lot of variety. Look for special hours during town events when Annie's Attic stays open later.

Farris Wheel Antiques and Collectibles is a house turned amazing antique shop. Kitchenware, board games, country decor, and primitives all have a place inside this large two-story antique store. The store is a chalk-paint vendor, and many items of furniture have been gloriously redone.

Need a fancy new dress or a tux for a special event? Lillian's Prom and Fashion Boutique is it. One of the top-ten dress shops in the state, it is classy, well organized, and absolutely amazing. Although this is a prom destination, there are plenty of dresses for those past prom age who need a new gown or cocktail dress. Find accessories, undergarments, and a tall wall of formal footwear.

Rat-a-tat-tat: it wouldn't be unusual to hear the sounds of instruments playing at Peru Music Center. For more than twenty years, Peru Music Center has been serving the community. Anyone needing instruments from violins to baby grand pianos to guitars to drum sets should make the visit. Find lessons and workshops, too. Drum sticks, sheet music, and gently used instruments are all right here.

NOTABLES

John Dillinger and his gang robbed the Peru police department armory back in 1933. They got away with two Thompson submachine guns, two Winchester rifles, two shotguns, four .38 revolvers, and a half-dozen bulletproof vests.

A 1913 flood sent water splashing along the main street at speeds of up to twenty miles an hour. The estimate for damages was a staggering $3 million.

Martin J. McNally nabbed a $502,500 ransom on American Airlines Flight 119 in June 1973. After he parachuted from the back of the Boeing 727, area residents found not only a machine gun in a cornfield but the entire forty-five-pound bag of money. For four days, 150 Federal Bureau of Investigation agents scoured the Peru area, looking for the man. He was found in his Michigan home days later and brought to trial.

Peru-born Cole Porter (1891–1964) composed for stage and screen, achieving lasting fame and celebrity with his musical flair. His childhood home is owned by a local civic theater group and is part inn and part museum. He now rests in Peru's Mount Hope Cemetery.

20

Porter

The first few buildings in Porter were combination home and store in the early 1850s as well as the addition of a railroad. A post office quickly followed, but in 1872 the post office was moved one mile away to the new town of Hageman. That apparently didn't sit well with the Porter folks because the next year a new post office was installed in their town. Imagine the confusion of such close proximity. Porter won that battle—the Hageman post office eventually closed.

Bricks were once a big business in Porter. In fact, Porter bricks were sent to Chicago to rebuild after the Great Chicago Fire of 1871. Lacking any major industry, Porter does possess a smattering of shops and an excellent restaurant.

☼ play

Although the park is open year-round, wait for the warmer months in order to get inside of the Joseph Bailley Home. Joseph Aubert de Gaspé Bailly de Messein (1774–1835), a fur trapper, and his family settled the area thirty years before building the home. Finally constructed in 1834, the home was in the possession of a member of the family until 1917. See the two-story log house, a storehouse, and a summer kitchen turned chapel. The family cemetery is an easy and short three quarters of a mile walk away.

🍴 eat

Enjoy patio seating surrounded by gorgeous flowers and plants in the summer or cozy indoor seating at Santiago's Mexican Restaurant. This downtown restaurant boasts so many delicious homemade items on the menu. Keep it simple: start with the tortilla chips and nachos. Both are freshly made. Go for the steak nachos, the chimichangas, or the wet burrito.

Bigg's Violin Shop, Porter.

shop

Bigg's Violin Shop restores, deals, and crafts violins—and for some big names, too. Beginning his apprenticeship in Chicago, Richard Bigg learned how to repair and make these fine instruments. Handling such rare and unique pieces for private individuals and symphonies has certainly kept him busy. Violins are in the shop ready to go. Need something else? He'll even special order.

21

Remington

Remington's beginning traces back to 1860, but at that time it was known as Carpenter Station or simply Carpenter (after the local creek). No one is exactly sure why Remington changed its name, but it has been suggested that Remington was the name of the shopkeeper at the second store that opened up during its early years.

No matter what it is called or how it got its name, Remington is big on community spirit. Visit Remington's Water Tower Days for a taste of wholesome small-town life. The list of events may include water ball, a cornhole tourney, candy-throwing parade with float judges, free hot-air balloon rides, a petting zoo, carnival rides, and even camel rides.

 play

Draft horses once occupied the 1919 red barn. Built by the owner's grandfather, it now serves as the stylish home of Carpenter Creek Cellars. Racking up the awards, Byron's Vineyard contains the first vines planted on the property by father and son, now a touching memorial for son Byron. Savor sips that run the usual range in the spacious tasting room. Dry-wine lovers should seek out the award-winning Gunny Red.

Remington's 1897 Water Tower really does tower over the town. At 120 feet tall, with a 20-foot diameter and 2-foot-thick brick walls, it's a neat throwback to the early days of public water utilities. During special town events, it's possible to take a peek inside the building.

eat

"Buttery" is an old-fashioned term to describe a pantry, a fitting way to describe Homestead Buttery and Bakery. They may carry Amish-style bulk food items that range from spices to nuts, but there's far more than plain packaging inside this charming retail shop and café. Serving breakfast and lunch, they do things a bit differently when it comes to bread. Grinding their own whole wheat flour for fresh 100 percent homemade whole wheat bread brings the term "homemade" to a whole new level. This delicious

Carpenter Creek Cellars, Remington.

bread forms the base of panini sandwiches. Browse the bakery case for available items of the day and hope that the lemon cream pie or turtle pie are still available. The cup of coffee is always "on the house." Check the freezer section for goodies to take and bake.

🛍 shop

Mini Measures Antiques and Collectibles is part antique shop and part resale shop. In business since 1998, it's not difficult to see why. There's not a flea market–type atmosphere here. Instead, explore excellent vintage office supplies like typewriters and adding machines, as well as scrapbooking stickers and stamps, collectibles, books, and board games.

22

Rensselaer

Before Rensselaer was Rensselaer (and should, perhaps, have been Yeoman), the Yeoman family arrived in the area and decided to settle. They built the first cabin, conveniently near the Iroquois River. During the winter, a man by the name of James Van Rensselaer, a New York businessman, entered the area. He was kindly invited to spend the winter with the family. As time passed, Yeoman confided that he had been lax in officially claiming the land for his own. Van Rensselaer left—

Jasper County Courthouse, Rensselaer.

and then claimed it for himself, naming the town Newton. He returned, kicked the family out of their home, and took it over for himself. The town name was changed to honor the "original" founder. A plaque sits near the cabin site, mentioning Yeoman as the first person to build here, but leaves out the rest of the story.

In what may seem like an odd move, considering that Hoosiers tend to lean toward names that highlight historical figures, trees, and presidents, a few streets in the heart of town reflect the names of females. Angelica, Susan, and Grace Streets are located around the downtown. These streets were named by Van Rensselaer to acknowledge his daughters and wife.

The past is in the past, and the Rensselaer of today emphasizes

community. It's clearly evident from the numerous festivals and events that often take place around or at the stately Jasper County Courthouse. Rock the Arts is a new addition to Rensselaer's festival lineup, celebrating Rensselaer's artsy vibe with a day of live music, food, and hands-on projects for the kids. Autumn brings a festival that is so sweetly small town it is not to be missed.

Occupying the courthouse lawn on all four sides, the Little Cousin Jasper Festival has loads of food booths, vendors, a parade, a teen dance, and performances on a makeshift stage (including a town talent show). This is one feel-good, family-friendly festival that's especially fitting for younger children.

☼ play

Exhibits change frequently at the Carnegie Center. Situated in the old 1904 Carnegie Library, it's long been converted over to an appealing art gallery, the Lillian Fendig Gallery. Owned by the Jasper Foundation, the Prairie Arts Council occupies lower-level offices. This nonprofit group holds a summer art camp, children's summer theater, and other events throughout the year.

Embers Venue is not only an event hall, but also a community gathering place. Featuring live music in all genres, from pop to country to gospel, it's come a long way from town eyesore to stunning focal point. Originally, the building was a hardware store and then a magazine distributor. The owners removed seven thousand pounds of metal and twenty-five hundred pounds of papers and magazines for recycling. That was just the beginning. After 875 days of renovation, it shines. The wood flooring is

Mathew's Tree Farm and Pumpkin Patch, Rensselaer.

from the old school gym, the bar is made of reclaimed materials, and the decor mixes modern with traditional in a style that is all its own. Past performers include Charlotte Sometimes, Tanner Walle, American Opera, and Wild Adriatic.

Admire the 140-foot tower with a clock face on each side. Marvel at the marble tile and detail abounding inside the 1898 Jasper County Courthouse. At this commanding, imposing stone building built from 1896 to 1898, do head into the lower level and read the sometimes tragic history of Rensselaer boys lost in the war.

Time a visit for the second Saturday of the month to catch the Jasper County Historical Society and Museum. Presenting rotating displays, occasional events, and a wealth of local history, it's a fascinating way to get to know the town from the beginning.

Pumpkins aren't just orange or white; they are also black, pink, green, and even blue. Smooth or warty, speckled or plain, mini or enormous, the variety at Mathew's Tree Farm and Pumpkin Patch is like a page out of a fairy tale. Pie pumpkins, honey from hives located on the property, and ornamental gourds are also available. When the weather turns, the tree farm is open for business.

Down a gravel road, and then some, the Sayler Makeever Cemetery, periodically referred to as the Old Settlers Cemetery, is a neat little off-the-beaten-path cemetery that is the final resting place for pioneers who first settled in Jasper County. The cemetery was established in 1838, and the gravestones are aged, often crumbling, and surrounded by cornfields. Locate the pioneer couple who both lived to be more than one hundred years old.

 eat

Lively and comfortable, Ayda's Mexican Cuisine is a local favorite. An excellent inexpensive menu makes it a prime lunch or dinner option. Homemade tortillas and salsa are made fresh. The monster burrito, nachos, and taco combo are outstanding choices. Finish up any meal with an order of banana fry.

Seasonally open with outside-only seating, Busy Bee features weekly soft-serve specials like German chocolate, cake batter, or strawberry. Opt for a tornado, the specially blended ice cream treat. The s'mores tornado with vanilla ice cream is particularly good.

Memories Café, also known as Martin's Restaurant, is off the square. Open for breakfast and lunch, this large restaurant greets locals at the same times each week. The servers always know who will order what—and sometimes have their usual beverages all ready to go for them before they even sit down. Homemade biscuits and gravy, Deana's special omelet, hot cakes as big as the plate, handmade burgers, and a crave-inducing peanut butter milkshake make it difficult to decide when to visit. Cross-table talk and teasing are common and lend an amusing atmosphere.

There's a drive-through window, local sport memorabilia on the walls, and even locally made custard ice cream at Schmidy's

Pizza Palace. Of course, there's no forgetting the pizza. Specialty pizzas include the buffalo chicken and the chicken alfredo pizza. There are quite a few crust options, from thin to hand-tossed to fair, stuffed crust, or gluten free. The place fills up during the lunchtime buffet.

Delicious coffees are poured out at the Willow Switch. Locally oriented names like "Rensselaer Makes Me Crazy" and "Bomber Black" (a dark-roasted nod to the high school mascot, the Bomber) add a clever touch. Choose among a small assortment of teas, fresh pastries, and novel drinks on the irresistible menu. The peach smoothie, dark chocolate raspberry truffle coffee, and the frozen mocha are delightful. This is more than a coffee shop, so sip something satisfying and peruse the large pick of country home decor that includes linens, furniture, and even local art.

🛍 shop

In operation since 2008, Greene's Exit 215 Antique Mall has well over one hundred vendors. There's no crowding here, either, with twelve thousand square feet of space. Each booth is different. Some specialize in a particular period or type, while others display collections like dishware, tin signs, or books. Together, it's a sprawling, well-lit, and extremely navigable shop.

It's hard to believe that up above the drop ceiling lies the engine hoist from when Long's Gifts and From the Needle's Point charming shop was a garage at the turn of the century. As the name implies, it is full of gifts, including a room full of kitchen essentials, plenty of home decorating accents, and a delightful toy room for all ages. Meander to the back of the shop for fabric, scrapbook necessities, and hobby supplies. Free gift wrapping is a wonderful little bonus.

Estate baubles of all kinds, watches for kids and adults, precious stones, and dazzling diamonds are found at this more than fifty-year-old family affair. Steffen's Jewelry boasts a registered watchmaker, jewelry, and diamond setter on site. It's a full-service shop with an ever-changing selection.

Cheerful, bright, and all around lovely, Unique Finds carries a superb mishmash of clothing for girls and women with loads of funky accessories. Purses, jewelry, tutus, wall art, Christian items, and whimsical hand-painted furniture all have one thing in common: they are quirky and fun, much like the shop itself.

NOTABLES

Eleanor Stackhouse Atkinson, Rensselaer born in 1863, was a writer best remembered for her 1912 novel turned 1961 Disney movie *Greyfriars Bobby*. A retelling of an oral tradition that began in the 1800s, it featured a Skye terrier rumored to guard the grave of his owner for fourteen years until his own death.

Rensselaer native Dan Brandenburg (b. 1973) went on to play for the Buffalo Bills from 1996 to 1999.

Charles A. Halleck (1900–1986) was a practicing Rensselaer lawyer before he moved on to become the Republican leader of the U.S. House of Representatives from the 1940s through the 1960s. He is buried in Rensselaer's Weston Cemetery.

No Indy 500 opening in Indianapolis, Indiana, would be complete without a round of "(Back Home Again in) Indiana" by Rensselaer-born resident James Frederick "Jimmy" Hanley (1892–1942). Released in 1917, it is one of many songs composed by Hanley for film and theater. It has been said that this song was written for his time spent in the town of his birth.

Born in the house on 118 South Weston Street back in 1919, Thomas Dudley "Tom" Harmon (1919–1990) later became the 1940 Heisman Trophy winner while at Michigan State University. After sustaining injuries in World War II, he had only a brief year of football with the Los Angeles Rams upon his return. Relying on his experience, Harmon became a well-known sportscaster.

Silent-film star Augustus Phillips (1874–1944) was born in Rensselaer, later starring in more than 130 films.

James Whitcomb Riley (1849–1916) once expressed the virtues of Rensselaer in his poem "Little Cousin Jasper."

23

Roann

Stockdale Mill, Roann.

Joseph Beckner first came to the area and settled down in 1836. After platting the town in 1853, he opened up a tavern. By 1866 the post office had moved in. Although some sources believe that Roann is named for Roanne, France, no one knows for sure where the name came from. There are numerous town legends that try to explain it. One such story is that of a Native American woman named Ann who used to take settlers across the river when they would call, "Row, Ann!" With a population under five hundred, Roann is one town that has embraced its history. Few towns of this size can boast of not one, not two, but three fabulous historical landmarks. Community is a big deal to this little place.

☀ play

With sharp Craftsman-style architecture, the Roann Carnegie Library is a beauty. Inside, there's even original furniture. See that large rolltop desk in the circulation area? Yes, that's original, too. Out of all the Carnegie Libraries in Indiana, Roann was the smallest town awarded the grant.

Rub elbows with the locals at the annual Roann Covered Bridge Festival. A big four-day festival that occurs the weekend after Labor Day, this one obviously requires a lot of planning. Organized entertainment and activities include carnival rides, a car cruise-in, an antique tractor and lawn mower show, a tractor pull, a cake walk, and even kids bingo. It is family fun on the cheap.

Wabash County once boasted twenty-nine covered bridges. Dwindling in numbers over the years, one of only two bridges

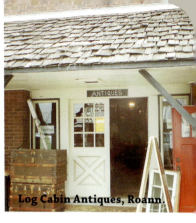
Log Cabin Antiques, Roann.

remain right here. A Howe truss design, the Roann Covered Bridge was originally constructed in Ohio. It was then taken apart, transported to Roann, and put back together again, where it is still in use today.

Stockdale Mill was one of seventeen grain mills in the county. Built between 1855 and 1857, it is now the only one left. Forty years it sat, slowly falling apart, until the mill changed hands—and a 2002 renovation restored the tilting mill to ship-shape condition. Open seasonally, it even works. See the mill's gears turning and belts moving on all three levels. Learn about the mill's contribution during the Civil War and marvel at the fact that only one person worked the whole thing. Packages of Stockdale Mill wheat flour and cornmeal are available for sale.

¶¶ eat

Looking for a patty melt or Angus burgers like no other? Lynn's Restaurant has been a town staple since the 1950s. Share the fries with a friend—they arrive on a huge plate. Of course, with such a small town, everyone knows everyone else, so expect an entertaining dining atmosphere.

shop

Retro wall art, fishing poles, and books are readily available at the Barn Antiques and Collectibles. Wide aisles and well-lit booths make hard-to-find items that much easier to spot. Look for the collection of bottles from almost every state.

Destined to become a favorite shopping destination, Log Cabin Antiques retains an exciting assortment of vintage items. Decked out in wood beams and flooring, that's about the closest to a log cabin that this gigantic shop gets. The furniture selection alone is worth any drive. Don't miss the dollar room in the back.

Riffle through the mix of items at Mom and Pop's Jazzy Junk. It's the kind of place where wonderful treasures are lurking, waiting for someone to take the time to look for them. Vintage lunch boxes, rolling pins, and records are a hint of what's available.

24

Roselawn

Platted in the beginning of 1882, Roselawn began as a hunting town. Three businessmen opened a store along the path of where the Monon Railroad was to pass. Originally named "Rose Lon" by combining two of their names, Orlando Rose and Lon Craig, the spelling was changed in 1893 to Roselawn. With the town's location near the swampy area once loved by hunters and fishers, hunting clubs popped up. One hunt club, the Diana, still remains, though it is now a private home.

It's not exactly a sleepy town: Alternet, an alternative news and information source, ranked Roselawn the number-one kinkiest city in 2011, most likely due to the two nudist colonies. Anyone who has actually visited Roselawn knows that the local residents are usually mild, typical clothes-wearing Hoosiers.

⑪ eat

It all started in 1986. Now that the original owners of J&J's Pizza Shack have retired, their children have taken the reins. Expect affordable, tasty pizza and sandwiches. Truly big appetites may want to take on J&J's Challenge, a humongous "kitchen-sink" deep-dish pizza topped with bacon, Canadian bacon, green peppers, ham, mushrooms, olives (both black and green), pepperoni, sausage, and cheese that must be finished in one hour. It's a small space with limited seating, so expect a tight squeeze if visiting during traditionally busy hours.

Start with the onion rings at Jordy and Jax BBQ. Pair nicely seasoned pulled-pork sandwiches with a baked sweet potato or the whiskey baked beans. Follow it up with homemade cheesecake drizzled with chocolate or caramel or topped with strawberries.

Sycamore Drive-In, Roselawn.

Hurry in for treats prepared with frozen custard at the seasonally open Sycamore Drive-In. Made daily, with a rotating assortment of flavors, it's always fabulously fresh. Pick the marshmallow fluff–topped banana split, the Hot Turtle, or the Hot Tin Roof sundaes. Those in need of real food will want the local favorite, lemon rice soup, or typical drive-in food like hot dogs and sandwiches.

NOTABLES

Pay respects at the touching roadside memorial on County Road North 400 East. Sixty-four passengers and four crew members lost their lives when a buildup of ice on the wings caused American Eagle flight 4184 to crash in a Roselawn field.

25

The original residents of the 1859 platted town Scarboro or Scarborough were not fans of the name. By 1862 they succeeded in changing the name to Star City. In the 2000 census, Star City was shown to have fewer than four hundred residents. Considering that this small village holds both a restaurant and a farm turned attraction, it becomes a worthwhile destination.

☼ play

Jones Robotic Dairy is high-tech and cow friendly. Robotics technology creates a comfortable milking experience for the cows. Apparently so, because some cows (like number 29, Betty) return to the machine before it's time. The robot, however, won't be fooled and simply ignores the cows. Eventually, the cow wanders away, back to the open air and dirt or the covered barn area. If it is time for milking, the robot will clean off the cow, play the sound of a baby cow in its ear, and complete the whole process in under six minutes. More than just a fancy milker, the machine can tell if a cow has weight loss or weight gain, reveal production values, and even analyze the parts of the milk. Like with tablets and cell phones, regular updates are available to keep the dairy running smoothly. It is a working family-owned farm: please call ahead for tours.

¶¶ eat

The only dining spot in tiny Star City, Oak Grove Restaurant is, fortunately, a great place to eat. It's kid friendly, so expect coloring books and a whole bag of crayons. Locals will heartily recommend the broasted chicken, but check the daily specials for other tasty options—including the available homemade desserts like chocolate cream pie or apple cobbler.

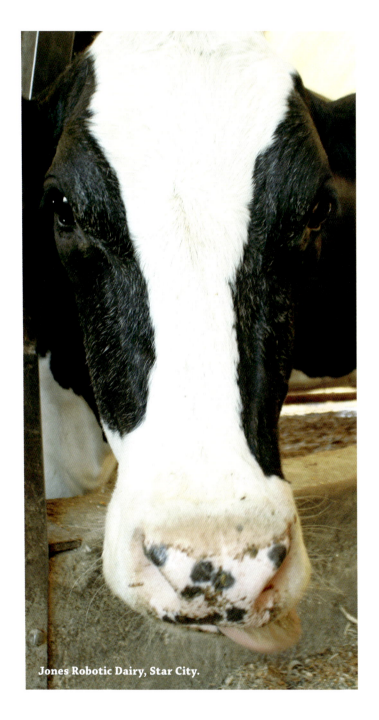

Jones Robotic Dairy, Star City.

26

Wabash

Wabash County Courthouse, Wabash.

More than ten thousand people gathered around the Wabash County Courthouse on March 31, 1880. Wabash made history by becoming the first electrically lit city in the world. Still making history today, Wabash holds the largest chili cook-off east of the Mississippi River each autumn.

Pacing is the key here: it's a massive one-day event. Receive a set number of tickets with paid admission. For each booth, taste a medicine cup–size sample of chili. There is white chili, beef chili, and chili that might have french fries, corn chips, or even orange soda in it. If it's really something, place a ticket into their bucket. If it's not, move along—there's more than one hundred to try. Some booths will bribe "voters" with trinkets or candy and outlandish decor to gain the people's choice award at the end of the day. It's a scrumptious, goofy event for charity that is like nothing else.

🛏 stay

Charley Creek Inn is a fashionable downtown boutique hotel. Luxury and comfort are found in every nook and cranny all the way to the rooftop garden. Amazing custom-made beds and elegantly appointed rooms mean a restful night's sleep is oh so close. More than lodging, enjoy the lower-level piano bar, restaurant, and shops. Candy, art, even wine and cheese are within easy reach.

☀ play

Plush red velvet–covered doors inside Eagles Theater are the first clue that something magical is about to take place. The two balconies pretty much seal the deal. Yes, there are three floors of seating inside this graceful and huge theater. Dressing rooms, offices, and a ballroom fill out the other three stories. Once upon a time, twelve hundred people could fit inside. Now, with space for not quite five hundred, and eight handicapped-accessible areas, a rather sizable crowd can still enjoy the latest movies on the cheap.

Large crowds gathered at the Wabash County Courthouse in 1880, heralding the new electric era to come. Step inside the stately courthouse that sits on top of a tall hill and see one of the original brush-arc lamps originally found on top of the courthouse. Excellent architectural details abound inside. Take note of the unique fire proofing in a room on the second floor.

Expecting display after dry display and signs of "Look, but don't touch" at the Wabash County Historical Museum? There are displays, all right, but everything here is interactive and engaging. Flip the switch and shed electric light over the courthouse. Pull the rope and hear the train whistle blow. Dig for fossils in the sand. Marvel at the miniature town and the hobby train track zipping through it. Hit the second floor for the rotating displays that change each month. Watch history come alive.

🍴 eat

When Mexican cuisine is the only thing that will do, try Aztecaz Mexican Grill. Downtown and oh so vibrant, all the standard favorites are here. Sip on something different—browse the extensive tequila menu. For meals, try the chicken and rice, garlic shrimp, tamales, or the chile rellenos.

Market Street Grill, Wabash.

Expect generous portions and excellent homemade food at Market Street Grill for those age twenty-one and up. Drunk'in Chicken (a buttermilk-soaked chicken sautéed in Sauternes wine and butter), burgers, barbecue ribs, and rib eyes are all popular. No matter how many courses have been consumed or how uncomfortably tight those pants have become, save room for pie. These aren't tiny little portions but slabs of creamy, fluffy, and delectable pie. The peanut butter pie is a Market Street Grill classic, and so too is the coconut cream, but really anything here is a win.

Elephants are on parade at Modoc's Market. Don't worry—this time they aren't rampaging. Back in 1942, the Great American Circus was setting up its last show of the season at Wabash High School. Barking dogs panicked Modoc, an Indian elephant, and away she went—right toward downtown Wabash. On her way she gulped down freshly baked pies cooling on a windowsill. Then she saw her: a woman leaving a building wearing a full-length raccoon-skin coat. Perhaps Modoc thought she was part of the act, for she followed the woman down the street, unbeknownst to her, until the woman opened the door of the Bradley Brothers Pharmacy. A glorious aroma filled the air: they roasted their own peanuts. Modoc rushed in, took out the door frame, and rolled a patron around on the floor, gobbling peanuts while frantic folks dodged out of the way, before she took off out the back door—frame and all. Across the way, two drunks sat in the bar. One of them happened to look over and saw an elephant's head. He proclaimed, "And that's the last drink I'm ever going to take." After five days, and losing eight hundred pounds, Modoc was finally captured. It's easy to see why elephant sculptures surround the sidewalks, are on a large painted exterior mural, and are seen all over the inside, too. Find a selection of coffees, teas, and snacks, both fresh and prepacked, inside this big memorabilia-filled shop.

Artistica Gallery and Woods Framing is the best of both worlds. One side, Woods Framing, focuses on all the essentials for any artist, professional or beginner. Paints, papers, pencils, custom framing, and even workshop space lie across from the traditional fine-art gallery—with quite a centerpiece. Dozens of local and regional artists' work in pottery, jewelry, sculptures, mixed-media pieces, and art glass are featured. Watch for special events scattered throughout the year.

Anyone who believes that antique shops are dusty and dirty needs to pop into the sparkling-clean Crow's Nest Antique Mall. Somewhere around thirty vendors contribute some of the most unique items. They could range from the large acquisition of a person-

Precious Gems and Metals, Wabash.

al collection containing 250 sad irons to an old-fashioned rocker washer. One thing is for sure: there are always terrific vintage items.

It doesn't get more hip than the Dorothy Ilene Gallery. Pieces of furniture are transformed into groovy usable items that add a punch of color to any room. Local artists stock their wares in everything from wall art to jewelry. Special events include live music and local wine. It's a terrific artsy hub.

Sparkling chandeliers, warm wood floors, and elegant decor at Ellen's A Dress to Impress mimic an upscale big-city boutique but with far more reasonable pricing. Racks of gently used and new dresses for cocktail parties, proms, and even weddings are available. It is a wonderful find for anyone celebrating a special occasion.

Want to save a buck and have fun in the process? Jack in the Box is a children's consignment shop that boasts more than one hundred thousand items and more than a thousand consigners. In other words: this place is so big, it has everything kids need (and even more that they don't). Clothes, toys, books, games, baby seats, swings, cribs . . . the list could go on and on. Although the vast majority are gently used items, there is a selection of

Reading Room Books, Wabash.

new clothing and shoes at the front of the mammoth shop.

Oh the shiny: Precious Gems and Metals is a classy jewelry store that's just full of amazing finds. Vintage brooches are attractively pinned to a fabric-covered board on the exposed brick wall. Glass cases contain precious gems and diamonds, while open shelving holds new jewelry for men and women. Buying and selling estate jewelry since 1979, this store has an eye for the beautiful.

Floor-to-ceiling shelves of used books await at Reading Room Books. Comfortable, cushy chairs are strategically positioned around the shop. For more than thirty-five years, this bookstore has kept locals well supplied. The selection of cookbooks and children's books is extensive and really well done.

Thriftalicious is kind of like the best part of a yard sale: it's everything there is to love about the hunt but without having to sift through all the castoffs. To think it all began as a Facebook page. The couple started selling things off the social networking site, expanding and growing enough to warrant a really large brick-and-mortar storefront right downtown. Furniture, books, even vintage video games are all within easy reach.

NOTABLES

Loren Murphy Berry (1988–1980), born and raised in Wabash, developed the *Yellow Pages*. During his younger years he even wrote for the local newspaper, the *Wabash Plain Dealer*.

Wabashian John W. Corso worked with John Hughes as the art director on 1980s classics such as *Ferris Buehler's Day Off, The Breakfast Club,* and *Sixteen Candles* (among others). He was nominated for an Academy Award for his work on *Coal Miner's Daughter* (1980) and received an Emmy Award for his direction of *Tales of the Gold Monkey.*

Electrical engineer (and Wabash-born) John P. Costas (1923–2008) invented the Costas loop and the Costas array.

Wabash-born Jimmy Daywalt (1924–1966) was the 1953 Indy 500 rookie of the year. He placed sixth.

Acting in more than fifty films, Charles Dingle (1887–1986) played the bad guy or, at least, no-nonsense businessman. His last stage appearance occurred in *The Immortalist* (1954)—and it was the last time on stage for James Dean as well.

Long-haired country singer Crystal Gayle (b. 1951) was raised in Wabash.

Offensive lineman Bobby Jones (1912–1999), Wabash born, was part of the Green Bay Packers in 1934.

Sticking closer to his Wabash home, Major League Baseball player George Joseph Mullin (1880–1944) pitched for the Detroit Tigers for fourteen years. He played for the Washington Senators in 1913 and then the Indianapolis Hoosiers (Newark Peppers) in the Federal League from 1914 to 1915. He once pinch-hit for Ty Cobb and got a triple.

A former middle-relief pinch hitter, Keith Wayne Shepherd (b. 1968) played from 1992 to 1996 for teams that included the Philadelphia Phillies, Colorado Rockies, Boston Red Sox, and Baltimore Orioles.

U.S. Army poster girl Margie Stewart (1919–2012), a Wabash native, appeared in a series of twelve posters during World War II, with ninety-four million copies distributed in order to encourage servicemen to buy war bonds. She even appeared in twenty RKO films, though her roles were often uncredited.

27

Wakarusa

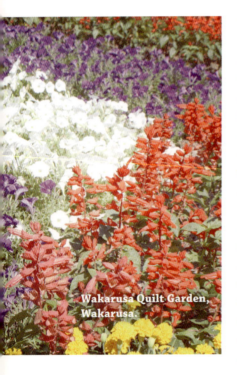

Wakarusa Quilt Garden, Wakarusa.

With another Salem already in Indiana, residents abandoned their first idea in favor of Wakarusa in 1859. No one knows where the name came from, but some believe it's a Native American word that means "knee deep in mud." Contrary to its origins, the short downtown is so charming.

Flowering baskets hang from vintage-looking lampposts. People stop on the sidewalks to chit-chat. It's all so pleasant. From the Wakarusa Bluegrass Festival held in June to the yearly spring Wakarusa Maple Syrup Festival, this small town looks for any excuse to get together and socialize.

☼ play

If the smell of flowers seems stronger than it seems possible, look for the Wakarusa Quilt Garden nearby, a free attraction. Volunteers carefully plant blooms to match the year's pattern. A hand-painted version stands nearby for comparison from the end of May to the beginning of October.

🍴 eat

Get the stromboli sandwich. There are other choices inside Cook's Pizza like, well, pizza, but the assortment of stromboli sandwiches with ham, pepperoni, sausage, or ground beef has made this tiny diner an area favorite. In true small-town style, local farmers were given a key to the place to let themselves in, make coffee, clean up, and lock up well before the usual business hours. It is part of what makes this such an ideal place to visit.

🛍 shop

Mom and Me Floral Boutique may sell fresh flowers, but the largest section of the shop holds antiques. Mostly pieces of furniture, dishware, a few primitives, and a gift section, there are a lot of interesting traditional pieces in excellent shape.

Feel like a kid again in Wakarusa Dime Store. Nostalgia candy like gummies, candy buttons, and Blackjack gum are hard to resist. But that's not what has made this 1907 small-town candy shop internationally known. No, it's all thanks to the giant jelly beans. Snacked on by President Ronald Reagan as a tool to stop smoking, they dwarf the traditional jelly bean. Offered in just as many flavors, there are typically samples available.

Most hardware stores don't have a place in a guide of things to see and do, but most hardware stores aren't Wakarusa Pro Hardware. This has been a hardware store since the turn of the century, and it's as obvious as the doors in the wall. An entire section of wall holds floor-to-ceiling drawers of all shapes and sizes. Some have marker scrawled across the front that lists the contents inside. Others have product taped to the outside, and still others are a mystery. The narrow hundred-year-old ladder

Cook's Pizza, Wakarusa.

Wakarusa Pro Hardware, Wakarusa.

helps employees reach the tippy-top. It's a nonenviable aspect of the job, but a really neat slice of Indiana history.

In the mood for a bit of antiquing? How about a lot of antiquing? Two buildings hold antiques at Yoder Brothers Mercantile. In this shop that was once a department store, the last hand-operated freight elevator in town is near the back. It's closed off, so politely ask for a peek. At the front of Yoder Brothers, notice where the wood dips a little where the department-store register sat for decades. Note also where the wood flooring is worn smooth from the feet of clerks over decades of pacing. The basement holds an embalming table . . . but that's a story for a different day.

NOTABLES

Feeling a big rush of patriotism at the start of the Civil War, some Wakarusa residents, according to legend, left farm implements and even a plow in the field in their rush to join the war effort.

Gale Sayers (b. 1943), former running back, was a career player for the Chicago Bears from 1960 to 1969. Sayers's autobiography was turned into the movie *Brian's Song* in tribute to Brian Piccolo, a fellow player and friend who lost his battle with cancer.

28

Walkerton

Corner Cup Café, Walkerton.

Founded by LaPorte resident James H. Walker in 1856, the banker responsible for construction of the Cincinnati, Peru, and Chicago Railway, the town itself was actually plotted by railroad surveyors. It took three tries before Walkerton became an incorporated town in 1877. An old Native American path served as the street for the first general store, owned by Charles William N. Stephens, in Walkerton. Doing business for forty years (while also serving as town postmaster), Stephens, it is said, took in more than thirteen hundred dollars in one day. Even in today's terms, that was a busy small business. He is credited with expanding the town of Walkerton. Things are a little quieter now.

☼ play

The Heritage House Museum is the repository for town images, artifacts, and collections of oral and written histories. Situated inside a donated 1885 home used as a doctor's office for thirty-eight years, it also handles Walkerton and North Liberty newspaper articles on microfilm.

Annette Hester's family, the LeBlancs, settled the area in 1832. Now Hester's Log Cabins becomes a site for historical reenactments and turns into a campground for the crowd. The Spring Fling each May celebrates pre-1840 life. The June Berry Feis is an event celebrating medieval times to 1840, Freedom Fest is during the Fourth of July, and the Fall Americana 1800 is an annual October event that again exhibits pre-1840 life. Tour Hester's Log Cabins: outbuildings that resemble a one-room school, an Irish family's home, the big barn, and the old cabin.

Locals hurry in for home-cooked food from this mother-and-daughter team at Corner Cup Café, open for breakfast and lunch. The dozens of flavors of coffee, panini sandwiches, and homemade desserts change with the seasons to keep things fresh. As if that weren't enough, there are Indiana-made chocolates, too.

The kitchen is the heart of the home and should have the decor to match. The New Kitchen Store carries absolutely everything needed for cooking, baking, and decorating. From linens to glassware to cookbooks to gadgets, there's no doubt that it is here. Cooking classes teach various international flavors like French or Italian techniques throughout the year.

NOTABLES

Chad Blount (b. 1979), a Walkerton native, has driven in the Nextel Cup Series, the Busch/Nationwide Series, and the Craftsman Truck Series. He is the winner of eight Automobile Racing Club of America races.

Walter LaFeber (b. 1933) is a Walkerton-born noted author and a Marie Underhill Noll Professor Emeritus of History and was a Stephen H. Weiss Presidential Fellow in the Department of History at Cornell University until his retirement in 2006. He has served on many scholarly boards and organizations.

Harold C. Urey (1893–1981), the winner of the 1934 Nobel Prize in Chemistry for his discovery of deuterium, was born in Walkerton.

29

Wheatfield

JT's Shrimp Farm, Wheatfield.

There's more than corn in Indiana; there's also wheat. Wheatfield was most likely named for its location in the Wheat Belt. Wheatfield was laid out in the 1880s around the Plymouth, Kankakee, and Pacific Railroad line, later known as the Indiana, Illinois, and Iowa line. Fewer than nine hundred people make Wheatfield their home. There is, however, one giant fall festival that celebrates the arrival of flocks of annual visitors: the sandhill cranes. The yearly Sandhill Crane Festival and Car Show holds all the usual booths and food vendors. More than one hundred cars alone turn out for the car show. Live entertainment and plenty to do for the kiddos create a memorable small-town day.

☼ play

Jasper County's only shrimp farm, and one of but a few in the state, JT's Shrimp Farm offers fresh, chemical-free saltwater shrimp year-round. This agritourism business allows individuals and groups to tour the shrimp barn for a nominal fee. Nine pools capable of housing six thousand shrimp provide plenty of tasty, quality shrimp for everyone.

¶¶ eat

Huge and savory, the garlic rolls at Marcella's Pizzeria are fairly dripping with real minced garlic and butter. Fresh ingredients are the key ingredient here, so pile the toppings over thin-crust or Chicago-style pizza. Specialties include the Mama Mia, the Philly cheesesteak pizza with homemade alfredo sauce, or the fresh margherita pizza. Nibble on sandwiches, pastas, soups, and salads. Indoor and outdoor seating, a beer and wine menu, plus homemade chocolate cake make Marcella's Pizzeria one delicious dining option.

The folks at Schnick's Good Eats, located in the old downtown, know their way around a kitchen. The beef Manhattan and meat loaf are popular items, but the Italian beef is really something. To locals, no meal is considered complete without the peach cobbler. The cobbler is a consistent sellout, but new batches are frequently churned out during the day. Take advantage of the outdoor seating. Enclosed and shaded, it's a lovely space.

30

Williamsport

The first resident, William Harrison, founded the town of Williamsport. In order to boost his ferry business, he created a short canal, giving the town the nickname Side-Cut City. When the western portion of the town was opened up to public sale of lots, the county joined in the celebration, footing the bill for free whiskey.

☼ play

Indiana's tallest free-flowing waterfall, Williamsport Falls, happens to be right downtown. There's a bit of grumbling regarding the "tallest" status, but at ninety feet high, it certainly sounds impressive. At times, it is. Farming has changed the landscape and turned the falls into more of a trickle at times. Sometimes, it doesn't

Williamsport Falls, Williamsport.

even do that, earning it the unfortunate nickname of "Dry Falls." To see it in action, time visits for after a rainstorm or the snowmelt. The overlook area is covered and complete with seating.

NOTABLES

James Frank Hanly (1863–1920), the 1905–1909 governor of Indiana, was a vocal supporter of Prohibition and vehemently against gambling and political corruption. Once a Williamsport resident, he had a law office downtown for twenty years, from 1879 to 1896. His grave site is in Williamsport's Hillside Cemetery. Look for it on the northeast side of town.

31

Wolcott

A series of horrible fires in 1969 left Wolcott residents gloomy and on edge. A few folks remembered the fun of the 1961 centennial and decided to re-create that same spirit with Summer Fest, a delightful Fourth of July celebration. It's not hard to miss: it spans the lawn surrounding stately Wolcott House as well as Town Park. Toes tap to live music performances, while delicious smells waft from food booths interspersed around a paved track. Contests and activities are centrally positioned between the park and the home. Locals always gather for the big fireworks show, ending with a band.

☀ play

The top-level observatory of the Anson Wolcott House is impressive. Construction began in 1859 by the founder of the town but was not finished until after the Civil War. Originally a lawyer, Anson Wolcott once appeared in front of the New York Supreme Court and the U.S. Supreme Court. But Indiana land was calling. Purchasing two thousand acres, he succeeded in arranging a railroad and plotted the town, all by 1861. Featuring curved walls and eight fireplaces (though not in the maid's quarters), it may be toured by appointment. Left to the town by the grandson of Anson Wolcott, it has been actively restored since the mid-1970s.

🍴 eat

Piping-hot pizza with all the fixings is readily available at Bell's Pizza. What's more, they've got the wings, sandwiches, and even ice cream to go with it. Rather than the usual breadsticks, Bell's Pizza does something a little different that's just fantastic: fried puffs of pizza dough. Soft and satisfying, they are delicious dipped in the accompanying cheese sauce. It's kind of like having a taste of the county fair all year-round.

Situated in front of what was the old movie theater, Wolcott Theater Café is conveniently located downtown. Daily features include changing specials, but the star of the show has got to be the homemade pies. At this favorite diner with the locals, try the counter seating to join in the chatter.

Wolcott House, Wolcott.

shop

Everything is positioned just so inside Timeless Treasures. Groupings of like items enchant in the nooks of this two-story building. Shabby-chic gifts, vintage items, new home decor, and a section of things for the garden, including iron items and glass globes, dazzle in eye-catching arrangements.

NOTABLES

Back in 1923, while on a road trip, a family lost their two-year-old Scotch collie and English shepherd mix in Wolcott. Returning to Oregon, they were shocked when, six months later, their dog, thin and with paws worn to the bone, appeared at their doorstep. Bobbie the Dog traveled between twenty-five and twenty-eight hundred miles of mountains, plains, and even desert during the winter to return to his family. Now that's loyalty.

Central Indiana

32

Arcadia

Founded in 1849, Arcadia has a unique history surrounding glass. When natural gas was found during the gas-boom age, Arcadia was thriving. With what seemed like a never-ending supply of gas, D. C. Jenkins opened a second sister business to his Kokomo factory in downtown Arcadia in 1894. Known for wearing white flannel suits and donating large quantities of glassware to churches, he even ran for Senate, so the rumor goes.

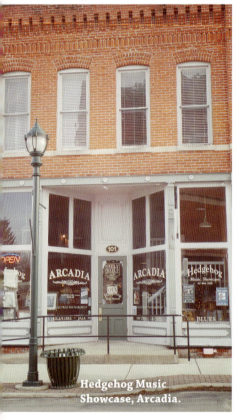

Hedgehog Music Showcase, Arcadia.

Chipped or uneven products, anything not up to retail standards, were sent home with workers. Many residents have stories to tell about that one. But all good things must come to an end. The gas ran out, and the business went under in the 1930s. The business long since abandoned, the glass vat and furnace are both still visible today.

☀ play

Facing demolition in the 1970s, the 1869 depot was moved and is now home to the tidy Arcadia Arts and Heritage Depot, off the downtown. Once used as a town library, the compact building now houses old documents, images, and artifacts. Arcadia

Glass sparkles everywhere. Case after case of glass highlight patterns, many of which are labeled, from the glory days of the town.

Some pretty big names and even Grammy Award winners have performed within the doors of Hedgehog Music Showcase, boasting live music every weekend. Expect a variety of music genres, from country to jazz to swing. Reasonably priced, it's an up-close and personal live show.

🛍 shop

Hartley's Interiors and Antiques occupies an enormous building. Antique linens, books, and toys are nicely priced. Although antiques occupy a decent portion, a full half of the first floor is devoted to furniture. The entire upstairs level contains rooms of furniture as well. Stunning vintage headboards are also tucked away upstairs.

Arcadia Arts and Heritage Depot, Arcadia.

Nationally renowned, Tabby Tree Weaver is a fiber-arts destination. Owner Linda Adamson began sewing when she didn't want to wear the same clothing as everyone else. Weaving and spinning ensure individuality. Glittering, hand-painted, or dyed, the yarns run the gamut. Spinning wheels and looms are up for sale. Workshops are offered for a variety of subjects like weaving rugs, felting, and even wool dyeing.

33

Battle Ground

Eye Opener Café, Battle Ground.

Those bypassing tiny Battle Ground in favor of the nearby city of Lafayette may want to think again. This town, with a population not even fifteen hundred strong, once played a pivotal role in the conflict between Native Americans and settlers. The Shawnee brothers, Tecumseh and the Prophet, were working to get tribes to band together and fight the settlers. But not if the government could stop them first.

Tensions ran high. William Henry Harrison gathered together a group of soldiers to deal with the Native American attacks on settlers. General Harrison arranged a visit with representatives of the Prophet with a list of demands from the government. There was to be a discussion the next day, but General Harrison didn't believe it. Informed by Harrison to sleep with their uniforms on, the men set up camp, complete with night guards to keep on the alert. Before dawn, the Native Americans launched a massive surprise attack. After a raging battle, the Native Americans were defeated. The Battle of Tippecanoe was the turning point, marking nearly the end of the Native American wars in the Midwest.

 play

View more than fifty long guns and rifles on display at the Tippecanoe Battlefield and Museum. Though they don't seem to pertain specifically to the period of the Battle of Tippecanoe, it is impressive nonetheless. A lot of plaques and information are found inside the museum and out.

Wolf Park is a behavioral research facility with an emphasis on education and conservation. Open to the public, Howl Night is an impressive evening program. In addition to hearing an interesting lecture, complete with a question-and-answer session, visitors are encouraged to howl and listen, as wolves in various packs around the preserve respond. Day tours offer guided sessions to look at the red foxes, gray foxes, coyotes, and bison also located in the habitat.

Shoup House Antiques, Battle Ground.

🍴 eat

The Eye Opener Café is cash only, but with that kind of inexpensive pricing, it's easy. Dine on a Saturday morning and listen to local music playing while munching on breakfast favorites like homemade biscuits and gravy, Steph's Stacker, or pancakes. It's nothing fancy, but everyone is chatty, local papers sit on a table in the center, and it is nigh impossible to leave hungry.

🛍 shop

Step inside the 1860 built Shoup House Antiques and expect to stay for a long while. There are so many rooms of the most beautiful antiques and things, anyone in search of home decor, primitives, and furniture has never had it so good. Each room is wonderfully themed, but locals say that to really see it shine, a holiday visit should be in order.

34

Cambridge City

Huddleston House, Cambridge City.

Cambridge City is part of the National Antique Trail for a reason. Delightful storefronts contain one antique shop after another. Propped-open doors tease at what is inside. Surprisingly, even with so many shops in one area, they differ greatly from one another.

A canal and railroad town, both contributed to Cambridge City's past growth. Join in celebrating this canal heritage with the yearly Canal Days Festival. A five-kilometer walk or run, golf tournament, fishing contest, volleyball tournament, and even gospel tournament are a few of the events during previous years. With more than forty years of Canal Days fun, every year just gets better.

🛏 stay

The Lehman House is so beautifully renovated that it doesn't seem possible it dates back to 1836. Two comfortable guest suites with private baths are available. Relax in the common area downstairs or the flower-filled courtyard. Be sure to stop inside the carriage house turned antique shop known as the Courtyard Studio, a welcome sight for any shopper.

☀ play

Most libraries don't possess a museum, but most libraries aren't the Cambridge City Public Library. Well lit and protected in glass-front cabinets, Overbeck Pottery was made between 1911 and 1955. It is the work of four of the five Overbeck sisters. Using a pottery wheel or hand-built methods (some of which show finger marks) and original glazes, they focused on quality, producing only a few hundred pieces annually. Find oodles of objects in the grotesque style by the Overbeck sisters in the basement.

Long-ago pioneers once trudged past the eighty-acre Huddleston Farmhouse built in 1841. Some pulled in to the farm for a break. After all, the farm was built with just such a purpose in mind. Folks traveling the Historic National Road found a restful and free stopping point, as pioneers were welcomed into the home of John and Susannah Huddleston (and their eleven children). Even the barn was open to travelers and their animals. Ramble through the first floor of the old farmhouse, furnished with some of the Huddlestons' original possessions. Downstairs, excellent interactive exhibits detail travel along the Historic National Road. The old barn is currently used for art. Time visits with the seasonal farmers market that occurs in the parking lot of the Huddleston Farmhouse Museum for a well-rounded destination.

Lumpy's Café, Cambridge City.

¶¶ eat

One amazing breaded pork tenderloin sandwich is found at Lumpy's Café. Bigger than the bun and almost as big as a dinner plate, it's crisp, crunchy, hand cut, and tender. In fact, one regular loves Lumpy's pork tenderloin sandwich so much that he stops by with a cooler before continuing to Florida for the winter to fill it up with thirty sandwiches for a taste of home, anytime. This is a family destination, and toys, coloring books, and crayons will keep kids busy and entertained.

Hilltop Drive-In might carry a selection of ice cream concoctions, but it holds its own when it comes to real food. Locals point to the chicken cutlet and the breaded pork tenderloin for those wanting a lunch or dinner option. But flurries, ice cream and topping swirled together, are irresistible. One look at the menu, and it is easy to see why: chocolate-covered cherry, turtlette, and peanut butter cup are but a small sampling of popular flavors.

The old No. 9 Lodge has been given new life as the No. 9 Grill. This lively atmosphere has a beer and wine menu. Burgers (like the Blues Burger) or steak are excellent entrées. Arrive early to avoid a long wait. More parking is located behind the building.

🛍 shop

Pull into the gas station turned Amish Cheese Shop since 1983. Although not Amish owned, this family business does source more than sixty cheeses that are made using Amish cows' milk. Refrigerators span the walls to hold not only the cheeses but sample cups and toothpicks as well. At the Amish Cheese Shop, samples are encouraged. Memorable flavors include blueberry cheddar cheese, smoked horseradish cheese, Danish dill havarti, and two-year-old Swiss cheese. Be sure to try the green onion. Browse the jars of pickles and relishes, the jams and jellies, and Indiana products like honey and maple syrup.

A place for everything and everything in its place seems to be the motto for sparkling-clean Building 125. Designed to mimic a series of country-themed rooms, the store's tables, chairs, beds, and other furniture capture the imagination of anyone with a decorating bug. The primitives here are unbeatable.

At more than one hundred years old, Indiana's oldest (and maybe even only) stuffed chihuahua is on display at the Doublehead Trading Company. That's just a hint of the type of unique items found inside. Believed to be the largest collection of Ball jars anywhere, they occupy an entire room. Vintage

Doublehead Trading Company, Cambridge City.

doorknobs, bicycles, furniture, jewelry—there's plenty here to peruse, pick through, and admire.

Dusty Rusty Stuff, previously This 'n That Antiques, is located in the former Howard Funeral Home building. It may have had a name change, but it still holds the varied range of neat antiques and primitives. Don't miss the Picking Room in the back that's chock-full of items ready for a little TLC.

The aisles might not always be the easiest to get through, but any shopper can forgive the squeeze when it's due to vintage finds like the ones at Hole in the Wall Antiques. It's all within reach, too, with these wallet-friendly prices.

Standing out on the main drag, Log Cabin Antiques occupies an actual log cabin that dates back to the 1800s. There's a lot of history within these walls, for this building has had a variety of purposes—including a stint as one of the earliest inns in Wayne County. Today, explore two floors and a basement of excellent antiques plus Indiana art and gifts.

Composed of more than eighty-five vendors, the National Trail Antique Mall will keep shoppers busy. There are more than twenty thousand postcards alone. That's just the beginning inside this sprawling antique shop. Visitors have two floors to peruse.

Once perfectly positioned between the former intersection of the National Road (U.S. 40) and the Whitewater Canal, the former three-story hotel turned Vinton House Antiques is amazing. Two floors of antiques are displayed in the gorgeous 1847 building. When it comes to shopping, primitives are in no short supply. Baskets of vintage wooden blocks, crocks of wooden spoons, pottery, baskets, and a small-town museum on the third floor result in plenty to see and explore.

NOTABLES

Move over Buffalo Bill, Buffalo Ben (1843–1884) is in town. Otherwise known as Benjamin Stalker, this resident hosted a Wild West show that toured the country. When not shooting his rifle or performing tricks in the saddle for crowds, he and his troupe wintered in Cambridge City. His entire family, including all six children, appeared in the show. Drawing on the skills Buffalo Ben learned while growing up in the West, the show toured for more than twenty years.

Born in the town, Larry Crockett (1926–1955) participated in Indy car racing for ten starts in 1954. That same year he qualified for the Indy 500, finished ninth, and was named rookie of the year. Sadly, he was killed while racing at Pennsylvania Langhorne Speedway early the next year.

Recruiting men for a volunteer regiment of infantry, Solomon Meredith (1810–1875) became the first colonel of the Nineteenth Indiana—though he lacked military experience. Meredith eventually became commander and part of the Iron Brigade of the Army of the Potomac, leading men into the Battle of Gettysburg. Losing a campaign to win a seat in the U.S. House of Representatives in 1864, he instead became a surveyor of Montana for a few years before returning home to his Cambridge City farm. Known for raising award-winning cattle, horses, and sheep, he lived a quiet life until his death in 1875. He is buried at Riverside Cemetery.

Single G (1910–1940) was a harness racehorse that raced for fourteen consecutive seasons before retiring. During his racing days, the Cambridge City–born horse placed in 418 of the 434 heats, accumulating more than one hundred thousand dollars in prize money—more than any other pacer in harness history. Find his larger-than-life mural downtown.

35

Centerville

Cannon hole at old Wayne County Courthouse, Centerville.

B arely twenty-five hundred people live here, yet it boasts a surprising number of buildings on the National Historic Register. Platted back in 1814, Centerville was deemed quite the up-and-coming town—and fit to be the county seat. That didn't sit well with folks of the (now nonexistent) town of Salisbury. They dished out a challenge: build a courthouse better than this one, and we'll go along with the switch. Centerville got to work, but when officials were comparing courthouses, Salisbury wouldn't let them inside. So they resorted to a bit of math. By counting the courthouse bricks, they could see which one truly stacked up. Centerville won, and the county seat was moved in 1818. But in 1873, Richmond decided that it should grab control of the county seat. Centerville residents were angered and locked themselves inside the courthouse to prevent Richmond folks from hijacking the official county records. Centerville citizens then fired a cannon toward the outsiders standing in the courthouse doorway. The door was blown from its hinges, but fortunately (and surprisingly) no one was hurt. Soldiers were brought in the next day to oversee the relocation. The records were taken, and the county seat was officially moved. To physically see this bit of history, look for the hole from "Black Betty" above the door.

That's not the only unique bit of history found in Centerville. The architecture here is different from anywhere else in the

Centerville Arches.

state. Two hundred wagons a day traveled on the Historic National Road, U.S. 40, that runs right through Centerville as they headed west. Originally one hundred feet wide, the main drag was shortened to sixty-five feet when locals added on to the front of their homes. To avoid the dust and dirt of the pioneer path, residents created archways in 1823 and 1826. These single archways lead to lovely backyards and, in some cases, are double arches just the right size for a horse. Known as the "City of Arches," Centerville's five archways may be viewed within a few blocks of each other. Grab a town map from area merchants and hit the sidewalk.

☀ play

Cemeteries aren't typically destinations, but in the case of Doddridge Chapel and Cemetery, exceptions have to be made. On the National Register of Historic Places, it's quite scenic. Although the current Italianate church wasn't constructed until 1876, Christians once worshipped here, with their Native American neighbors, all the way back in 1814 when a small group of pioneers from Pennsylvania (including a six-week-old baby born along the way) decided to end their journey and put down roots. Feeling more comfortable outside, the Native Americans would gather around to listen. Pioneers and the Native Americans are both buried here. Native American graves are at the western edge of the cemetery.

Americana Pizza is where locals celebrate sports victories and birthdays. The "Americana" pizza is really loaded: green peppers, hamburger, pepperoni, sausage, onions, mushrooms, and black olives are generously scattered across this crust. Park it outside and watch Main Street go by.

Pastries, cookies, donuts, homemade fudge—it's all made here at Cinnamon Spice Bakery. Have a seat outside in the rocking chairs or pick a table. Don't forget an apple fritter.

People watchers will love the location of Stone Hearth Café— it's right in the middle of the Warm Glow Candle Company Outlet Store. The economic downturn threatened the survival of this business, originally located downtown. In a stroke of luck, Warm Glow offered Stone Hearth Café the opportunity to move in with them. It's been a great match ever since. As their own entity, this café dishes out excellent homemade entrees. Order the pizza or the family-recipe beef brisket. Save room for a towering slice of the choco loco cake or the coconut cream pie.

shop

The Centerville Antique Mall, formerly known as Webb's Antique Mall, spans eighty-five thousand square feet. Once an old casket factory, it's now the perfect place for an antique shopper on the hunt. Expect more vintage items and less flea market–type finds from the more than five hundred vendors.

The Enchanted Sleigh might sound like a seasonal decor shop, but

Cinnamon Spice Bakery, Centerville.

there's more to this shop than the name implies. Two daughters are heralded for their differing artistic talents, such as papier-mâché, folk art, and painting, easily keeping their mother's shop well stocked. It is also the home of Bear, the sweet shelter-rescued Maine coon and ragamuffin-mix cat who would love attention.

In an 1835 home turned cozy antique shop, explore inviting rooms of engaging items at Mockingbird Antiques. Rare and vintage books are in abundance. So, too, are beautiful pieces of furniture and smaller items like cameras, clothing, and art.

Admire the usable objects like bowls, vases, and plates from Scott Shafer's Stoneware Pottery Studio. Nationally known and recognized for his work and making pottery for more than thirty years, he certainly knows a thing or two. Hand thrown, every piece is one of a kind. The airy, light studio is a definite boon to the town. Look for the short sign out front that reads "Shafer Pottery."

Not exactly a small business anymore, but still made in Indiana, the Warm Glow Candle Company Outlet Store isn't hard to miss, not with the presence of the world's largest candle. Inside, more than eleven thousand square feet are full of more than seventy different scents. But it's not all hand-dipped candles. Discover home decor here, too. The Watering Can, an adjacent building, is everything garden.

Restoring or renovating a historic property? White River Architectural Salvage and Antiques includes scads of fireplace mantles, some with an opening taller than the average man, light fixtures from all periods, tables, cabinets, cupboards, and so much more. Children will receive the choice of a noisy toy. If adults get caught up in browsing, children can't really wander when it is so easy to hear them. The potential for accidents is reduced, and kids get a new plaything. That's a win-win—and so, too, are the quality of items found here.

NOTABLES

Bloomberg Businessweek deemed Centerville the best place to raise children in 2011.

John A. Burbank (1827–1905), Centerville native, became the fourth territorial governor of North Dakota. He was not popular with the people due in part to leaving the state too often and for a scandal involving the railroad. Returning to Indiana, he became the U.S. post office inspector in Richmond.

Born and raised in Centerville, Major League Baseball pitcher Barry Louis Jones (b. 1963) racked up 250 strikeouts over the course of his career. Before retiring in 1993, Jones played for (in order) the Pittsburgh Pirates, Chicago White Sox, Montreal Expos, Philadelphia Phillies, and New York Mets.

"Uncompromising" was one word used to describe Centerville-born politician George Washington Julian (1817–1899). A member of the U.S. House of Representatives from Indiana's Fourth and Fifth Districts in the mid- to late 1800s, he was loudly opposed to slavery, was once a vice presidential nominee, and adamantly called for the hanging of former Confederate leaders after the Civil War.

The territories of New Mexico and Arizona were not going to be turned into one large state if Centerville-born sixteenth territorial governor of Arizona Joseph Henry Kibbey (1853–1924) had anything to say about it. But the title that made Kibbey most proud was that of "judge." After studying law in his father's Indiana law office, Kibbey became associate justice in the Arizona Territorial Supreme Court and preferred that title to any other.

36

Cicero

10 West, Cicero.

Founded in 1835, Cicero may have received its name in a unique though seldom-remembered way. A surveyor had brought his son along as he was surveying the area. His son went to drink water out of the creek when he somehow fell in and drenched himself. His father named the creek Cicero Creek in teasing. Later, the town was named for the creek, so it too is named for the boy who only wanted a drink of water.

 play

Between the small town of Cicero and the city of Noblesville, Morse Reservoir provides a bit of lakeside fun. Boating and swimming are allowed in the man-made seventeen-hundred-acre lake in specific places.

eat

Incredibly stylish for a small town, 10 West glitters. With a restaurant on one side and a bar on the other, it is a fabulous dining destination. In true Hoosier fashion with a twist, the bacon-wrapped pork tenderloin is worth a try. Dessert is eye appealing and palate pleasing no matter what the option.

Alexander's on the Water has so many flavors of hard-packed ice cream that it is hard to make a quick decision. Homemade waffle cones are a delightful addition to the menu. There are kid sizes and a dog dip, vanilla ice cream in a cone, or a cup for hot pups.

It's not every coffee shop that leaves visitors raving about not only their coffee but also their sandwiches. Nevertheless, that's the way it is at Cicero Coffee Company. The applejack, a turkey, colby cheese, and apple sandwich, is really good. Coffees from around the world are represented. Daily flavors may change, but the classic salted caramel and the always available Columbian supremo are wonderful.

Mornings shine a little brighter at Erika's Place. Breakfast items like the Greek omelet and Joe's Frying Pan are great, although locals really dig the fried bologna. Conversation is encouraged and friendliness a staple.

Lake views are easy when there's an abundance of windows like at Lazy Frogg. Attentive service makes for a sensational start, and so do the appetizers like bacon-wrapped jumbo prawns and roast-chicken nachos. Follow it up with the black-and-blue burger or the fish and chips. It's a supremely satisfying meal.

shop

Leaving the corporate world behind, the owners of Upscale Junk and Antiques have decided that vintage items are the only way to go. Occupying an immense space, the store offers a huge range of vendors that each seems to have its own special focus. Put it together and it is one incredible browsing experience.

NOTABLES

"The Kids Are All Right" episode from television's Supernatural series was set in Cicero.

AIDS activist Ryan White (1971–1990) is buried at Cicero Cemetery.

Lazy Frogg, Cicero.

Lazy Frogg, Cicero.

Upscale Junk and Antiques, Cicero.

37

Covington

Official formation of the town and achieving county-seat status marked 1826 as a busy first year for the town of Covington. After completion of the courthouse a year later, the murmurings of discontent with its current noncentral location in Covington grew louder. In fact, an 1831 act demanded relocation of the courthouse. The matter was talked over by both sides, but the arrival of the railroads quickly ended the issue of inconvenience and Covington got to keep their county-seat status.

Locals still take advantage of their courthouse square by throwing Apple Fest, an annual one-day event each autumn. Local bands play, events are organized, and everyone has a chance to gather together outdoors before the cold of winter sets in.

Snoddy's Mill, Covington.

☼ play

Not every small town has the foresight to save and reuse its more unique features. The Circle Trail Bridge system, however, incorporates a bridge that's more than a century old on the 3.2-mile trail. This bridge, known as a Pratt pony truss, once spanned the East Fork of Coal Creek. Eventually, six miles of smooth, paved, handicapped-accessible trail will encircle the town, creating a family-friendly path for a variety of uses.

The Fountain County Clerk's Building was once the office of author Lew Wallace. With the construction of a new courthouse, the building was obsolete and sold as a private home. It was then moved on logs two blocks down the street in 1859. It now houses pieces of the original "yard of bricks" from the more than three million pavers used to craft the 1909 Indianapolis 500 track (manufactured in nearby Veedersburg), notes on the cost of Fountain County travel by road in 1826, and a coverlet from the only nineteenth-century professional coverlet weaver, Sarah LaTourette.

Inspired by Nature
Sand Bar Indoor Beach,
Covington.

Essentially unchanged, the Fountain County Courthouse is a marvelous example of Art Deco architecture. Built from 1936 to 1937, the courthouse cost $246,734 for a design by Louis R. Johnson, from Fountain County, and Walter Scholer, of Lafayette. Scholer is well known for his design work on buildings around Lafayette and even the Purdue campus. The courthouse's flourishes, like those above the heavy strong doors, were crafted with Rostone, a synthetic substance used for the places between the pillars. Inside, murals specifically designed for the courthouse by nationally recognized artist and sculptor Covington-born Eugene Savage cover every wall. In fact, more than twenty-five hundred square feet of murals are found within the courthouse doors. Coincide visits with government hours to get inside.

Marrying a farmer who doesn't like to take vacations made this small-biz owner get resourceful. Inspired by Nature Sand Bar Indoor Beach is the only one of its kind in the entire United States. Hauling in sixty-three tons of sand, this small business owner turned an empty building into an indoor beach—and brought the beach to her. Complete with sand toys, beach volleyball, and specially themed events, search the sand for shells, shark teeth, and starfish for freebie souvenirs. What color shell will Edward the hermit crab choose today?

🍴 eat

It seems as though the entire town of Covington could dine at once inside the huge Beef House restaurant. Its famous homemade yeast rolls were made for slathering on berry preserves or apple butter. Steaks are cooked over hardwood briquettes on an open-hearth charcoal broiler in plain view. Tip: steaks are unseasoned, so consider giving them a dash of salt to up the flavor. Those on a budget may want to go for lunch.

Snoddy's Mill, Covington.

Snoddy's Mill hand-breads one of the most amazing pork tenderloin sandwiches ever invented. Add a slice of homemade peanut butter pie for a transcendent meal. Ample space inside—and out.

Mimicking an old-fashioned ice cream parlor, the seasonal Sundae Shop is so cute inside. Offering hard-packed and soft-serve ice cream, there are different flavors on special. Peanut butter cup razzles are always a good idea. Consider it for a light lunch, too.

🛍 shop

Off of Highway 136 lies a sign with an arrow pointing the way to Covington Antique Company. This country store occupies a huge heated barn. Books and glassware, as well as toys and memorabilia, are numerous. It's a fine beginning or end to a day spent in Covington.

Hand-picked antiques lie in wait inside the elegant renovated building that houses Glorie Bee Antiques. The owner, a choosy picker, makes sure only the best of the best makes it inside. Sometimes she even knows the stories behind the items, like the case of a dresser from Virginia that was brought to Indiana via covered wagon. Search through lace collars and cameos, pretty portraits, and lovely china.

Nothing smells better than the candles inside Holly's Scent-Sations. More than forty fragrances keep boredom at bay. Made of soy, her all-natural product line also includes melts, deodorant, soaps, and lotions. It's all made in the United States—and many of them are Indiana made.

Hue carries quite the range of packaged foods, including pastas and seasoning. The bottled beverages, however, are a bit unusual and certain to elicit a laugh, what with names like "Kitty Piddle."

The site of Jake's Farm served as the local hardware and implements store more than a hundred years ago. Now it's a shop devoted to all things repurposed and gently used, specializing in vintage furniture and everything that goes with it. See what a little cleaning and sometimes even a bit of paint can do.

NOTABLES

Edward Hannigan (1807–1859) was a presidential hopeful . . . and a longtime alcoholic. When his brother-in-law approached him regarding the effect his drinking could have on his budding political career (he was a U.S. representative and later a senator), Hannigan exploded, grabbed a cane dagger, and killed the man. This occurred on the steps of the white house across from the Methodist church downtown. Needless to say, his political career was over, although it took him a few years to realize it.

Lew Wallace (1827–1905), general, eleventh governor of New Mexico Territory (1878–1881), U.S. minister to the Ottoman Empire (1881–1885), and author, was a Covington resident from 1832 to 1837, relocating to Indianapolis when his father became governor. After becoming an adult, he moved back to Covington in 1849 and opened up a law firm. It is where he would live for the next five years. Some believe he penned his first novel, *The Fair God*, during his time in the town.

38

Cutler

John A. Cook laid out the town in 1871 during construction of the Logansport Crawfordsville and Southwestern Rail Road. Trees, hills, and curvy roads are the constant beautiful backdrop of this unincorporated town.

☀ play

Post-and-beam construction, hand-hewn logs, and shaved wood pegs make up the Adams Mill, built in 1845. For more than a hundred years, Adams Mill produced flour. Up until a big flood in 2003, it was still operational. Remarkably preserved, three of the four floors are open for tours. There are scads of items left over from the mill's productive years as well as other period pieces. Time visits for one of the music-filled, canoe-riding, kid-friendly events.

Adams Mill, Cutler.

Adams Mill, Cutler.

39

Danville

Daniel Clark built a log cabin on the future site of Danville in 1824. Four men each provided twenty acres of land to form the beginnings of the town. Driving a stake into the ground where the parcels met became the site of the Hendricks County Courthouse. Other settlers began pouring in, so much so that it justified the building of a school. Officially laid out the same year, the town's name is a mystery. Although the town was marshy in spots, its beauty kept drawing new settlers in. Danville was off to a roaring beginning, and it hasn't stopped since.

Hendricks County Courthouse, Danville.

Those soggy days are over. Danville has a walkable downtown that was made for festivals. Danville holds the Short Film Festival each year, the only one of its kind in the Midwest. Summers also bring the Mayberry in the Midwest Festival, two-days of Andy Griffith Show–themed fun. There is always something going on.

stay

The Marmalade Sky Bed-and-Breakfast is nothing if not comfortable. Each room of the 1860s home boasts a different style, reflecting the personalities of the couple's four daughters who grew up within its walls. Close to downtown and a local park, the bed-and-breakfast conveniently enables visitors to do as much, or as little, as they desire.

☀ play

Seasonally open, Beasley's Orchard began with tomatoes sold out of a little red wagon next to U.S. 36. Now, it's a massive operation. The barn, built shortly after the Civil War, features peg-and-beam construction. It holds an awesome retail market and a cider mill. Look for the Heartland Apple Festival, held the first two weekends in October, or Christmas at the Orchard, an old-fashioned event that features arts-and-crafts booths and Santa.

The Twin Bridges are not the easiest place to visit. An iron bridge built in 1877 once spanned the space the concrete bridge now occupies. Built in 1906, the mammoth concrete bridge replaced the much smaller iron bridge. Some say that this is the portion of the smaller metal-truss bridge that was saved and now sits beside it. Together, they make up the Twin Bridges. For the less adventurous, drive under and past the massive stone bridge. Marvel at its size and slightly creepy factor, complete with its own tales of ghostly happenings. Those not afraid of zipping traffic or local legend may pull off to the side of the road next to the smaller iron bridge and cross it on foot.

🍴 eat

Using local ingredients whenever possible, the Beehive is an organic market and café. Avoiding processed sugars, this quaint dining venue turns to honey. Smoothies, espresso, and a tea bar as well as build-your-own soft-serve frozen yogurt with a whole slew of toppings to choose from make snacking easy. Gluten-free items, crusty hand pies, homemade soups, and salads are also available. Try the hazelnut latte, chicken casserole, or Italian wedding-ball soup.

Cozy and cute, the house turned Bread Basket Café and Bakery boasts a gorgeous selection of house-made desserts. Outrageous chocolate cake, snickerdoodle cake, and peanut butter pie are but a small list of carefully designed but delicious treats. For real food, consider the portobello mushroom sandwich or the excellent chicken salad croissant. Pair with the soup of the day, made with seasonally available local produce.

Golf balls, Victorian shoes, ornaments: no more are they items to use or sit around—not inside Confection Delights anyway. Clever chocolate treats are abundant in this shop that has relocated downtown. Hand-dipped chocolates are available as truffles or creams. Handmade fudge and chocolate-covered pretzels are but a few of the snack offerings inside this shop that's sure to bring instant joy to anyone with a sweet tooth.

Frank's Place has been a dinner destination for Italian-food lovers since 1999. The owner immigrated to the United States

Mayberry Café, Danville.

from Sicily back in the early 1970s, gaining experience making pizza in New York before moving to Danville and setting up shop in slightly upscale digs. The restaurant features Italian favorites, and locals look for the spinach lasagna as a daily special, petto di pollo principessa (chicken topped with asparagus and mozzarella cheese), or Tony's Chicken, featuring ham, provolone cheese, and red roasted sweet peppers over chicken.

The 1962 Ford Galaxie 500 police squad car parked in front of Mayberry Café is just one way of capturing the essence of the fictional town of Mayberry. Decorated like a typical home of the time, but with walls of autographed celebrity photos, it's the one place where The Andy Griffith Show reruns are always playing. Locals enjoy the fried chicken, meat loaf, and breaded pork tenderloin sandwich. At this family-friendly spot, kids gain a token when they order from the kids' menu. The token may be redeemed for a toy from behind the register at the front or for a sundae. Gomer, Goober, and Charlene Darling have all made an appearance here.

🛍 shop

Nostalgia candies, vintage copies of popular toys and stuffed animals, faith-based decor, and even local honey are tucked inside Carla's Creations and Gifts. The gift-basket queen, this Danville gal has turned gift giving into an art form.

Gallery on the Square is a co-op of local artists. Art mediums of all kinds are welcome here, such as pottery, photography, jewelry, fibers, wood, and metal. There's so much talent. Workshops and classes are taught by the artists themselves. Wine tastings and live music are a few of the events that occur inside the stunning gallery.

Name-brand gently used clothing, accessories, and even shoes are waiting inside Jane's on the Square. It's a stylish boutique devoted to making consignment shopping fun—and beautiful. New handcrafted jewelry and lovely consignment pieces are charmingly arranged. Other locally made items make an appearance here, too.

Rustic style and repurposed pieces make Outta the Shed an experience. Look over the items displayed in the front window and on the sidewalk. Seasonal items, Christian decor, candles, and a scattering of antiques intermingle inside.

Those who have boats, cars, or furniture to upholster will want to visit Raders Fabrics. Fabrics are piled into mountainous heaps of color and texture that seem to almost touch the ceiling. It's hard not to run down the aisles in a big game of tag. Drapery, foam, vinyl, curtain rods, tiebacks, lace, and threads are available in a huge variety.

When custom jewelry orders kept coming in, it only made sense for Sarah Stogsdill, the owner of Seize the Night Designs, to open up a brick-and-mortar shop. Discover darling Indiana-themed accessories, vintage clothing, home decor, and upcycled pieces.

NOTABLES

A graduate of Danville high school, John W. Cravens (1864–1937) stayed in the town to earn his bachelor of science degree from Central Indiana Normal College in 1884. That same year he co-founded the Danville Gazette, becoming the youngest newspaper editor in the state. In 1885 he left Danville behind to serve as the superintendent of Monroe County Schools, where he served until 1890, when he was elected clerk of the Monroe County Circuit Court. Five years later he was appointed the registrar of Indiana University. Although he carried multiple job titles at Indiana University, he held the record for serving the longest term as registrar—a total of forty-one years.

In third grade Bob Snyder was performing with the Danville high school band. As an adult, his musical career included playing with the Tommy Dorsey, Ted Weems, Motown Recording, and Lionel Hampton orchestras, along with the WJR Radio Band.

Danville-born right fielder Samuel "Big Sam" Luther Thompson (1860–1922) may have been recognizable for his long handlebar mustache when he played for Major League Baseball in 1884–1898 and again in 1906, but his hitting skills are what really set him apart., His 1,887 runs batted in remained an unbroken record until Babe Ruth came along in 1921. Thompson, however, still carries the record for the most RBIs in a month—unbroken since 1894.

40

Dayton

Buck Creek Pizza, Dayton.

Folks first settled the area in 1823, but it wasn't until 1827 that the town was given a name—and it wasn't Dayton. Instead, they called the town Fairfield. The name was changed to Marquis because of another town named Fairfield (now lost because of the Federal Reservoir Project of the 1970s). In 1830 David Greggory added another addition of lots to the town, promising to donate land for a school if the town name was changed to Dayton. Residents eagerly agreed, and today Dayton Elementary School occupies the same land it was originally donated not quite two hundred years before.

☀ play

Wander over to Dayton's Historic District. It is bordered by Harrison, Pennsylvania, and Walnut Streets.

🍴 eat

Zippy little cars deliver pizza to locals and sometimes even to farmers busy in their fields. For everyone else, find plenty of indoor seating at Buck Creek Pizza. With a lodge feel, there's a lot of wood inside: the walls, ceiling, floor, chairs, and tables. Fresh out of the oven and served with a choice of dipping sauce, the breadsticks are a must. Pick the barbecue, sausage, or everything pizza.

41

Delphi

Delphi possesses a rich history due in part to its unique transportation-related past. Settlers first appeared in 1824. Two years later, a "state highway" was laid out along the Wabash River, from the National Road at Terre Haute to Fort Wayne. Though not exactly meeting the standards of today's roadways, it made it easier for settlers to access the new town. General Samuel Milroy moved into the area, occupying eighty acres with his large family. Just a few years later, he had the authority to organize the town and named it Delphi, using one hundred acres of land donated by settler William Wilson in order to create the county seat for Carroll County. Milroy's log cabin is long gone, but a historic plaque marks the spot.

Carroll County Courthouse, Delphi.

Officially becoming a town in 1835, the completion of the Wabash and Erie Canal in 1840 gave Delphi access to Fort Wayne and, by 1843, made even Toledo accessible. Ten years later the canal would connect Delphi to ports that ran from Ohio to Louisiana. It wasn't much longer before railroads appeared. Both the Wabash and the Monon Railroads ran through Delphi, making it a hub of transportation. The canal, with only seasonal access, was doomed. By the 1870s the canal became a part of history. But it's this canal heritage that adds to Delphi's uniqueness.

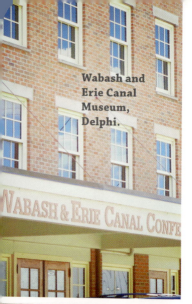

Wabash and Erie Canal Museum, Delphi.

Delphi Opera House prior to renovation.

Of course, there are many other ways that this old canal town sets itself apart. The Old Settlers has been an annual event since 1855. Occurring Wednesday through the second Saturday in August, it traces its beginnings back to an early pioneer gathering. Other canal-centered festivals include Canal Days, celebrated during the Fourth of July weekend, and Old Fashioned Christmas, a re-creation of mid-1800s holiday festivities—with homemade apple dumplings. In addition to themed entertainment, historic sites are open, and the canal returns to the sort of hustle and bustle once common during the time when canals reigned supreme.

☀ play

With such an incredible parade of businesses centered on the downtown square, an Architectural Walking Tour only makes sense. It's a walkable loop that highlights points of interest along the way, of which there are many.

Situated near a section of the largest man-made canal in the country, the Canal Interpretive Center and Museum is a superb destination. Pick up heavy tools used in the construction of the canal. Learn about the role of animals when the canal was in operation, and discover how canal boats floated through locks with an excellent water-play feature. Little ones won't want to leave. Step inside the life-size replica of the living quarters on a canal boat—complete with a rocking, swaying motion. Finish up a tour with a ride on the seasonally available canal boat, The Delphi, or turn the children loose outside at the canal-boat play structure.

Visit during the week when the Carroll County Courthouse is open. Various monuments are dotted around the building. Marvel at the lovely domed window (just like the Spencer County Courthouse in Rockport, Indiana, also built by Elmer Dunlapp), the marble-lined walls, and the amazing mosaic tile floor. Legend has it that before the first floor was completed in 1914, silver coins were collected from workers at the site, placed in a mason jar, and stuck underneath the floor and have been hiding there ever since. The courthouse was built with a town museum in mind. Look for it on the lower level. On the southwest side of the Carroll County Courthouse lies a longtime community drinking fountain. A unique outdoor sculpture, the Murphy Memorial Drinking Fountain, was a gift to honor the husband of Clara G. Murphy and herself. Crafted in 1918 by the Blakley Granite, Marble, and Tile Company (an Indianapolis business) with sculptor Myra Reynolds Richards, it is made of Vermont-quarried Barre granite. Featuring a young girl holding out a chalice in her right hand, it is one of the few original outdoor sculptures by the artist that still remain.

Built in 1865, the Delphi Opera House was the place to go for entertainment. Stairs were crafted to accommodate women's hoop skirts, and the wooden seats had a place underneath to store men's hats. The balcony, story-tall windows, and stage created one gorgeous performing space. Backstage, view the names, dates, and sometimes even drawings of the actors and actresses who passed through here. James Whitcomb Riley took to the stage on more than one occasion, though his signature has yet to be found. Shut down in 1915 due to a lack of other escape routes in case of fire, the Delphi Opera House has slowly decayed over the decades. After recently completing massive renovations, it once again provides a glamorous space for entertainment.

Reed Case House, Delphi.

Just down the path from the Interpretive Center, Noble Bikes and Concessions offers bicycle rentals for kids and adults. Although typical bicycles are available, so too are models built for two and bigger bikes for a small family or group. Take them on the trails that span out from Canal Park. Hot day? Try the paddle boats or kayaks offered for rent. With the canal at no more than four feet deep and lacking a current, it's a safe way to learn a new skill.

Tour the Reed Case House during special events or by prior arrangement at the Wabash and Erie Canal Park. The 1844

Federal-style home was constructed by Reed Case, a contractor for the majority of the area canal. As his business ventures increased, he built a second home in Delphi, turning the original home into an inn for canal travelers. Furnished with period style, such as the Pennsylvania-made grandfather clock that journeyed from Virginia to Carroll County in the early 1800s, the home is surrounded by other period buildings.

Carroll County held an international competition for commissioning of the Sailors and Soldiers Monument back in 1887. There is currently a debate as to the identity of the winner. The year of installation is also in question, but there are a few things that are known: it is a tall, stately work of art that bears a bronze relief on all four sides on the grounds of the courthouse. Each side displays a different snapshot of various battles of the Civil War and the soldiers who fought it. These include the Battle of Shiloh and Battle of Stones River, the Battle of the Wilderness and Battle of Cedar Creek, the Siege of Vicksburg and Battle of Champion Hill, the Battle of Antietam, and the Battle of Gettysburg.

eat

Andy's Place, just a hop away from the downtown square, has an array of mouthwatering homemade items. Located in a wonderfully renovated Civil War–era building, the restaurant's changing daily specials keep things interesting. Fresh local produce is used whenever possible. Breakfast fare is satisfying: homemade biscuits and gravy, fresh donuts, and even scones. Lunch and dinner options include hand-breaded pork tenderloin sandwiches and freshly cut fries, along with three soups each day. Roasted in-house, coffees from around the world are in no short supply. Grab a scoop or two of an Indiana-made ice cream before leaving. Visit on a Friday or Saturday evening and enjoy local mic night like the residents.

Take a seat at the U-shaped counter (only a couple of tables fit inside), and prepare to order a phenomenal reuben sandwich at the Sandwich Shop. Word on the street declares their fries the best in town. It's the kind of place where locals and the help tease each other, slinging gentle insults and sarcastic comments. It's all in good fun. Order right from the table and prepare to be amazed.

With a bit of a scandalous history pointing to whisperings of long-ago use as a brothel, the Stone House Restaurant and Bakery is a dining destination right downtown. Crafted from recipes that have been handed down from the owner's great-great-great-grandma, baked items are truly memorable. Ask for dining recommendations from the server, as the menu occasionally receives updates.

🔒 shop

Bill's Rock Shop isn't a cleverly named jewelry store but an actual rock shop. Inside, find fossils and rocks of all kinds. Some sit on the counter, some sit inside the counter, while others are in baskets underneath. It is a rock collector's dream. It's seasonally open, so call before heading out. Search for a different kind of diamond in the rough with the antiques for sale in the back of the shop.

NOTABLES

William Fritz Afflis (1929–1991), born in Delphi, was a lineman for the Green Bay Packers in the 1950s. But his claim to fame became his wrestling career. "Dick the Bruiser," as he was called, inspired David Letterman to name his studio band after him. Multiple championship winner Afflis was known as the "World's Most Dangerous Wrestler," so Letterman named his studio band the "World's Most Dangerous Band."

William Vincent Lucas (1835–1931) became a member of the U.S. House of Representatives in 1892. He may have been born in Delphi, but he was representing South Dakota.

A graduate of Delphi High School, John Doxie Moore (1911–1986) went on to play basketball at Purdue University in 1930 when John Wooden was coach—and was a part of the 1932 big championship win. His basketball career didn't end there. Moore went on to coach the Sheboygan Red Skins, the Anderson

Packers, and the Milwaukee Hawks. As if that wasn't enough, he served as an administrative assistant to Indiana governor George N. Craig and became the first president of the Hall of Fame Foundation (of which he became a part in 1978).

Navy rear admiral and thirty-first governor of American Samoa John Gould Moyer (1893–1976) spent his childhood in Delphi.

From 1940 to 1981, forward-thinking Delphi-born Robert H. Shaffer (b. 1915) was renowned for his insight. Awarded an honorary doctorate from both DePauw and Indiana University, he changed the face of student affairs.

Elizabeth Watson (1912–2001) was a prolific author on food and cooking. This Delphi resident was a journalist working for Edward R. Murrow during World War II, but because she was female she never received the recognition or respect that other male writers received. Doing freelance work for CBS, she was making her way to Norway when the Nazis invaded. Hiding from border guards, hitchhiking, and even hiding in a field during an air raid were but a few of the hazards she faced in order to get the story. She was once held as a prisoner by Germans in Greece. It still wasn't enough. Dismissed from CBS, she turned to writing books, producing twenty-four of them over the course of her career.

Who would have thought that Delphi resident Clarence Whistler (1856–1885) would become a champion Greco-Roman wrestler? The oldest of eight children, he began wrestling in 1879 and would until almost the day he died, a short six years later. After winning the championship in Australia, Whistler reportedly bit off the tops of champagne bottles, even eating champagne glasses whole. He passed away from pneumonia, and possible other complications, a month later.

42

Fairmount

James Dean Gallery, Fairmount.

Log cabins popped up in Fairmount in the 1820s by North Carolina Quakers, but it would be thirty years before the town was "official." It would be another sixty years before folks would rush into the town, with the discovery of "Jumbo," a gas well named for Barnum's famous elephant. Drilled in 1887, it was said to be the major gas deposit in Fairmount. Several glass factories moved into the town, as did new residents, lured by the cheap cost of gas.

No one would know it from wandering the town, but the Scott Opera House, though completely unfurnished and devoid of a stage, sits unoccupied right downtown above an auto-parts shop. Opened in 1884, it even attracted the attention of James Whitcomb Riley, who not only performed there in 1886 but also took on a Fairmount resident as his stage manager. When the gas boom ended in the late nineteenth century, so too did many of town's industries.

Fairmount lived on, and during the last full weekend in September residents and visitors can really see the town brought to life. Mark the calendar for the James Dean Festival and James Dean Run Car Show at Playacres Park. With more than two thousand cars on view just for the car show, that single event alone almost rivals the population of the town.

Garfield Trail,
Grant County.

The Fairmount Historical Museum contains several different exhibits highlighting not only town history but also the more famous locals of days past, like Jim Davis, the creator of Garfield, and actor James Dean. Complete with fossils, photos, and even military uniforms, it is remarkably well rounded. Garfield items fill a room, but the real treasure trove is found within the James Dean portion of the museum. A set of Dean's footprints and handprints cast in concrete from when he was eleven are here. So, too, is a rocking chair, a part of the family since at least 1887, accompanied by an image of Dean sitting on it. They seem to have everything—including his New York apartment sink. It's an excellent tribute to the small-town boy who made it big.

Leave a kiss on James Dean's simple headstone like so many before. The bright lipstick prints are all over it. It's easy to find; just follow the signs situated inside Park Cemetery.

🛍 shop

Absolutely massive and completely packed with incredibly unique vintage items, the D&M Variety Shop is laden with different collections. Milkshake mixers and letter jackets, yearbooks and vintage cameras—the range of items inside is truly astounding.

Downtown
Fairmount.

Indiana's oldest record store, Hi-Fi Stereo Shop, is a vinyl lover's dream. In business since the late 1960s, this place has thousands of records. Featuring new and vintage records from current and classic musicians, along with CDs, eight-track cartridges, and everything else that's music related, this shop is fun to explore. They even special order. Folks from around the world, as far away as Germany and England, leave their signature in the guest book—make sure to sign, too.

What does a man do with all the James Dean items he's been assembling since 1974? He opens it up for public viewing. Declared to be the world's largest collection of James Dean items, the James Dean Gallery boasts artifacts that range from international newspaper clippings to personal items and movie props. Move to the back for Rebel Rebel, a 1950s- and '60s-style antique shop.

NOTABLES

The Smithsonian Institution in Washington, D.C., holds a piece of Fairmount history. Three residents—Orlie Scott, Charles T. Payne, and Nathan Alpheus Armfield—invented a horseless carriage in 1888. The big test run was exciting—especially when they realized they forgot to add brakes and crashed into a rock. Discouraged, Orlie Scott sold their invention to Kokomo resident Elwood Haynes. Haynes drove the buggy for the first time on July 4, 1894.

One October day in 1900, four thousand people patiently waited at the Fairmount depot for President Theodore Roosevelt to pass through. Arriving by train, he gave a stirring ten-minute speech before continuing on.

The family farm in Fairmount had twenty-five cats. It's no wonder that cartoonist Jim Davis (b. 1945) developed the idea for Garfield. A multiple Emmy Award winner, Davis has also received the Distinguished Hoosier Award, the Indiana Journalism Award, Sagamore of the Wabash, the Reuben Award for Overall Excellence in Cartooning, and plenty more. Not bad for a comic involving a lasagna-loving fat cat. Hunt for the lazy feline along the Garfield Trail scattered over Grant County.

Fairmount grad James Dean (1931–1955) didn't have an easy childhood. After his mother passed away from cancer when he was nine years old, Dean was sent by his father to live with an aunt and uncle on their farm in Fairmount. Although he tried acting in high school, he wasn't a standout performer—at least not yet. After changing college majors and dropping out of school entirely, Dean snagged small roles in film. Four years after his high school graduation, he received his big break, starring in East of Eden, a film based on the John Steinbeck novel. His improvisation in the mostly unscripted film earned him another starring role, Rebel without a Cause. Enjoying fast cars, Dean got into racing, but during filming for his role in Giant, the studio kept him from participating in any races. As soon as filming was over, Dean hit the road to break in his Porsche 550 Spyder, crashing head-on with another car on the highway just hours after receiving a speeding ticket, ending his life. His funeral was held at the Fairmount Friends Church in Fairmount with an estimated three thousand people in attendance.

Phil Jones (b. 1937) always knew he wanted to be a broadcast journalist. During his youth, he practiced reading the news in the storage section of a chicken house. After he graduated from Fairmount High School in 1955, he left for Indiana University and its blossoming broadcast program. Gaining experience through a Minnesota television station was just the beginning for the IU graduate. He went on to work as a CBS correspondent, winning multiple Emmy Awards, conducting high-profile interviews on CBS's 48 Hours, and covering a slew of major news events from Vietnam to Watergate up until his retirement.

Another 1955 Fairmount High School graduate, meteorologist Robert Sheets (b. 1937) was the director of the National Hurricane Center from 1987 to 1995. He was also a member and later the director of Project Storm Fury, a failed project launched by the U.S. government that ran from 1962 to 1983. It attempted to weaken tropical storms by flying aircraft into them and lacing the clouds with silver iodide. Although it didn't have the intended effect, the project did help meteorologists better predict where a hurricane would move—and how intense it would become. He may have retired in 1995, but for many years Sheets has served as a special-situation hurricane analyst.

After playing in Major League Baseball for eight years during the 1880s, William Ashley "Billy" Sunday (1862–1935) left the field to evangelize, hitting Fairmount in 1902, holding a four-week Christian revival.

Author Mary Jane Ward (1905–1981) moved away from Fairmount after high school graduation. Focusing on writing, she attended college and worked as a book reviewer. After a nervous breakdown, and what many deem a false schizophrenia diagnosis accompanied by hospitalization and treatments that included electric shock therapy, she penned The Snake Pit (1946). It was later revealed to mimic her experiences at the institution. It became a Random House Book-of-the-Month Club offering and an Oscar Award–winning movie starring Olivia de Havilland.

43

Farmland

Quaker Eli Hiatt Sr. was the first to move into the area in 1837. The year 1852 and the completion of the Indianapolis and Bellefountaine Railroad led to the founding of Farmland. Said to be named for its abundance of fertile farming land, the name could also be the result of the town's original platting of 152 lots on two family farms, the properties of Henry Huffman and William Macy. The post office opened for business a year later. Farmland officially became an incorporated town in 1867.

Chocolate Moose, Farmland.

☼ play

Pull on those sneakers and grab some water. McVey Memorial Forest is a public park and animal sanctuary. Comfortable and with wide walking trails, this is truly a beautiful stroll. For dedicated hikers, the trail after the bridge becomes smaller and more rugged.

🍴 eat

The Chocolate Moose possesses 1950s-style soda-fountain counter seating, in addition to booths and tables inside and out. Using locally sourced meat really makes a difference. Opt for the hand-breaded pork tenderloin sandwich or any of the burgers. The cowboy burger, one-third pound of locally sourced

Chocolate Moose, Farmland.

beef, gourmet barbecue sauce, cheddar cheese, and beer-battered onion rings, is downright tasty. Don't forget the homemade chips and milkshake.

🔒 **shop**

Bright Ideas Stained Glass may specialize in the repair and installation of church stained-glass windows, but there are pieces found inside this spacious glass-filled shop that will dazzle and delight. Inventory changes as items are sold or repaired.

Farmland General Store.

Its exterior architecture makes Farmland General Store look the part. It's an old-fashioned-looking candy store on one side, with glass jars and barrels holding popular bulk candies. A wall of coffees from around the world will tempt grown-ups. On the other side is the general store: a pleasant mix of antiques, games and toys, garden supplies, and tin signs.

NOTABLES

Robert R. Retz was responsible for the erection of the Farmland Airport, built on the Retz family farm. Approved in 1934, it featured three grass runways. Unfortunately, Retz was killed in a flying lesson gone wrong in May 1937.

After retiring from farming at the age of eighty-seven, Ansel Toney (1887–1987) wanted something to do to keep busy. Teaching himself how to use an old sewing machine, he began to create his custom nylon kites for children. When he flew his kite over the fields, it was a sign to let the kids know they were welcome to join him. He gained the attention of national news outlets, appearing on television and in print.

44

Fortville

"Fortville" rolls off the tongue a bit easier than "Walpole," one of the original names for the town. Francis Kincaid first platted twenty-four lots in 1834. Due to Main Street and the Greenfield-Noblesville Pike (State Road 238) crossing over it, the area became known as "the Crossroads." The post office, named "Walpole" for politician and attorney Thomas D. Walpole, from nearby Greenfield, and a general store opened for business, though the area was now termed Phoebe Fort. Forward-thinking Cephas Fort was convinced that the railroad would run through his property, so he platted the town in 1849. Three years later he got his wish, and the town was named Fortville in his honor.

Once the home of the largest flour mill in the United States with a one-hundred-barrel capacity, Fortville hasn't ventured too far away from its agricultural roots—though flax is no longer its main crop. This town is on the rise. Residents frequently gather for enjoyable seasonal events that range from Wednesday-night cruise-ins during the warmer months to a Christmas extravaganza each winter that always includes clever events. One year a fantastically timed flyover by Santa in a plane marked the start of the parade through the downtown. For warmer months, there's Indiana Bastille Day. The French national holiday celebrates the day that France overthrew its oppressors and embraced the new Enlightenment way of thought. In Fortville it's a day of French-themed fun. From a petanque tournament (a traditional French game) to a waiters race, puppets or the lantern procession, it is a July celebration that is anything but run-of-the-mill.

stay

The comfortable Ivy House Bed and Breakfast, a 1920 Dutch colonial built by a respected town doctor, was once a Prohibition-era gambling operation. Locals insist it was frequented by Al Capone. Finding gambling-related remnants inside basement and garage walls clued the current owners in to the home's intriguing past, snagging it a feature on HGTV's If Walls Could Talk segment.

play

Piney Acres Christmas Tree Farm and Pumpkin Patch holds more than fifty acres of Christmas trees. An autumn destination, Piney Acres also sells pumpkins. Two corn mazes entertain every member of the family. The first is an eight-acre maze that winds through woods, while the other maze is rightly sized for the younger crowd, at a mere two acres. The newest attraction, the Haunted Loft, is a bit of spooky fun for preteens and up.

Studio 309, Fortville.

Long tables are situated on one side of the window-filled room of Studio 309. Art of all kinds is displayed on the walls. Sheri Jones, a Herron School of Art grad, teaches art, hosting special ladies nights or kids parties in or out. On the other side, Mom teaches the kids to play the piano. But the space wasn't always so wonderful. Before renovations, the home turned studio lacked heat, air, walls, and even the ceiling. Delve into art in a comfortable, cozy setting.

eat

So chic and with a modern flair, Indulge Ice Cream Parlor and Café has created a really magical space. Once the location of

Heche's Five & Dime Store, the original (and amazingly well-kept) soda-fountain counter still remains. Although known for the Pink Elephant, a generous pink ice cream and soda confection, they have since developed new flavors like the Woolly Mammoth and Fluffalump. While ice cream and other frosty treats are delicious (get the butterscotch ice cream sandwich), the California wrap or the chicken salad on a croissant is incredible.

Indulge Ice Cream Parlor and Café, Fortville.

Using Indiana roasted coffee, Java Junction is a coffee shop with enticing selections. Wake up with the triple-wide eye and its three shots of zippy espresso, the bourbon barrel blend coffee, or the white chocolate strawberry hot cocoa. Panini sandwiches and the taco soup are popular in this friendly family-run business.

"Love the rub" at R-Smokehouse, a barbecue joint that's just as big on style as it is on flavor. Using rubs, referred to as "Texas style," the restaurant's smoked meats are certainly amazing, but don't skip the coleslaw. Delightfully different, the nachos are a tasty alternative.

🛍 shop

Blending together home decor and vintage-inspired pieces, Best of What's Around focuses on Indiana artists. Repurposed furniture or shabby-chic embellishments, this shop is whimsical, playful, and sweet. Seasonal items are adorable.

There's no excuse for frumpy with easy access to the spacious and bright Gypsy Chicks Boutique. Sizes run the range. Let these ladies put together a look to fit any need. Shopping for clothing, accessories, and undergarments is finally enjoyable.

Whether you have unfinished projects or new beginnings, Palette & Paper provides space and instruction. Settle in the comfortable space with a nice beverage and loads of inspiration—just look at the walls for a mental jog. Whether it is an all-day creative session or finishing up personal incomplete projects, this is the place to go to finally get it done while picking up art supplies, paper, and stamps.

Simply More is simply elegant. Once the site of a bar (and, a long time ago, possibly a brothel), the space underwent massive renovations to expose the brick walls and ductwork. During renovation the four owners discovered handwriting on the ceiling. Apparently, bar customers would get a little rowdy and scale up the firefighter poles to leave their mark. New, revitalized, and vintage furniture offers big style in a stunning atmosphere.

The Stable Tack Shop is a unique retail store in that they've got everything needed—for a horse. Saddles (both new and consignment), brushes, blankets, clothing . . . they do mean everything. Dog lovers will also want to step inside and check out the selection of accessories for canines.

The Studio is spectacular. Specializing in primitive home decor, the space is elegant yet purposeful. Self-taught cross-stitch artist Stacy Nash receives international acclaim for her patterns. Find them (and special events) in her charming shop.

45

Fountain

Originally thought to become a major player on the upper Wabash River, this unincorporated town didn't quite live up to those grand expectations. Platted in 1828 as Portland, Fountain experienced a fair bit of growth before slowing down to something a little quieter. Located in an area so lovely and green, it does not look like "typical" Indiana.

☀ play

There's no gate to go through or parking permit to purchase at Portland Arch Nature Preserve. Ramble over an eighth of a mile trail loop that covers only a tiny portion of the 293 acres of preserved forest. Pass through different ecosystems and see a different kind of Indiana. A bridge, rock formations, aged trees—they are all here, waiting. Bring a pair of shoes or boots in case of mud as well as plenty of bug spray.

Portland Arch Nature Preserve, Fountain.

No matter what it's called, Portland Arch Cemetery, Bear Cemetery, or Portland Cemetery, this pioneer cemetery is worth a visit by history lovers or genealogy hunters. The headstones are intricate and numerous. Some are in their original positions, while others are propped up against trees or even inside a prickly briar patch.

46

Fountain City

Fountain City has had a few name changes. Platted as New Garden in 1818, it experienced a name switch in 1834 and was called Newport. It wasn't until the late 1870s when undergoing incorporation that a name was found that wasn't a duplicate of another Indiana town: Fountain City. It seemed a natural fit with the freshwater springs, or fountains, once present in the area.

The entire town turns out for Levi Coffin Days, held the third weekend in August. Somewhere between four and five hundred arts-and-crafts booths set up shop. Including carnival rides, a parade, ball games, planned events, and the tremendously popular kids' dig for treasure, this annual free event has brought the community together since 1968.

☀ play

The Federal-style home built in 1839 may appear to be a simple brick home, but in its past the Levi Coffin House was considered the "Grand Central Station of the Underground Railroad." Building the home with hiding slaves in mind, the family was committed to helping others on the path of safety. Constructed to help hide the runaway slaves, the house possesses a lower-level kitchen and a secret room. In all, Levi Coffin, the "president of the Underground Railroad," as he was termed, and his wife, Catharine, are believed to have helped as many as two thousand escaped slaves make their way to freedom. Catharine even set up a sewing circle in her home in order to help clothe the runaways who passed through their doors, as many runaway slaves were without proper clothing or even footwear. The dining room possesses not only the original horsehair plaster but five doors to provide easy escape when needed. Informative tours and original belongings of the Coffins make the Levi Coffin House an excellent historical stop.

Of the many escaped slaves who are said to have passed through the doors of the Levi Coffin House on their way North, William "Billy" Bush was but one. Traveling in a box on a buggy to the home in a pair of wooden shoes (also on display in the Levi Coffin House), he took on the last name of "Bush" in honor of Mr. Coffin. Some say it was due to the bushy appearance of Coffin's beard. In fact, Bush chose to stay on at the house and help others along the way. Find the William Bush headstone at Willow Grove Cemetery and

Levi Coffin House, Fountain City.

Wooden Shoes
Made and worn by
escaped slave William Bush
Donated by granddaughter Ina Bur[...]

those of his descendants intermixed with the Quakers buried here, an unusual action during the time period since most cemeteries took a more segregated approach. For Quakers, however, it was a nonissue.

NOTABLES

In his autobiography, Reminiscences of Levi Coffin, Coffin (1798–1877) wrote of a slave woman from Kentucky. With her infant in her arms, she crossed the Ohio River by jumping on hunks of ice. Her name, Eliza Harris, served as a basis for a character of the same name in Uncle Tom's Cabin by Harriet Beecher Stowe.

47

Gas City

It only takes a moment to notice the small oil derrick street signs to realize that there's got to be an interesting backstory. Laid out in 1867, and named Harrisburg by founder Noah Harris, the new town exploded with population after the discovery of natural gas in 1887. In a short three-month period, eight factories moved in, lured by the prospect of free gas. Five years after the discovery of what seemed like an endless gas supply, officials changed the name of the town to Gas City. It grew so quickly that a tent and shanty community sprang up of families waiting for their houses to be completed. By 1900 the population had increased to almost twenty-five times its 1890 population count. When the gas ran out, so too did the factories and businesses that had popped up almost overnight. Gas fields switched over to cornfields.

Payne's Custard and Café, Gas City.

Gas City may not be the bustling metropolis of twenty-five thousand people that early town founders had envisioned and hoped for, but it is an excellent, friendly small town. Yearly festivals, including the new National Bacon Festival, and summer concerts in the park typically occur at the "Beaner" Linn Memorial Park.

¶¶ eat

Boasting locally sourced foods, pasture-raised meat, Indiana beer, and an on-site organic garden, Payne's Custard and Cafe British-American cuisine serves simple, delicious food. The cozy interior features unrestored antiques, menus tucked inside antique books, and decoupage tabletops of Indiana maps or vintage cookbook pages. Local suggestions include British chicken curry with Naan bread and the Indiana-raised duck with red-wine blackberry sauce. Follow it up with an order of the owner's mother's delicious recipe for bread pudding that's packed with dried fruits and caramel sauce or the sticky toffee pudding. Either option is ooey-gooey satisfying.

🛍 **shop**

Children can't resist the wall-to-wall selection of balloons inside of Balloons, Flowers, and Gifts. Cavernous and stocked with everything to throw a party, this store even sells fresh flowers and plants.

Mama Pearson's Soaporium, Gas City.

Dragonfly Cottage is a must for any shabby-chic lover. Like the shop sign reads, "A little shabby, a little chic, always unique." Once-lackluster furniture is redone, repurposed, and beautifully arranged. Tossed pillows, knickknacks, and vintage items are placed on furniture, on shelves, and in baskets. It's hard to know where to look first.

Bottles of sauces and seasonings cater to the spicy-food lover at Hotheads Pepper Store. Barbecue sauce or rub, jam or condiment, their goods definitely add the special something. They sell gluten-free, all-natural, and hard-to-find items too.

Once a farmers market test, Mama Pearson's Soaporium has grown to become a sweet-smelling brick-and-mortar business.

All-natural fresh scents have clever names: Dirty Hippie, Little Black Dress, and Maple Bacon. Getting kids to clean up has never been so easy—there are even soaps with toys inside.

Twenty years in the antique business has made Mick's Flea Market jam-packed with booths. It's inexpensive and eclectic, and bargain hunters will love searching through boxes, combing through shelves, and wandering around the enormous first floor. Furniture shoppers should head upstairs for the desks, tables, and vast quantity of furnishings. View neat vintage town photos at the register area before leaving.

Not a typical thrift shop, Rescued Treasures' profits fund a local men's shelter. Well organized and almost cavernous, this huge shop features clothing, housewares, books, and toys. Expect supremely low prices and a shipshape range of things.

48

Greencastle

English American Ephraim Dukes founded Greensburg and named it for his home, the Pennsylvania town of the same name. College Avenue was long ago named Ephraim in his honor. Officially becoming a town in 1849, Greencastle's county-seat status followed soon after, although it wasn't without its own share of rivalry. Putnamville also wanted a chance as county seat. As time passed, Putnamville had a better location in relation to the new highway, but although they raised a little fuss, it never amounted to much. Greencastle hung on as county seat.

Greencastle did become the site of Indiana Asbury University in 1837, a school for men. It wasn't until 1867

Oakalla Covered Bridge, Greencastle.

that women were allowed within its doors. Now, it is better known as DePauw University, a campus noted for its stunning architecture and liberal arts curriculum. With more than a dozen buildings not only at the college but also in Greencastle, it's listed on the National Register of Historic Places.

🛏 stay

Peace and quiet is easy at 3 Fat Labs Bed and Breakfast. Away from the downtown, this country setting is perfection. Roam twenty-six wooded acres or spread out in the

Almost Home Restaurant, Greencastle.

seven-thousand-square-foot home. Settle in the theater room, explore the nearby Oakalla Covered Bridge, and hope to sample the owner's soft ginger cookies handed down from an old family recipe.

☀ play

Just down the road from 3 Fat Labs Bed and Breakfast is a single-span wooden bridge built in 1898. One of many bridges built by Joseph J. Daniels, the Oakalla Covered Bridge is a beauty. Look south to try to see the old interurban railroad bed.

Outside of Putnam County Courthouse lies the World War II buzz bomb, one of only two in the United States. The other buzz bomb is housed at the Smithsonian Institution in Washington, D.C. It's a guaranteed hit with kids and history lovers.

🍴 eat

Almost Home Restaurant serves pretty food, what they term "stylish comfort food." Indeed it is. Try the pork tenderloin sandwich with homemade potato chips. The dessert tray is enticing, but bypass it all for a slice of the award-winning strawberry pizza.

Casa Grande Mexican Restaurant doesn't look like it would be amazing on the outside, but there's no beating the service. It's all good here. End the meal with a giant sopaipilla. It's big enough to share.

🛍 shop

Since 1908 Eitel's Florist has provided the area with fresh flowers and plants.

Almost Home Restaurant, Greencastle.

But the gift selection is definitely worth a peek. With gifts like this, even a Monday may be cause for celebration.

Attention getting from the outside, Isabella Marie's Antiques and Things has an enormous collection of stuff. Children's gently used and vintage toys are especially abundant, though the dishware selection is also ample. Look for her spontaneous clever sales for a little fun and a bit of extra savings.

NOTABLES

Greencastle was a 2008 Stellar Communities winner, receiving funding for improving the courthouse square and improving the quality of life in the town with capital for a number of projects.

Born in Greencastle, Amalia Küssner Coudert (1863–1932) would later move to Terre Haute and become known for her miniature portraits. She traveled to Europe and painted royalty, including Czar Nicholas II of Russia and King Edward VII.

In 1910 Greencastle-born William Michael Crose (1867–1929) became the seventh naval governor of American Samoa.

John Dillinger (1903–1934) and his gang robbed the Central National Bank of Greencastle, nabbing $74,782.09 before fleeing the scene. It proved to be his major grab and one of only two banks he robbed in Indiana.

Samuel Holland Rous (1864–1937), also known as S. H. Dudley (not to be confused with the African American vaudeville performer), was a recording-studio pioneer and also born in Greencastle. He put together sessions at Victor Records, created monthly and yearly catalogs that would be used to sell records to shops, and became assistant manager of the company's artists and repertoire division.

Alexander Campbell Stevenson (1802–1889) was a Greencastle farmer, physician, and politician known for helping to establish the Indiana State Fair and for breeding shorthorn cattle.

Jesse W. Weik (1837–1930), born and raised in Greencastle, published the first biography of Abraham Lincoln with William Herndon in 1889. It was the result of years of interviews with anyone he could track down who knew the former president.

49

Greens Fork

For more than seventy years, Greens Fork was known as Washington. Historical documents point to an earlier time when it was known as Westfield, though where that name originated is a mystery. But for seventy years after that, Greens Fork was titled Washington. The discovery of a second southern Indiana town named Washington prompted officials to change the name. Unlike some places named in honor of community founders or other notable people, the town was named for Greens Fork, the nearby creek. The creek was named for a member of the Delaware tribe known for being as fierce and mean as he was shrewd. The spelling of Greens Fork varied from person to person until 1968, when the original town documents were looked over and the town officially adopted the correct spelling.

☀ play

It's hard to find a small-town museum more committed to preserving its town than the Clay Township Historical Society Museum. A population of barely four hundred people has managed to dedicate a sharp 1848 Federal-style home to town preservation. Folks from all over the world visit the museum and one of its more unique features: a room devoted to the old Greens Fork High School. Due to school consolidation, the high school graduated the last class in 1962. Currently used as a fire station, the old Greens Fork High School has had much of its character stripped away, as wood boards cover what must have been amazing windows. Relics from the school, including desks, chalkboard, and trophies, have made their way here. Framed class photos line one wall. Save time for reading, browsing, and admiring the way a town of so few has preserved the past for so many.

NOTABLES

Born in Greens Fork in 1850, when it was still known as Washington, Johnny Ringo and his family moved around a bit. Tragedy struck on the way to California in 1864. Ringo was fourteen when his father accidentally shot and killed himself with his own shotgun while stepping out of their wagon. The family continued to California. Reports differ as to Johnny Ringo's teenage years, some reporting him to be a drunk and troublemaker, while others mentioned only that he was a farmer. His first bit of documented trouble occurred on Christmas Day 1874, when he shot his pistol in Burnet, Texas. Although his trial wasn't until July, the Mason County War, also known as the Hoodoo War, changed everything. German settlers and U.S.-born men were in hostile dispute over cattle ownership. Johnny Ringo and his friends wreaked havoc on German folks in the area before they were rounded up and thrown in jail—though they later escaped. Parting ways with his friends to avoid capture, the solo Ringo made his way to a saloon, where he shot a man for refusing a free drink of whiskey. The man survived, but Ringo was intent on causing trouble. Evading the law, and U.S. marshal Wyatt Earp in particular, while still robbing and killing, Ringo was alone and still on the run when he ended his life in 1882.

Clay Township Historical Society Museum, Greens Fork.

50

Hagerstown

Abbott's Candy,
Hagerstown.

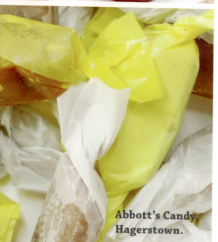

Abbott's Candy,
Hagerstown.

Located on the northern terminus of the seventy-six-mile Whitewater Canal, Hagerstown marked the beginning of the connection from Indiana to Ohio. After the state went bankrupt, Hagerstown financed and built its own canal, connecting itself to Cambridge City and becoming a part of canal history. When the railroad moved in, the old towpath found new purpose.

☀ play

Those busy canal days may be only a memory, but pride for this tiny community is still strong. Nowhere is it more apparent than the second-largest vintage-plane air show in the United States. What's been called the longest, smoothest grass runway in America at four thousand feet long and two hundred feet wide, the Hagerstown Airport hosts an annual fly-in known as the Hagerstown Flying Circus. Precision landing and fun events like cutting a roll of toilet paper three times after it's been dropped five thousand feet or the target drop for bags of flour make a fantastic family event.

🍴 eat

William Clay Abbott was a traveling candy salesman. Tiring of the road, he opened a restaurant and then set up two side businesses in his garage. One was selling homemade candy, and the other was ice cream. Business for the restaurant was booming, but he decided to stop everything and focus solely on candy. Abbot's Candy has been in

Bowman Bakery, Hagerstown.

business since the 1890s. Up until 1985 it was even in the same location: William Clay Abbott's backyard. Originally built as a Presbyterian church, the space now serves as retail shop and chocolate factory. Take a tour and don't skip the caramels.

Somewhere around eighty-five varieties of donuts are made available each day, and that's just the tip of the cheesecake—another item that Bowman Bakery specializes in. At three and a half pounds each, these cheesecakes are hefty. With close to sixty-five kinds of seasonally produced cheesecakes, it may take a while to get through this list. Whether buying by the slice or whole, check the refrigerated case for that day's selection or call ahead and place an order.

🛍 shop

Originally built as the 1880 Lodge hall, the Hagerstown Arts Place is a combination of art gallery and workshop space. Open painting classes, free violin lessons, and access to area artists who lead each particular class of their choice make it one excellent addition to the town. Other small towns should take note.

Delightful dishware and other antique necessities are located inside Main Street Antiques. Sheet music, class yearbooks, and old copies of the Hagerstown Exponent newspaper are just a sampling of the marvelous picks here. Kerosene-lamp collectors might want to pay a visit.

Payne's Music and Recording Studio is the place to buy or repair music instruments. In fact, there's even a recording studio inside. This is not a "look but don't touch kind of shop." Pick it up and play. With a bit of luck, even the owner, a professional musician, may select a guitar and start strumming away.

NOTABLES

Gyroscopes are made in Hagerstown by Tedco Toys, a scientific and educational toy manufacturer. They are shipped internationally.

51

Kirklin

The early bird gets the worm, as they say, and for the founder of Kirklin, Nathan Kirk, that would certainly prove true. Alone in the county for three years, his cabin served as a needed stopping place for anyone passing through. New Castle Road (stretching to Lafayette) was completed, and Michigan Road, set to cross through it, was not yet opened. Folks waited anxiously to view the location of the crossing of the road so they could be the first to lay claim to the land. Everyone thought it would prove to be an important location.

Nathan Kirk wasn't going to leave this one to chance. He hid a horse in the woods so he could see just where the Michigan Road would cross over. Then he took off for Crawfordsville to lay his claim. The area was originally known as Kirk's Crossing, and Kirk opened a tavern there and later a mill. Other buildings slowly sprang up. But it wasn't until the Monon Railroad passed through the town in the 1880s that Kirklin saw real growth.

Clementine's Antiques and Accents, Kirklin.

The Kirk's Crossing Festival, held the fourth weekend in June, pays tribute to its early history. Town-wide yard sales, a parade, a baked-goods auction, and a car show are a few of the events typically scheduled. Join the fun at this free event since 1972.

For shopping bargains more than once a year, head downtown for the Kirklin Flea Market, occurring every second Saturday of each month from May to October.

☀ play

Not many small towns can boast of possessing a comic-book art gallery, but that's exactly what guests will find at Kid Domino Museum. Daniel L. Mann is the creator of the graphic-novel series Forgotten City. His original art, and that of other noted comic-book artists, lines the walls in this unique space with high tin-covered ceilings.

Kids of all ages will revel in a stop at Kirklin Park. There are multiple places to romp in this play place that's crafted with two separate yet connected areas for different ages. Surrounded by ball fields, it is obviously a big part of town life.

🍴 eat

Booker's Bar and Grill has that family-friendly atmosphere down pat on its all-ages side. Serving traditional Hoosier favorites like pork tenderloin and reuben sandwiches, burgers, and a much-anticipated Sunday brunch in a lodge sort of setting has

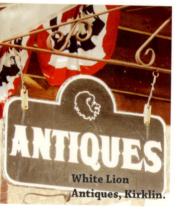

quickly made this a favorite local hangout. End any meal with a slice of homemade triple-layer chocolate cake.

There's no cutting corners at Empire Pizza. Everything is freshly made of high quality. Even the mozzarella cheese is made in-house. Start with the antipasto platter. Then opt for the unusual BLT pizza or the Hog and Heifer, for the meat lovers. End with a pizza cookie, their soon-to-be-famous dessert. Kirklin residents even receive a discount.

White Lion Antiques, Kirklin.

🛍 shop

The store 3 Stray Cats Vintage is a spin away from the typical antique shop. Bold pops of color draw the eye from ceiling to shelving to furniture and rugs. Retro glassware, aprons, and far-from-ordinary home decor are plentiful. There's nothing quite like this one.

Quantities of chairs, vanities, and tables are heaped with wonderful rustic touches like country candles and handmade soaps. The Black Crow has a remarkably cozy shop. They feature a nice faith-based decor and seasonal selection.

3 Stray Cats, Kirklin.

Clementine's Antiques and Accents feels like a shabby-chic magazine spread. This gal has got an eye for arranging—and for giving vintage items new purpose. Whether browsing birdcages or primitives of all sizes, it's just about impossible to walk away empty-handed.

Vendors, vendors, vendors: there's booth space galore inside of K&G Time Traveler's Antique Mall. Items run the range, but the Victorian pieces of furniture and the vintage toys are really something.

Old Bank Antiques occupies a unique niche. Sure, there are some really lovely furniture pieces, wall art, and other decor, but there's also an extensive selection of fair-trade items. Representing more than thirty countries from around the world, from Afghanistan to Zimbabwe, this old bank turned antique and fair-trade shop covers a lot of ground. Discover coffee beans, jewelry, and even clothing. Don't forget to check out the two old bank vaults, complete with working vents.

In the market for antiques? For more than twenty-five years, White Lion Antiques has been the go- to destination for fabulous primitive finds. A large shop to begin with, items are displayed floor to ceiling high. Wander to the back and find another section full of furniture, vintage advertising, and one of a kinds. Truly unique, it's no wonder White Lion Antiques has been a longtime fixture in this tiny town.

This is primitive paradise. Wikerdoodles has a bit of this and a bit of that. Somehow, it all comes beautifully together. Repurposing picture frames turned clothespin picture frames or wicker baskets of needful things, the chatty owners of this shop keep visitors coming back for more.

52

Knightstown

Believed to be the only Knightstown in the world, Knightstown was named for Jonathan Knight, a well-known man in his day when the town was platted in 1827. He was one of the chief engineers of the National Road, the first federally funded highway in the country, which served as a gateway to the West for pioneers. It was an immensely popular project around the time the town was platted. The National Road was (and still is) the main street that runs through the center of the downtown. Old writings reveal that as late as 1830, bears would come up from the riverbank and then end up chased through the streets and out of town.

Though the days of deep woods and bears are gone, this town of two thousand people manages to attract international travelers. But that's what happens when an unused town building becomes the scene of a celebrated movie.

☼ play

A place of community fun in the 1920s, the Hoosier Gym was a place where professional and college basketball players created their own teams; the gym even expanded, thanks to Works Progress Administration funding in the 1930s. Changing times and a bigger, newer gym led to its closing in the 1960s. Like too many small towns with a lack of foresight, it, too, could have been torn down and lost, yet something miraculous happened: it became the site of the 1986 film Hoosiers. Pulled back into public attention with movie fame and enduring 1950s design, the gym offers visitors tours of the locker room. See movie memorabilia in the lobby, and even shoot hoops on the old wooden floor. Check out the annual Hoosier's Reunion All-Star Classic, a doubleheader composed of top Indiana high school seniors, for a taste of what it was like during its glory days.

Knightstown Diner.

eat

Amazing pork tenderloin sandwiches and burgers beckon from the Knightstown Diner. The homemade potato chips and fries are phenomenal—and definitely rank as some of the best in the state. Resistance is futile. Remember to save room for dessert. The bakery case is always loaded with appealing items.

shop

Bittersweet Memories is so full of different nooks that it takes a significant amount of time to poke through it all. Excellent vintage toys, the likes of which are not commonly found, are abundant. Tin signs and vintage books in the back add to the picking perfection.

How does five thousand square feet of antiques sound? Glass Cupboard Antiques is a delightful shop that's big on space. The store is painless to navigate, so browsing is a treat.

NOTABLES

Charles A. Beard (1874–1948), professor, historian, and author, was born in Knightstown.

Gerard Montgomery Bluefeather (1887–1963), better known as Monte Blue, a silent-film actor who transitioned to character work, received a star on the Hollywood Walk of Fame.

U.S. secretary of agriculture (1969–1971) Clifford Morris Hardin (1915–2010) was Knightstown born and raised.

Actor Forrest Lewis (1899–1977) grew up in Knightstown. Appearing in film and TV, his work ranged from The Absent-Minded Professor to appearances on The Andy Griffith Show and My Friend Flicka.

Medal of Honor recipient William Zion (1872–1919) was Knightstown born. He received the award for his conduct during the China Relief Expedition, the rescue effort and later suppression of the Boxer Rebellion.

53

Maplewood

Polly's Freeze, Maplewood.

Like so many small Indiana towns, Maplewood also possessed a different name in its early days. The post office called itself Progress back in 1880. Renamed Maplewood a year later, for the heavy maple forest once located there, the tiny unincorporated town couldn't support the post office forever. It was closed in 1912. Sometimes referred to as Georgetown, sometimes referred to as Maplewood, and sometimes called Anderson, this small town with too many names has something here worth tasting.

🍴 eat

Since 1952 seasonally open Polly's Freeze has been a local landmark. After all, it's hard to miss the retro green neon parrot sign. The menu is also unexpected: there are homemade ice creams and sherbets here from banana to strawberry to black raspberry. Homemade orange sherbet is always on the menu, while other flavors are shuffled in. With so much outside seating, it must be able to hold more visitors than there are people in the town!

54

Martinsville

Martinsville has had more than a few claims to fame. It was once the "Goldfish Capital of the World." Inheriting a piece of soggy, swampy farmland, two brothers developed a brilliant way to put it to use, opening Grassyfork Fishery in 1889. This was just a few short years after the Chicago World's Fair Japanese goldfish reveal when the masses became goldfish obsessed. Operations expanded and carried on until 1970, when the fishery was bought out and the fishy showroom, once attracting thousands of visitors each year, was closed. At one time, Grassyfork Fishery supplied 75 percent of the world's goldfish. The showroom built in 1936 still stands today and is worth a drive-by.

Beginning in 1888, when Martinsville resident Sylvanus Barnard was drilling for natural gas, he made an unexpected discovery: the presence of mineral water. That was enough. Beginning a craze that would last for the next eighty years, folks came from everywhere to indulge in the "healing waters." It's easy to find traces of Martinsville's resort past. Right downtown a neon sign proclaims "Martinsville City of Mineral Water" on the site of what was once the National Sanitarium. This central Indiana town formerly boasted eleven different resorts.

Although those bustling resort days are long gone, this Hendricks County town has so much to offer that it is still a destination in its own right. The Morgan County Courthouse is a real beauty. Redbrick and in the Italianate style, it may look familiar for frequent small-town travelers. If not for a few 1970s additions, it is almost identical to the Jennings County courthouse, both of which were designed by the same man. The rest of the architecture downtown is equally as attractive.

☀ play

The site of a former Methodist church, Art Sanctuary is now an incredible studio space for twenty artists. Photography, painting, quilting, handmade jewelry, and then some have a place here. Look for special events or purchase local art right here on the second Friday of each month.

Large found items like doors and windows are creatively turned into something new at Art Work by Elizabeth. The owner handcrafts items to make them usable and heirloom quality.

Regional artists and amazing jewelry are situated inside the Sterling Butterfly. It's a sweet little spot for Indiana items, artisan jewelry from Pam Hurst, and accessories.

Martinsville Candy Kitchen.

Find a tasting room and brewing facility at this satellite shop from Three Pints Brewing. Fill a growler with a house brew, like the Martinsville Pale Ale.

🍴 eat

Open for lunch and dinner, Café 166 Smokehouse and Deli smokes its own deliciously tender meats. Opt for either the Sicilian sandwich or the pulled pork with the restaurant's own special sauce. Every choice is a good choice.

During the holiday season, people come from all over to visit Martinsville Candy Kitchen, founded in 1919 by Greek immigrant Jimmy Zapapas. The recipes have been passed down from owner to owner through the years. Best known for their homemade candy canes available all year, they boast more than a dozen flavors at Christmas. Though not everything is made in-store, what is made might still use Zapapas's own gas stove, copper pot, marble slab, and metal hook. Visit during the Christmas season to watch the production of handmade candy canes. During warmer months, sit at the diner-style seating and decide between more than twenty flavors of ice cream.

If candy canes weren't enough, pop inside Mimi's Fatcakes. Made with Morgan County fruits and farm eggs, the pies and pastries frequently sell out. Don't skip the chicken pot pie. Everything here is scratch-made and mouthwatering.

🛍 shop

Art Gallery and Framing is a longtime art gallery, retail space, and workshop provider well stocked by local artists. With jewelry crafted by a local or pottery made from area clay, there's plenty to enjoy with this kind of artistic range. The entire wall full of art is certainly a showstopper.

No shopping excursion would be complete without a visit to Berries & Ivy Country Store. Absolutely enormous, this shop is the home decorator's dream. Featuring seasonal items as well as the everyday and new and antique treasures, in country and shabby-chic styles, it's not all home decor. Find new boutique clothing, brand-name handbags, and even jewelry.

Rolling hills dotted with fluffy sheep seem more like Ireland than Indiana. A knitter's paradise, Sheep Street Fibers has an assortment of fibers, including wool from their own flock. Learn how to get started or take a class in advanced techniques. Looms and spinning wheels are also available for purchase.

NOTABLES
Famed basketball coach John Wooden (1910–2010) moved to Martinsville in his teens.

55

Matthews

Judging from the extra-roomy main street through the center of town, it is obvious that the founders of Matthews expected big things. It's hard to believe that this town of not even six hundred people was once eyed as a potential site for the state capital in the early 1820s—but it was. The founders strategically positioned Matthews on the Trenton Gas Field, the chief natural gas deposit at that time. This gas deposit is what began the Indiana gas boom, launching the founding of many other small towns around the county. Unfortunately, the gas supply peaked in 1900, ending entirely by 1910. But Matthews held on.

Listen for the crowd. Labor Day weekend brings the yearly Cumberland Covered Bridge Festival. For more than forty years, there have been music, food, and plenty of laughs for a nominal entry fee. Head to the covered bridge to join in.

☀ play

At 181 feet long, the Cumberland Covered Bridge lies northeast of town and spans the Mississinewa River. Just imagine the horror in 1913 when floodwaters kept rising, eventually carrying the bridge away downstream. The informational plaque located on site states that the bridge was listing at a 70° angle, with the north end pointing the way down the river, until just past the Matthews Cemetery. It hit a tree, did a 180° turn, and hung on to the south bank until the flood dissipated. Like so many bridges before, this could have been the end of the Cumberland Covered Bridge. Fortunately, it was deemed usable, so, with the help of horses and rollers, it made the quarter-mile trip back where it belonged. After a few fixes, it has stood fast against subsequent flooding.

Cumberland Covered Bridge, Matthews.

56

Morgantown

First settled in 1828, Morgantown wasn't laid out until March 1831 by Robert Bowles and Samuel Teeters. Settlers slowly trickled in, and by 1836 roughly seventy people called Morgantown home. Apparently, the original platting wasn't quite right, so it was changed to include things like wider streets and different lots.

In a festive twist, Morgantown doesn't have a festival to pay honor to its first settler or founders, but instead the town celebrates an early entrepreneur, pastor, founder of the first Baptist church, and one of the key people involved in changing the town plat (as the story goes): Colonel John Vawter. In fact, this English transplant was also the founder of Vernon, Indiana; spent time as a U.S. marshal in Madison, Indiana; and even served as a frontier ranger for a few years. It's been said that he was completely against slavery, even buying slaves to let them go as free people. Every third Saturday in September, Colonel Vawter Days, an almost thirty-year tradition, celebrates this successful merchant and activist with music, booths, crafts, a pet parade, a car show, and even a flash-mob dance.

Bernie's Barbecue, Morgantown.

¶¶ eat

Ask anyone where to head for homemade food, and they'll reply,

"Bernie's Barbecue." Don't pass up Rajean's coleslaw, Bernie's pork brisket sandwich, or the fresh-cut sweet-potato fries. Paired with a dab of apple butter, it's a bit unusual but totally works. Homemade desserts are available, of course, so go for the apple pie à la mode.

🛍 shop

Antique Cooperation occupies the old hardware store. The tall ladder still stands, only instead of stretching upward to provide easy access to nails, bolts, or tools, it offers access to antiques. Vendors display an excellent assortment. Primitives, advertisements, art, architectural items—it's all here and then some.

Jeepers Dollhouse Miniatures, Morgantown.

It's not necessary to own bees to appreciate Graham's Bee Works. Beginning on their own property in 1992, this beekeeping couple decided to expand their business and moved downtown in 1994. There are items to help with the care and maintenance of bees, educational materials, and even beeswax products for personal use or display. Sit in on workshops that teach the art of raising bees.

Chairs, beds, food, and even houses combine to total more than twenty thousand items in stock. Don't worry—there's plenty of room when everything is scaled down to size like it is at Jeepers Dollhouse Miniatures. Glass cases fill the middle of the shop. Stocked with tiny detailed items, there's even a selection of imaginative, locally made dollhouse wares.

57

Mulberry

Founded in 1858, Mulberry currently contains just less than 1,300 people. Interestingly, its plat was somehow misnamed Glicksburg by a surveyor. In 1938, with a population of only 817, Mulberry was considered the wealthiest town of its size in the whole United States.

For so small a town, it manages to throw a big downtown event. Mulberry Fest, the fourth weekend in June, features live music, a pizza-eating contest, a parade, and one phenomenal car show. See the whole town turn out for the family-friendly fun.

The best reason to visit Mulberry is Southfork Restaurant and Pub. This area favorite begins with a menu that's actually fun to read. Mulberry history, Indiana history, and even trivia are a way to get acquainted with this standout small-town restaurant. Among the sizable fish selection, walleye and fresh catfish are popular items. No matter what the entrée, begin the meal with the hand-cut, hand-dipped onion rings or, as they should be called, World Famous Onion Rings. Watch for specials like all-you-can-eat fried chicken that's served until it runs out . . . and it will.

NOTABLES

Robert D. Gaylor (b. 1930) spent most of his childhood in Mulberry. As an adult, he had the distinction of becoming the fifth chief master sergeant with a specialty revolving around enlisted soldiers' well-being. He advised Secretary of the Air Force John C. Stetson and Chiefs of Staff of the Air Force General David C. Jones and General Lew Allen Jr.

Channel 6 television host and Mulberry native Curley Hickenlooper (1920–2013) had a Saturday-morning TV program with friend Harlow through the 1960s until 1973.

Mulberry-born songstress Amanda Overmyer (b. 1984) placed eleventh in the seventh season of American Idol. She is the only Indiana finalist so far.

Zerna Sharp (1889–1981), also of Mulberry, was an editor of the Dick and Jane books. Although she did not write them, she was responsible for choosing the stories, the clothing of the characters, and even their names.

Vesto Slipher (1875–1969), a Mulberry-born astronomer, was in charge of the group, which also included his brother Earl Charles Slipher, that discovered the dwarf planet Pluto in March 1930.

Russell Stairs received one of the first pilot licenses. In 1928 he turned fourteen acres of his Mulberry field into a flying field, training other young men who wanted to be pilots. His attendees included John Glenn and Roger Chaffee, both future astronauts, the latter lost in the Apollo 1 fire.

Southfork Restaurant and Pub, Mulberry.

58

North Salem

Platted in 1835, then incorporated as a town in 1899, North Salem is a quiet place—unless it happens to be during the big community celebration. Old Fashion Days, a much-anticipated festival on Labor Day weekend, boasts the largest parade in all of Hendricks County. Plenty to do for all ages since 1975, some of the more hilarious events include a bed race, an outhouse race, and a spaghetti-eating contest. There's all kinds of sloppy, embarrassing fun to be had at this festival with a focus on unique events.

¶¶ eat

Bringing family recipes with him all the way from Sicily, the owner of Perillo's Pizzeria has created the real deal. Seating inside and out adds a little more elbow room to this smaller establishment. It's cash only, but expect Italian favorites like spaghetti and meatballs, frutti de mare, or fettuccine alfredo. And the eighteen-inch pizza and sausage-filled calzones are really out of this world.

shop

Deals galore are found within Garden Gate Gifts and Flowers. A florist, gift shop, antique shop, and chic boutique all occupy a space inside this wonderful building. Candles, clothing, furniture, jewelry—it's all here. Look for the sweet pink and green exterior.

North Salem Antiques and Sundries was the site of a long-ago pharmacy. It still possesses the original soda fountain counter and seating. Purchase ice cream and scan the shelving for wonderful antiques. Kids will love the inexpensive vintage coins available for purchase at the counter.

Garden Gate Gifts and Flowers, North Salem.

59

Perkinsville

Spelling isn't always easy. Perkinsville should be named Parkinsville. The founders of the town, platted in 1837, intended to pay tribute to resident William Parkins, an active, early settler who arrived in 1825. Somehow the name was confused with Perkins, and the town has carried it ever since.

The phrase "Don't blink or you'll miss it" may be cringe-worthy to a small-town lover, but in the case of Perkinsville it is absolutely correct. Once the site of a bustling saw- and gristmill, said to be one of the best flouring mills in Indiana, it is now a true bedroom community. Even in its lengthy history, though, it has never had more than 500 residents. As of the 2012 census, the population hovered around a mere 128 citizens. It's the oldest town in Madison County, but there are few buildings remaining in the town from its early days. Yet it is still proof that there is always something to see or do in a small town.

 eat

A small sign high up on a telephone pole pointing the way to Bonge's Tavern is the only indication of a destination down the ditch- and tree-lined street. Serving as a hardware store built in the 1830s, it is now, at least for those age twenty-one and up, an American gourmet destination. Make reservations for weekend visits or expect to wait two hours to get inside. Bonge's encourages visitors to use the massive parking lot as a tailgate party, even providing a Port-a-Potty from May to September. Folks in the know bring their own chairs, music, and stocked coolers. Once inside, the simple chalkboard menu highlights the current entrées created by the father-daughter chef team. Everything is homemade. Go for the Harger duck, the applewood-smoked prime rib, or the Perkinsville pork. Be sure to try the almost famous tomato soup and the jalapeño cornbread. Follow it up with anything from the dessert list.

Bonge's Tavern, Perkinsville.

60

Romney

Romney, or Columbia, as it was once called, was founded in 1831. It was named after Romney, West Virginia, the home of some of the first settlers.

🛍 shop

The Romney Toy Shop is a toy collector's paradise. Find well-known and loved toys from popular brands throughout the years. Amazingly organized, it's a breeze to hunt for anything specific. Reasonably (and often surprisingly) priced, toy shopping might turn out to be as exciting for grown-ups as it is for kids.

NOTABLES

Foxton Farm began in 1968 as a fox-hunting barn. It served as the home of the Purdue equestrian team for many years and is now a multidisciplinary stable.

Romney Toy Shop.

61

Rossville

Solomon Miller and his wife entered the area in March 1828, cleared land, and welcomed their first child into the world in October of that year. Other settlers soon followed. The installation of the Monon Railroad in 1883 helped the town gain a bit of extra momentum. In its long history, it wasn't without its series of setbacks, like the 1912 fire that destroyed seventeen businesses, the 1913 flood that disconnected Rossville from the county, and the 1961 tornado. But as the Rossville town motto goes, "Rossville is a place where you feel at home." It's a friendly, tidy, and cute little town if ever there was one.

Downtown Rossville.

Since 1984 the main street, town park, and Rossville High School fill with folks eager to join in the fun of the annual Summer's End Festival. Occurring on the fourth full weekend in August, it is activity packed. The Hornet Hustle five-kilometer walk and run and town-wide yard sales kick off the events. The Laurell Hodson Memorial Car and Bike Show, live entertainment, and street fair only add to the appeal of this family-friendly festival.

☀ play

Marvel at the twenty varieties of apples that come from the two thousand trees at Skiles Orchard and Farm Market. Inside the market, expect fresh fruits and vegetables and gifts as well as various odds and ends, including handcrafted and locally made products. Outside, explore the handful of greenhouses bursting with fragrant flowers and bedding plants. Children will love the play area created just for them.

Dan the Man's Taco Stand, Rossville.

🍴 eat

Dan the Man's Taco Stand is a tiki-themed oasis right downtown. Hand-painted murals displaying beach scenes, a tiki-hut ice cream counter, and oldies playing on the radio are certainly a different approach to decorating than what is typically found in a small town. Clean and bright, this airy restaurant features more than excellent tacos. The freshly cut in-house pork tenderloin sandwich with a side of their incredible curly cheese fries is a must. Available in two sizes, even the smaller pork tenderloin sandwich is a hefty serving. Giant appetites may want to tackle Dan the Man's Food Challenge. Consume three beach tacos, large cheese fries, and a sixteen-ounce drink or a sixteen-ounce breaded pork tenderloin sandwich topped with nacho cheese–covered curly fries and a drink in thirty minutes or less, and the winner gets it free—as well as their picture added to the "Real Men" wall.

Flour Mill Bakery, Bulk Foods, and Cheese is Rossville's best-kept secret. No longer down a country road, it's now easy to find and impossible to forget. Fifty kinds of donuts await morning customers. The shelves in this snug little shop are full of bulk food items like spices, gluten-free mixes, and pastas. Check the refrigerated case for cheese, pies, and cakes. The lemon crinkle cookies and cream horns are worth writing home about.

Clean and Christian themed, the Lion's Den is another bakery and café mix. It's all scratch made, but the locals love the breakfast items. It's not your typical biscuits and gravy. Neither are the cinnamon rolls.

Gluten-free sensitivity or not, the Sweet Spot Bakery and Cafe is remarkable. An avid baker, the owner had to come up with new ways to bake after the discovery of a daughter's painful allergy to gluten. After those years of tweaking, tasting, and tweaking some more, the public can now enjoy sandwiches, cookies, cakes, cinnamon rolls, breads, and other freshly baked items so incredible, it's hard to believe they are gluten free. Definitely try the monster cookies. Better yet, check the freezer for take-home sweet treats and breads.

Catfish, blue gill, the hand-breaded pork tenderloin sandwich, and the prime rib are the specialties at Treece's Restaurant and Lounge. Look to the whiteboard for the daily specials. There are plenty of appetizers to choose among, but go with the onion sticks: crispy, different, and delicious. Wine and beer are available.

🛍 shop

Perfectly organized, Rossville Quilts is a quilter's dream destination. Bolts of fabrics run almost the length of the sizable shop. Sewing machines occupy a healthy section, as do sewing notions such as threads, patterns, and other essential accessories. Workshop space with cushy, comfy chairs welcomes fellow quilters participating in social circles and classes all through the year.

62

Swayzee

Roll into the small town of Swayzee, and the big sign is impossible to ignore: "Welcome to the only Swayzee in the world!" How do they know? Well, town legend shares that during World War II, a postcard was sent by a serviceman overseas to Swayzee. It did not contain the name of the state, or any other identifying address, other than "Swayzee." Residents decided that that had to mean that in all the world, there was only one.

Named for the father of the landowner where two train tracks crossed in 1880, it had a slow start—until it experienced a gas boom in 1887 with the discovery of natural gas. In just over a decade, forty businesses had moved into the town. But after the natural gas ran out in 1900, the remaining businesses experienced a series of setbacks that caused many more doors to close or relocate. An explosion occurred at the glass factory in 1901, and fires took the lumberyard in 1906, both churches in 1918, and the flour mill in 1926.

Those who remained have created strong ties to the community and each other. For a rip-roarin' good time, Swayzee Farm Days includes an antique tractor show, a car show, a town parade, booths, food, and Kiddie Land. Look for it near the end of July.

🛍 shop

Touches of blue on the outside of Swayzee Antique Mall are attention getting and easy to spot. It may not look so large on the outside, but looks can be deceiving. There's room for everything, with more than six thousand square feet of floor space. Furniture, collectibles, coins, jewelry, vintage fishing equipment, holiday decor, and dainty teacups are abundant. So much to see, so much to browse.

NOTABLES

Workers at the Pipe Creek Junior limestone quarry discovered the Pipe Creek Sinkhole in 1996. Considered one of the best-preserved paleontological sites in the eastern half of North America, it represents a range of creatures, including new discoveries. Uncovering fossils that date back five million years to the Pliocene epoch, it was an unexpected event that resulted in years of successful digs.

Also noted on the town's welcome sign is another of Swayzee's offbeat claims to fame: it is the state record holder for the most overtimes in a basketball game. The March 15, 1964, game at the Marion Regional versus Liberty Center went into nine over-

times. Swayzee finally pulled out in front, winning 65–61.

The first town ordinance in Swayzee passed in 1890. It set the maximum bicycle speed at four miles per hour.

Dr. Aaron Wesley Dicus (1888–1978), the inventor of the turn signal, an author, and a songwriter, grew up in Swayzee.

Swayzee is the hometown of Joni T. Johnson (1934–1988), a painter and founder of the Talbot Street Art Fair. Her work can be found in the East Room of the White House and many celebrity homes.

63

Upland

When John Oswalt caught wind of a possible canal passing through a particular stretch of land, he snapped up what later became Upland in the 1830s. In the 1860s Jacob Bugher, anticipating the new railroad that would connect Columbus and Chicago, platted the town. Upland wasn't named for a founder, nor was it a name to honor some well-known political or historical figure. Instead, Upland was thought to be the highest point on the rail line.

LaRita's Lodge Bed and Breakfast, Upland.

Another gas-boom town, Upland took off upon the discovery of natural gas in 1886 and reveled in newfound prosperity and an influx of new residents. Businesses relocated to Upland, and the town saw an increase in population from 150 in 1880 to more than 1,000 residents in 1890.

Financially struggling, Taylor University took advantage of inexpensive land rates and extra perks (like ten thousand dollars in cash and ten acres of free land) in 1893 and opened its doors in Upland. Although the gas boom ended in the early 1900s, the college continued, eventually recovering and consistently named one of the top regional colleges in the Midwest. Close ties to the town let students make a difference locally.

🛏 stay

Watch the sun set over the pink barns and gently rolling hills found at LaRita's Lodge Bed and Breakfast. The story goes that the setting sun in LaRita's original home in Oklahoma caused the barns to look pink. LeLand painted the barns to give his wife a taste of Oklahoma in Indiana. Known as the LeLaLo Farm, named for the first three members of the family, it couldn't be a more scenic or restful place. Wander the property or relax in a glider with a big old book. Photo opportunities abound, especially with resident bison, cows, bulls, and llamas.

﹗ eat

Part restaurant and part ice cream parlor (with its own ice cream–only line), Ivanhoe's Ice Cream and Sandwich Shoppe is where area students and residents have gone for superb food, treats, and conversation since 1965. As far as food goes, the pork tenderloin sandwich and the chicken salad are wonderful. Pair either with a mini shake to better sample something from the ample ice cream menu. The ice cream and milk shake selection is unbeatable: there are one hundred sundaes and one hundred milk shakes on the Ivanhoe's menu. Complete either group of one hundred and become a part of Ivanhoe's Ice Cream and Sandwich Shoppe 100 Club, snagging a free Ivanhoe's 100 Club T-shirt and ice cream immortality with a nameplate on the Ivanhoe's wall.

NOTABLES

Barton Rees Pogue (1891–1965), an author, poet, professor, and even preacher, resided in Upland. Two poems, "The Kid Has Gone to College" and "Fortunes and Friendship," are thought to be about his town. Each year in April, the community remembers this beloved resident with the Barton Rees Pogue Poetry and Arts Festival. Just like its namesake, who read his work three thousand times during a lecture circuit, the festival enables creative types to share their work through readings, competitions, art display, and workshops. The town library, where he worked, was renamed in his honor.

Ivanhoe's Ice Cream and Sandwich Shop, Upland.

64

Winchester

In 1818 early settlers donated land in order to gain a county seat. Thought to be named for Winchester, Virginia, this was yet another town to get in on the gas boom of the 1880s and 1890s. For Winchester, glass was especially big business in those days.

Although Winchester draws folks for its unique assortment of attractions, shops, or restaurants, it holds a neat-themed festival: the Mom, Baseball, and Apple Pie Festival. This one-day event at Goodrich Park has an apple pie–baking contest, an apple pie–eating contest, pony-chip bingo, an auction, and, in quaint small-town style, a community picnic. Look for it in August.

Randolph County Courthouse, Winchester.

☀ play

Find the oldest Civil War monument in the state on the grounds of the gorgeous Randolph County Courthouse. Completed in 1890, and dedicated two years later, this granite Soldiers and Sailors Monument is rumored to be the second (or third) tallest, coming in just after the one in Indianapolis.

Bogies, Winchester.

Four detailed bronze sculptures by thirty-two-year-old renowned Chicago artist Lorado Tate guard each corner of the memorial.

If county commissioners had had their way, the Randolph County Courthouse would have long since been demolished. Fortunately, a small bridge-playing group of senior ladies decided to do a little fund-raising. They posed in the buff with a strategically placed porcelain replica of the courthouse in order to sell calendars. The publicity, and the dollars, poured in. The 1875 courthouse was saved and renovated back into the stunning second empire building seen today, mansard roof, bell tower, and all.

⑪ eat

Bogie's Soft Ice Cream seasonally serves fast lunches, dinners, and cool treats. Fan favorites include the ultimate nachos, the pineapple fluff, and caramel shakes. Really, any milk shake is good at this long-time ice cream spot.

El Carreton Mexican Restaurant may get busy, yet service is fast, fast, fast. Meals start with fresh salsa and chips. Entrées are piping hot and irresistible. The chimichangas real and the nachos real (with beef) are excellent choices and nicely sized. Featuring a full bar but still family friendly, it's a wonderful choice for Mexican cuisine.

House of Flavors Café and Coffee Bar, Winchester.

Hand-painted
dishware at Meeks
Antiques, Winchester.

A coffee shop, ice cream parlor, and diner, House of Flavors Café and Coffee Bar is the best-kept secret in Winchester. The ice cream side of things features a page of creative sundae flavors such as German chocolate cake, fudge mint, tropical luau, and the delicious pretzel twist. Coffee drinks also boast a full-page assortment. The caramel coffee frappuccino is smooth and satisfying.

 shop

When the economy took a nosedive, Countryside Antiques and Collectibles didn't want to go with it. Thinking outside the box, the owner placed vintage items everywhere outside as well as fresh fruits and vegetables. Inside, there are so many one-of-a-kind and timeworn items. The old school paraphernalia like desks and maps are outstanding. Tables and hutches, dishware, and bottles are in generous supply.

Meeks Consignment and Antique Store appears to be a typical antique shop—but it isn't. Notice the multiple locations of vintage-looking plates, platters, and serving ware. A true artist, the owner has hand-painted each and every breathtaking piece. At one point, a well-known department store was interested in selling his hand-painted works of usable art, but, unfortunately, he knew that the time he put into them wouldn't keep up with the demand, so he turned down the offer. Yes, there are antiques here, but the hand-painted pieces are definitely the highlight.

Southern Indiana

65

Batesville

The John Callahan Trust Company acquired a fifteen-year-old 120-acre homestead in 1852, originally purchased by Teunis Amack back in 1837. So began the railroad's grand plans for expansion. Officially founded in 1852, Batesville had the new railroad run right through it. The first resident, Joshua Bates, was the town platter and a member of the John Callahan Trust Company—and where the name for the town is believed to have originated. For the next thirty years, the fledgling town's forests would be stripped for local industries, clearing the way for future farmland, the source of the town's main trade.

🛏 stay

Mary Helen's Bed and Breakfast couldn't be more beautiful. With scenic views of a peaceful pond and a fine-dining experience, intimate weddings are a happy, frequent occurrence. Everyone else enjoys the country quiet and comfortable cabin feel.

☀ play

New digs provide a lot of room for the many photographs and memorabilia composing the Batesville Historical Society Museum. Built in 1910, the building alone is a beauty. Upstairs or down-, view remnants of the town's early industries from caskets to hospital beds, long-ago sports memorabilia, and then some.

More peaceful surroundings would be hard to find. Ertel Cellars Winery is a family-owned winery located on 200 quiet acres. Producing wine grapes since 1999, it wasn't until 2006 that they quit the grape-selling business and began crafting their own award-winning wine. Step up to the sparkling wine bar for a taste or dine in the high-ceilinged room.

The Gibson Theatre is wonderfully retro. Built during the 1920s, the exterior of this first-run movie theater looks like it came straight off Route 66. Balcony seating is an unexpected find.

eat

Consistency is the theme at Lil' Charlie's Restaurant and Brewery. From the ales brewed on the lower level to the spectacular specialty burgers like the Bulldog or Brewhouse with onion rings upstairs, the friendly servers and staff aim to please. Sip craft beer on the spacious patio while live acoustic music plays.

Lil' Charlie's Restaurant and Brewery, Batesville.

Pizza Haus adds a bit of German flair . . . even to pizza. The addition of sauerkraut is one way they do things a little differently. As good as the pizza is, some folks travel awesome distances for the steak hoagie.

Back in 1963, Schmidt Bakery sold not only baked goods but pizza as well. Ditching the pizza part of things by 1970, they narrowed the focus to what they do best: donuts, pastries, and everything in between. Locals love the donuts—but everyone rushes in when it is time for the Cherry Thing-a-Ling,

Schmidt Bakery, Batesville.

a fried-cherry and cherry-glazed donut. Otherwise, look for the special donut flavor of the day or try the colorful T cookies.

shop

Two stories of new and used books create the Bookshelf, an independent bookstore sure to wow. Get lost in the winding, towering shelves. Yes, it has happened. Child or adult, there are beaucoup books for everyone, buy, sell, or trade.

The Turquoise Hen, Batesville.

Though it might be a full-service florist, the Gooseberry Flower and Gift Shop puts extra emphasis on the word "gift." Pick through the green plants. Then search the shop for locally made soaps, candles, and cute gifts.

Days of absolute boredom are over after a visit to Grinning Goblin Comic Books and Games, which is clean, organized, and oh so spacious. Break out a demo game from the towering shelves in the corner and settle in at one of the many tables. Pop culture, comic books, and amazing board games are waiting.

With forty thousand square feet of shopping at RomWeber Marketplace, visitors are going to need to pace themselves. There's almost no end to the books, furniture, art, and antiques. Fortunately, this cavernous destination also holds an ice cream parlor and arcade (where most games are only a quarter).

Elegant and stylish, the Turquoise Hen is glamorous yet hospitable. Repurposed with chalk paint, the furniture here is irresistible. Women's clothing, accessories, and home decor are lovely.

Six-year-old William Weberding was slowly recovering from an illness and turned to carving wood to pass the time. As the years went by, he didn't set his hobby aside but grew it enough to open Weberding's Carving Shop. Now run by three generations (two of whom are carvers), the space is twenty-two thousand square feet with something for everyone.

NOTABLES

Batesville became the first city west of Cincinnati, Ohio, to possess streetlights.

New York Times best-selling author Rachel Macy Stafford was formerly a Batesville teacher.

66

Bean Blossom

Beanblossom or Bean Blossom? The town is commonly spelled both ways. Like so many small towns, Bean Blossom had more than a simple spelling variation. It originally began as Georgetown, named for the first settler and founder of the town, George Groves. He had a gristmill and created the town in 1833. When the post office appeared in 1842, it took the name of Bean Blossom, the Native American translation of the nearby creek. Old town legend claims that the name stemmed from someone almost drowning in the creek: a settler, soldier, or Native American—no one is sure. But the story remains the same: a person with the name of Bean Blossom almost drowned in the creek and had the area named after him.

Bean Blossom Covered Bridge.

☼ play

One of not even a handful of Howe single-truss bridges, the Bean Blossom Covered Bridge dates back to 1880. Built by Captain Joseph Balsey, the charming red bridge extends over Bean Blossom Creek. It is a one-lane bridge, but there is an area on one side of the bridge to carefully pull over and park if needed.

Bluegrass and country music fans shouldn't miss the Bill Monroe Bluegrass Hall of Fame & Country Star Museum, a trove of memorabilia from big-name bluegrass and country music stars such as Johnny Cash, Dolly Parton, and Loretta Lynn. Time a visit to coincide with the Bill Monroe Memorial Bean Blossom Bluegrass Festival, the oldest continuously running bluegrass festival in the world.

shop

Nothing is haphazardly arranged at Plum Creek Antiques. Look for Katy Did, an awesome Model A all decked out in steampunk style. So many collections of things like jewelry, handkerchiefs, fans, bottles, and jars make it a win for many a collector!

Plum Creek Antiques, Bean Blossom.

67

Cannelton

L iving and working in the company town of Coal Haven, the handful of coal families were employed by the American Cannel Coal Company. A few short years later, fire broke out and destroyed a chunk of the fledgling town. Most families moved on. Even the original owners ditched the company. New stakeholders took over, including Francis Yates Carlile. Prior to surveying the town in the 1840s, Carlile allowed the remaining families to vote on a new town name. They chose from Huntsville, Hobartsville, Cannelburg, and Cannelton. Surprisingly, Cannelton was not the winner. Instead, Coal Haven became Cannelburg because of cannel coal, a highly volatile, oily bituminous coal mined here all the way up through the 1960s. By 1844 frequent confusion regarding the name was enough to officially switch the name to Cannelton.

Now living in a town of scarcely fifteen hundred people, Canneltonians come together in a festival devoted to arts and history. The Cannelton Heritage Festival offers hands-on arts-and-crafts projects for kids, artisans and craftspeople demonstrating their talents, plus live music with plenty of food. It's one day only, so look for it in October.

🛏 stay

Blue Heron Bed and Breakfast is tucked away down a country road and surrounded by gorgeous views. No sharing here: spread out and enjoy the whole farmhouse. Eat a delicious homemade breakfast at the barn overlooking the grapevines. Yes, the owners also possess nearby Blue Heron Winery. Tranquil, restful, and lovely, it's a peaceful retreat with convenient access to the Hoosier National Forest.

Blue Heron Winery, Cannelton.

☼ play

Way up in the hills, Blue Heron Winery is a lovely destination that features a tasting room and gift shop with items from local artists—including the owners. Multilevel decks overlook a view that's three hundred feet above the Ohio River. Focusing on American and French American grapes, like Chambourcin, Fredonia, and Marechal Foch, there are just under a dozen wines for sale—and tasting. Sample Four Stars, named in honor of four family members' military backgrounds. The winery is located on the same property where Gary grew up. Be sure to ask about the time his father asked his elementary school–age self to redirect traffic.

Once the largest industrial building in the United States west of the Allegheny Mountains, the Cannelton Cotton Mill was constructed from 1849 to 1851. Made of Indiana limestone, the mill provided jobs for almost four hundred people, mostly women and girls. It is said that it once produced two hundred thousand pounds of cotton batting and four million yards of cotton sheeting each year. The mill closed in 1954, was listed on the National Register of Historic Places in 1975, and became a National Historic Landmark in 1991. After languishing in disrepair for decades, the Cannelton Cotton Mill was converted into seventy low-income apartments. The exterior, though imposing with its two one-hundred-foot towers, is far more stark and severe than architect Thomas Alexander Tefft's original design yet is still considered by many to be one of the most impressive stone structures of the pre–Civil War era. It is a commanding presence just off the downtown.

Originally intended to move commercial traffic along the water, Cannelton Locks and Dam was a replacement project to streamline an aging structure. Costing $98,040,000 in 1962, the locks and dam have essentially created a 114-mile lake that runs

Celtic Cross, Cannelton.

from Cannelton to Louisville, Kentucky. It is perfect for water fun. Access the scenic overlook to view the Cannelton Locks and Dam from above.

The 20' x 22' x 4' sandstone rock was already there when Greg Harris got to work, six days a week for twenty-three months. He carved the Celtic Cross through winter snows and summer heat to complete what is believed to be the largest in situ (of its own stone) cross in the world. It's high up on a hillside, so four-wheel drive will be required to get to this one. Considered by many to be one of the seven wonders of Indiana, it is only a short distance away from Blue Heron Winery.

The Flood Wall Mural serves to protect Cannelton from river flooding while also revealing town-history highlights in larger-than-life murals. Scenes depict the steamboats, landmarks, and long-ago life along the Ohio River throughout its history in the 100'-long, 12'-high series of five panels. Although the wall blocks all access to the riverfront, it isn't without any reason. Disastrous flooding in 1937 spurred construction of the wall in the 1940s. Look for the waterline markings painted on buildings near the river to get an idea of what the town faced almost one hundred years ago.

What do roller-derby girls, Colts cheerleaders, Boy Scouts, and a bachelor's party share in common? They have all enjoyed horseback rides at Froehlichs Outfitter and Guide Horse Rides. After fourteen years of waiting to receive the proper approval, this family-owned business is the only authorized guide and outfitter of the Hoosier National Forest. Based on experience, riders are matched with the horses before taking off through the German Ridge Trail that bumps up against the property. Twenty-four miles of trail await. Drink in the wooded landscape and rock formations and, if the ride is long enough, even a cave. It's open year-round, so dress appropriately for the weather.

Flood levels, Cannelton.

There's room to roam at the 202,000-acre Hoosier National Forest. More than 200 miles of trails provide options for horseback riding, mountain biking, and walking. Geodes are a common site in certain places. Others bring along noncommercial equipment to pan for gems and flakes of gold in the streams. Caves, wildlife viewing areas, and even water recreational opportunities provide something for everyone.

What really happened at Lafayette Springs? Local opinion differs on the event surrounding the historic site named for General Marquis de Lafayette. The story goes that his steamboat *The Mechanic* wrecked on May 9, 1826, on the Ohio River. Some say that while on his way to Louisville, his boat hit Rock Island, a Cannelton rock formation. Others believe he was on the Kentucky side of the river. Either way, both stories agree that he lost a desk containing eight thousand dollars, a considerable sum in 1826, and important papers. Lafayette survived thanks to the deckhands. Some hold that a local family heard the noise and offered Lafayette a bed for the night. Others say that the sixty-five-year-old Lafayette spent the night on the riverbank. Eventually, a steamer, *The Paragon,* was spotted, and arrangements were made to carry Lafayette to his intended destination. If nothing else, everyone does agree that the site of this event occurred at Lafayette Springs.

Named after a favorite principal, Myers Grade School is the oldest continuously used school in the whole United States. Built in 1868, it was the first public school to operate in Cannelton. Originally called Cannelton High School, and later the Free School, it cost ninety-eight hundred dollars to build and offered grades 1 to 8. Today, the delightful building holds grades 2 through 6. It still possesses the original slate blackboards, stairs, cloakrooms, radiators, and woodwork. One of the two stairwells on the main floor, one for the boys and one for the girls, has an extra step. Which side has the extra stair? It is a favorite student debate.

The Perry County Museum occupies what was once the Perry County Courthouse. Switching the boundaries in 1859 made the county seat move from Rome, Indiana, to Cannelton, resulting

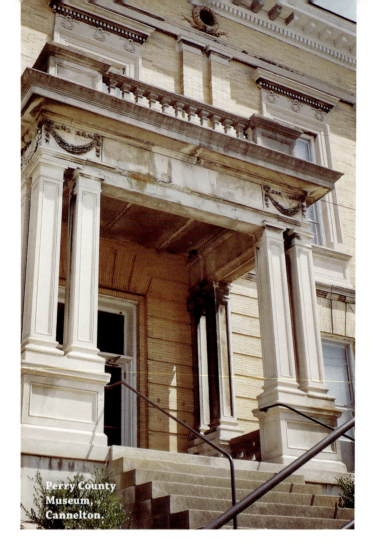

Perry County Museum, Cannelton.

in a makeshift courthouse in a Cannelton schoolhouse. Known to locals as the "Old Gym," the two-story school held a packed crowd for a big trial in 1893 when the floor suddenly shifted underfoot. It was time for a new courthouse. In 1896 nearby Tell City residents were determined to be the new county seat, and they began constructing a courthouse just four months after Cannelton. But Cannelton finished its courthouse first at a cost of thirty thousand dollars. Both offered county commissioners use of their not-yet-finished courthouses for one dollar.

SOUTHERN INDIANA

Canneltonians took it a step further. Deciding that they needed to take matters into their own hands, they waited until the Tell City county commissioner had left for the day. They had a bit of a wait. The commissioner had heard that Cannelton was considering moving documents into the offices as soon as they were completed, and he was on his way to the circuit judge to file a restraining order to keep that from happening. Little did he know that the town was watching. As soon as he was gone, townsfolk sounded the fire station bell, and somewhere around 350 citizens helped carry documents from one building to the next, thus securing its county-seat status. It continued its services until 1994 when Tell City built a new courthouse and took over the reins as county seat. The Perry County "Old Courthouse" Museum stands in a state of disrepair amid fund-raising efforts—yet is truly a remarkable small-town museum. From the cotton mill and pioneer items to Native American artifacts and Cannelton Pottery, the long history of this river town is brought to life.

Shubael Little Pioneer Village, named for early settler (and original owner of the land) Shubael Little, began in 2000 after the dedication of the Hinton Cabin. It is unlike any other pioneer village attraction. Prepare for rugged paths and thick woods dotted with 1850s cabins. Wander down trails that lead to various early cabins like the Adam Shoemaker Cabin, the Homer Hull Carter Cabin (built in 1858), and the James Falls Cabin. No walking by cabins here. Step inside and see history come alive. Letters, photos, vintage books, and furnishings highlight the purpose of each cabin and detail life in the early days of Indiana. The Edgar Carter Blacksmith Shop and Forge is exceptional—and it works. Discover an operational carpenter shop, sheep pen, the Millstone one-room schoolhouse, and the Troy Stone Jail. Other buildings, including the Oriole Methodist Church, are set to move or undergo construction or a bit of renovation. Time visits for the third weekend in October or the second Saturday in December to enjoy unique annual events not found anywhere else.

Rocky Point Waterfront Grille is a year-round local dining destination. With seating indoors and out, Rocky Point offers an unparalleled vantage point from the second-story deck that looks out over the Ohio River. A full bar, juicy burgers, and a seafood menu keep tourists coming back.

Dishing up hard-packed or soft-serve ice cream, Wall's Drive-In is a decades-old hangout. Famous for its Big Square Burger, there's a mix of food and treats here. Parking is ample and so is the selection.

NOTABLES

Honor those lost at the Northwest Orient Airlines Flight 710 Memorial. All fifty-seven passengers and six crew members aboard the Lockheed L-188 Electra perished when the plane disintegrated during the flight. The inscription reads: "This memorial, dedicated to the memory of 63 persons who died in an airplane crash at this location, March 17, 1960, was erected by public subscription in the hope that such tragedies will be eliminated."

Rock Island, a sand bar, was a favorite long-ago picnic spot. When Cannelton Locks and Dam moved in, Rock Island became submerged in water, and a piece of history was gone.

Cannelton-born William P. Birchler was a marine in World War I. Later elected to the Indiana House of Representatives on the Republican ticket in 1948, he served every year thereafter until 1963, when he lost reelection.

68

Corydon

Corydon possesses a remarkable past. The first territorial capital was not located in Indianapolis, or even Corydon, but in Vincennes. Deemed a more central location in 1813, as the majority of people lived in the southern part of Indiana, the capital was relocated to Corydon. In June 1816, forty-three delegates gathered to compose the first state constitution. Due to the Indiana heat, they discussed business outside under what has been referred to as the "Constitution Elm," a massive shade tree with a trunk that spanned five feet across. Although the tree has long since died, the trunk of it remains on the courthouse grounds and is protected. That autumn the first General

Corydon State Historic Site.

Assembly of representatives, senators, and the lieutenant governor convened in the new capital building. As of December 11, 1816, Indiana was officially a state. As for Corydon, it was the state capital until 1825, when Indianapolis was reasoned to be the more central location.

Nine buildings still stand from when Corydon was the state capital. They include the capitol building, Governor's Headquarters, First State Office Building, Adams-Payne House,

Cedar Glade (also known as the Kintner-McGrain House), Harvey Heth House, Posey House, Westfall House (the oldest building), and Branham Tavern. Public tours are available through the capitol building and the Governor's Headquarters.

🛏 stay

A historic home turned bed-and-breakfast, Kintner House Inn possesses an astonishing fifteen rooms. After the battle of Corydon on July 9, 1863, General Morgan turned Kintner House Inn into his headquarters. He learned of the defeat at Gettysburg from the innkeeper's daughter, Sallie, a Northern supporter. Lost to fire in 1871, the new inn was rebuilt bigger, better, and in a new location. Reopening in 1873, it is the same inn that stands on the corner today. On the National Register of Historic Places, the inn's rooms feature tall ceilings and fancy antique beds, yet they are child friendly. Perfectly situated downtown, it makes a first-rate home base.

☀ play

The only Civil War battlefield in the entire state of Indiana is found at Battle Park. The battle of Corydon, on July 9, 1863, although brief and generally considered a minor skirmish by Civil War historians, has certainly left a lasting impact on the town. Confederate general John Hunt Morgan charged into the outer edge of the town. Folks had spent the night preparing for the arrival of the 2,000 soldiers. Although not caught unprepared, they did not have much in the way to stop the more experienced Morgan and his men. The Harrison County Home Guard (known officially as the Sixth Regiment of the Indiana Legion) was made up of some 450 men who fought to keep Morgan at bay. They didn't last for more than thirty minutes before they panicked at the two cannons fired their way. Those who could fled. More than 350 men were captured though soon turned over for parole upon entering the town of Corydon. Morgan lost 11 soldiers, the Harrison County Home Guard lost 4, though many more from both sides were wounded. Stores, three mills, and the treasury had to turn over money to Morgan or watch their businesses go up in flames. Corydon businesses paid the money. Later that day, Morgan and his men finally left and continued northward. Annual reenactments of the encounter get the whole town involved. The Battle of Corydon Battlefield is now a public park. Tour the tiny log cabin. It's built to mimic housing styles (and sizes) of the nineteenth century. Look for the low-to-the-ground informational plaque and the six-pound field gun located on the grounds. So, too, are the recovered mooring post and anchor chain from the *Alice Dean,* the steamer boat sunk by Morgan's men before they arrived at Corydon. There is also the grave of a casualty from the skirmish, Georia Nantz.

This is the birthplace of Indiana. The 1813 Corydon State Historic Site held the first delegates who got Indiana approved as a state—though the structure was originally intended to be the courthouse for Harrison County. Made of local limestone, and using nearby poplar and walnut logs for the roof and ceiling supports, it's a well-built, rather dignified structure. Back when the state was in dire need of funding and on the verge of bankruptcy in the 1840s, folks auctioned off everything they could get their hands on . . . except for one item: the barrister bookshelves in the upstairs room wouldn't fit through the door. They are originals to the building. Amazingly enough, when the current courthouse was completed back in 1929, the town restored the capitol building, opening it as a state memorial in 1930. The doors are open year-round, and tickets are modestly priced.

Located next door, the Governor's Headquarters is a nice walk-through. It was originally a private home built in 1817 by resident Davis Floyd, then a member of Indiana's state legislature, but he lost it after the panic of 1819, the first U.S. financial crisis in times of peace. The state swooped in and purchased the property to house the governor, William Hendricks. He lived in the home from 1822 to 1825. Judge William A. Porter purchased the building in 1841 as his residence. Though only the first floor is available for tours, it is still enjoyable.

Finally, meander through the Porter Law Office, conveniently located next to the Governor's Headquarters. Constructed back in 1819 by Henry P. Coburn, then the clerk of the Indiana Supreme Court, it later became the office of Judge William Porter. He was also speaker of the Indiana House of Representatives. Many future Indiana lawmakers studied in this building.

Tee time! Rain or shine, grab the family and go to Golf Shores Fun Center for an inside or outside golfing extravaganza. Play an eighteen-hole round of mini golf outdoors or venture in for black-light mini golf. Bordered by murals painted by area schoolkids in exchange for pizza, it adds a personal touch.

The Binkley Cave System is Indiana's newest cave system. What's more, it is also the longest in the state—and eleventh longest in the country. It wasn't until 2010 that experienced cavers finally discovered an entrance to the thirty-eight-mile cave system that wasn't located on private property. Surprisingly, they also found a slew of Ice Age bones, one of the largest collections in North America, to go with it. Just two years later Indiana Caverns was open for business. Float along underground during the twenty-five-minute cave ride. Walk past the four-story waterfall. Bring walking shoes and a jacket to this year-round attraction. Even in the intense heat of a Hoosier summer, it stays a balmy fifty-four degrees. The truly adventurous may want to take the longer uDig Paleo Dig, an eight-hour stint working with the fossil excavation team, to dig up the many more fossils just beneath the surface. It's messy, thrilling, and made for those age ten and up.

Leora Brown School is a bit of history and a lot of heart. The last standing segregated school for African Americans left in Indiana, the Corydon Colored School (as it was originally named) was built in 1891. The school graduated its first class in 1897. It is named for Leora Brown, an African American woman who graduated from the school, attended a teaching college, and then returned to teach others for twenty-six years; it's a wonderful honor to the woman who helped shape a community. A section of the original blackboard still stands, its chalky scribbles forever protected.

Two hundred miles of trails await as part of the three thousand acres that compose O'Bannon Woods State Park. Along

Turtle Run
Winery,
Corydon.

with the usual outdoor activities like hiking, horse trails, fishing, and biking, there are also the mid-nineteenth-century blacksmith forge and the historic (and working) haypress at the pioneer farmstead.

Kick back and relax in an atmosphere that's inviting and hospitable. Perched on thirty-five acres of rolling hills and surrounded by forest, Scout Mountain Winery is easy to love. Owners Mike and Margaret have only been in business since 2009, but Mike has been crafting wines for more than twenty years. Even dry-wine lovers will enjoy the unique sweet wines available here. Discover delicious local goat cheese, Margaret's seasonal bread, and a lively atmosphere that's unpretentious and oh so comfortable. Look out for live music and special events scattered here throughout the year.

Sit at the tasting room inside Turtle Run Winery or visit during production hours and grab a seat there instead. It's a neat place to be a part of the action—and an easy way to chat with Jim, the winemaker and owner. Turtle Run Winery got its name from the once seemingly nonstop parade of turtles that moved from one

Alberto's Italian Restaurant, Corydon.

pond to another. After a small earthquake drained the ponds, the turtles disappeared, but the notable wines remain. They are crafted the French way, with no added sugar; even the sweet wines are sugar free. Tours are available.

♦♦ eat

Alberto's Italian Restaurant features fine dining in a casual, cozy space. This is the real deal. Award-winning Italian executive chef Alberto Papsodero uses local ingredients to prepare amazing, eye-appealing food. Local favorites include chicken piccata, seared mahi-mahi, spaghetti and meatballs, and bruschetta of every kind. In a fun twist: there is no separate kids menu. Children age ten and under may choose any item from the adult menu and have it perfectly portioned for them.

Opening its doors during the Great Depression, Emery's Premium Ice Cream was actually located in New Albany, Indiana. After the business changed hands, it moved and reopened in Corydon. Yes, the soda fountains, the counter seating, and even the vintage wall art all hail from that long-ago shop. Emery's still delights the area with its old-fashioned malts and fountain drinks, bulk candy assortment, and homemade ice cream flavors that include vanilla, banana, and raspberry peach.

Emphasizing homemade breakfasts and lunches, with the occasional themed dinner hours thrown in to keep it interesting, Frederick's Cafe is the kind of place that creates loyal forever fans. That just doesn't happen overnight. Each local has a favorite dish—and they all differ. It's homemade, so expect to wait for it, but oh, is it worth it.

🛍 shop

Bookworm Used Bookstore has been around a long time. This will be a hit with romance novel fans. Bookworms now holds somewhere around thirty thousand gently used books of all kinds.

Gifts and collectibles are combined at Collections of the Home Place. Wall art and seasonal decor, rag rugs and curtains, this shop covers all the bases. To put it another way, country decor is situated everywhere—and outstandingly organized.

Visit the Hurley D. Conrad Memorial Bandstand downtown near the courthouse. The local band leader, Hurley was also the son of C. W. Conrad, the man responsible for starting Conrad Music Service in 1890 with his son Claude (though it was known as Conrad and Son Piano Company). In 1925 the business passed to the second generation, and Hurley Conrad took the reins. Expanding the product line, he grew the business until passing it on to his twin sons, Charlie and Paul, in 1960. They changed the name to Conrad Music Service to reflect their expansion efforts. Handling thousands of instruments for school orchestra and band ensembles at the start of the school year is just the beginning. There are also private lessons, sales, and repairs. Admire the sheets of music, the shining instruments for sale, and the numerous accessories in Indiana's fourth-oldest family-owned music store.

Displaying an assortment of artisan products is just one part of Harrison County Arts and the Artisan Center, or HCA. This nonprofit organization provides art educations of all kinds. From workshops to after-school programs to large-scale community art-focused initiatives, this group has done it all.

Roam the rooms of goodies at Old Town Store Antiques. Since their opening in September 2012, they have expanded to include more than four thousand square feet of antiques. The young owners are passionate about their business—and are always on the hunt for "new" additions.

Browse the converted barn turned antique shop at Red Barn Antique Mall. Not one, not two, but three floors of vintage items and collect-

Art from the Artisan Center.

ibles await. In business for more than fifty-five years, they've got a fantastic selection of items in a range of styles. Say hello to Smokey the cat, who flits around the premises.

Red, Wine, and Blush is party central for grown-ups. Wines from around the world take the stage with a room devoted just to them. Also find specialty beers, gourmet foods, stemware, and accessories to cover all the bases.

Watch an artist work at White Cloud Window Stained Glass and Supplies. In this unusual shop for any city, let alone a town, completed stained-glass pieces are available for sale, or bring in a design and let owner Roni get to work. Restoration, repair, custom beveling, and sandblasting are a few of the services offered at this bright little shop. Participate in a slew of workshops for beginners, or even couples, in a particular design or technique.

There's nothing pretentious about Zimmerman Glass Factory. Watch a demonstration by the fourth-generation glass blower inside the ample workshop space. Innumerable Corydon residents possess a piece of this fabulous local art.

69

French Lick

French Lick Resort.

William A. Bowles laid out seventy-seven lots that marked the beginning of the town of French Lick on May 2, 1857. The area, however, had already seen settlers long before. Beginning as a French trading post due to its closeness to both the sulfur springs and a salt lick, by 1811 a secured ranger post became a part of the landscape. A few decades would pass until the budding community would appear on an 1837 map—and it was known as Salt Springs.

stay

French Lick Resort was up and running in 1845, decades before the town was even officially a town. But two things happened to really push the resort into the public eye: a championship golf course designed by Donald Ross and Pluto Water. Usually referred to as "Hill Course" or "Upper Course," the golf course has since been landscaped to mimic its long-ago design. "Pluto Water," on the other hand, was the term used for the mineral springs located on the property. Said to be restorative and healing, Pluto Water was even shipped internationally. Guests to the hotel would spend a month, enjoying the healing properties of "nature's greatest laxative," Pluto Water.

French Lick Resort.

Lost River Lazy River or the three-story water-play structure with a one-thousand-gallon dumping bucket? Water slides or floating lily pads? So many choices, what with forty thousand square feet of water fun at Big Splash Adventure Indoor Waterpark. Supremely family friendly, the park also has an outdoor pool, an arcade, and a couple of on-site restaurants in addition to lodging. Life jackets and lifeguards are provided, but parents should still remain with their child at all times.

Turn the kids loose at Shotz Laser Tag and Mini Golf. No one can resist a competitive game of laser tag. Head outside for a round of miniature golf on eighteen pleasantly landscaped holes, or stay inside for nine holes of black-light mini golf. Just don't forget the quarters: there are all sorts of arcade games here, too. New additions include a thirty-two-foot rock climbing wall and a three-station bungee trampoline.

⟨⟩ eat

Though technically not in French Lick, but close enough to count, French Lick Winery and the Vintage Café are an Indiana winery and Italian restaurant sharing the same spacious location that was once the site of

French Lick Resort.

the Kimball piano factory, where 250 pianos and 150 electronic organs were pounded out in a day. The Vintage Café features homemade Italian dishes. Pan bigio, or "gray bread" (named for its traditional use of unrefined flour), is a crusty Italian country bread paired with an herbed olive oil. Opt for either the thirty-two-inch thin-crust pizza made with wild yeast just like they did in Naples in the 1800s or the creamy ravioli. Finish it off with a hunk of wine cake, a nicely hued Bundt cake prepared with French Lick Winery's award-winning red wine. Then clink glasses with a friend at the lengthy wine-tasting bar. Most tastings are free. Coloring books and crayons are available for little ones to pass the time. There's a lot of seating both at the wine-tasting counter and at the café portion of the business.

NOTABLES

Both the Chicago Cubs and the Chicago White Sox held spring training in French Lick during World War II when travel was restricted.

Basketball legend Larry Bird played basketball at Springs Valley High School, leaving behind top scoring status. In his professional career, he was a twelve-time National Basketball Association All-Star and won three NBA Championships and two NBA Finals MVP Awards. He was a part of the "Dream Team," the 1992 men's gold-medal-winning Olympic basketball team.

70

Friendship

Friendship Bridge.

Friendship began as Harts Mill in 1837. The post office was already in business by the time William Hart laid out the town in 1849. Some sources say the town was also referred to as Paulson. But by 1868 the name was changed to Friendship. Local saying holds that it is because the local people were so, well, friendly. This unincorporated community may have only fifty or so residents, but they are just as friendly today. In June and September, however, the population always swells when it's time for the National Muzzle Loading Rifle Association shoots. More than just various competitions for muzzle-loading rifle, tomahawk throwing, pistol, shotgun, and knife throwing (among others), it is also part flea market. This open-air flea market sprawls across two parts of the town. Even this event is more than a typical flea market, with nightly campfires, live music, dancing, auctions, and on-site camping.

☀ play

Stone-arch bridges are few and far between. Here in Friendship spans one of the best and lengthiest examples of this bridge in the state. Built in 1909 by Henry Harman, Friendship Bridge, sometimes called Olean Road Bridge, is a 104-foot bridge possessing four arches across tiny Raccoon Creek. These bridges had their heyday until World War I and the discovery of concrete. Unfortunately, concrete has been added in places like the top of the railings and the retaining walls. Aside from these disfiguring blemishes, the bridge stands as intended.

71

Greensburg

In 1824 Greensburg was chosen as the county seat and named for a town in Pennsylvania of the same name by the wife of one of the first settlers, who also happened to be the mother of four daughters. The voting on the final name was put into the hands of mostly single unmarried men. It is no wonder that these bachelors wholeheartedly supported the town name.

Like most small towns, there's always a big festival. In Greensburg there are two. The new Tenderloin Throwdown event crowns the best-of-the-best pork tenderloins, while the September Tree City Festival has been around since 1979. A baking contest with a special kids competition, Battle of the Bands music event, talent show, watermelon-eating contest, and parade provide oodles of entertainment options for the whole family.

🚐 stay

Park it on the front porch swing at Nana's Bed and Breakfast. Delicious breakfasts might include a tasty parfait topped with fresh fruit and a generous slab of quiche. Hope for the dried-fruit-studded white chocolate chip scones.

☀ play

For fine art, turn to Art on the Square. Local artists represent a variety of media that cover the walls in a changing display, The ample workshop space provides a bit of hands-on fun.

Something isn't quite right about the Decatur County Courthouse. It's a bit

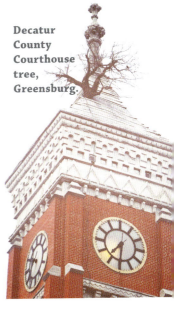

Decatur County Courthouse tree, Greensburg.

Carriage on the Square Smokehouse, Greensburg.

Funky Monkey Café inside It's Your Dime, Greensburg.

green, in fact. Towering high above the town below, the courthouse roof sports a Mulberry tree. Put there by nature, there's documentation of a tree (even, at times, multiple trees) making a home on the top of the courthouse since 1870. Records reveal that one tree reached a height of fifteen feet. After so many years, the trees die off, but a new one always takes its place. It's quirky, it's fun, and it's also why Greensburg is nicknamed "Tree City."

It began with a plate souvenir. The Last Supper Museum holds the famous painting in different re-creations from around the world from wood, banana leaves, and even cigar bands. The museum occupies an entire ranch house.

⑆ eat

Baby-back ribs have never been more fall-off-the-bone tender. Carriage on the Square Smokehouse smokes chicken, pork, and beef in what used to be an old carriage house back in the 1920s. Order the ultimate nachos, beef brisket, or the Walking Pony. Choose the homemade mac 'n' cheese as a side. Follow it up with graham cracker ice cream.

Homemade sides are hard to choose among at Cecil's Pork 'n' More, but the fried potatoes and onions are a must. Pair them with the brisket and find out where the term "hog heaven" really comes from. Indoor seating, homemade desserts, and changing daily specials combine for an excellent dining experience.

Like the owner of Dawg House Diner says, it's "where the only time being in the Dawg House is a good thing." All-beef hot dogs are served with a twist: unique flavor combinations and a menu boasting oodles of different kinds of hot dogs. Build your own hot dog or try the reuben or firehouse dog. Although there's a railing in place to keep it family friendly, it does have more of a bar feel.

The Funky Monkey Café inside of It's Your Dime serves coffee and cheesecake. Everybody raves over the specialty coffee drinks like German chocolate cake, PB o' Chocolate, and the morning monkey blend. Noncoffee lovers should try a hot chocolate with a shot of flavoring.

Perched on historic Pleak's Hill, Highpoint Orchard may hold more than thirty-five varieties of apples, pears, and peaches, but the renovated barn is more than just a market. Inside the lovely, spacious interior, find mouth-watering lunches at the café. Get the chicken salad, the soup of the day, or an appealing green salad and a slice of fruit pie—à la mode, of course.

The first Indonesian restaurant in the Midwest (and still the first in Indiana), Mayasari Indonesian Grill concocts memorable meals. Mango tea is a must. So, too, is the gluten-free pork tenderloin or the chicken satay. Welcoming and warm menu items, learn their unique story from the source. It involves a restaurant-owning grandma in Indonesia sending twenty-seven equally hardworking family members off to college.

Mayasari Indonesian Grill, Greensburg.

The "secret-recipe" pork tenderloin sandwich is a must when near Storie's Restaurant. But locals know to save room for one thing: graham cracker pie. Twenty-five pies are baked daily to keep up with demand. Many recipes come straight from a decades-old family recipe book. Taste the difference.

🛍 shop

Part honey bar and part women's clothing shop, Denim and Honey is one unique yet beautiful boutique. Tin ceilings, chandeliers, and touches of wood highlight the quality apparel. Raw-honey

Storie's Restaurant, Greensburg.

tastings offer a healthier way to jazz up beverages and baked items. Sample the orange blossom or fireweed honey.

Live music events or antique shopping, coffee shop or the new home of Christian's Kinderladen toy store, It's Your Dime is a friendly, bustling hub. With furniture, home decor, paint your own pottery, and antiques of all kinds, it stands on its own as a "must visit."

All towns need something like Little Frogs and Fairies. Consignment items for baby and kids have never looked so sparkling and neat. From clothes to toys to books, the range of items (and ages represented) is remarkable.

Holding bits of vintage, bits of shabby chic, and a nice assortment of quality furniture (especially tables), Magnolia Mercantile makes for quite the experience. New arrivals are common. Expect to take a bit of time getting through the nooks.

Old Picket Fence carries vintage and new shabby-chic items just waiting for a permanent home. Charmingly decorated pieces of furniture hold a smaller mix of retro or new items. Ask for help finding specific items, and they will get to work.

For anyone wanting to wander through an almost endless selection of antiques, Pickers Paradise is it. Vintage toy enthusiasts should definitely stop inside. For everyone else, the vast rows of odds and ends might prove tempting.

Rainbow-hued fabrics are just the start of Tree City Stitches. This quilt shop offers a vast selection of items for any level quilter. Workshops and other group sewing projects add to the fun.

NOTABLES

During the Civil War, local men camped on the courthouse grounds to defend Greensburg against Morgan's Raiders if they decided to try to take the town.

Stop in to see the hefty vintage cash register still in use at County Supply Company for ninety years.

An 1861 ordinance forbade hogs from running freely through the town to root for grubs at the courthouse—unless the hog had a ring in its nose.

72

Hatfield

Originally named Fair Fight, the new town was settled by a dozen families and possessed a blacksmith and occasionally portable sawmills by 1883. James Hatfield owned the first store and, it has been said, even the property that began the town. Now, more than a hundred years later, it holds roughly eight hundred people.

☼ play

Wander really far off the beaten path to drive across the longest bridge left of its kind: Boner Bridge. This iron bowstring bridge, sometimes referred to as Pyeatt's Mill Bridge, was built back in 1866. Three 50-foot arching red spans with a center span of 160 feet reach across Little Pigeon River to connect Spencer County with Warrick County. Mild local traffic takes advantage of this fabulous iron bridge that is located way out in the country.

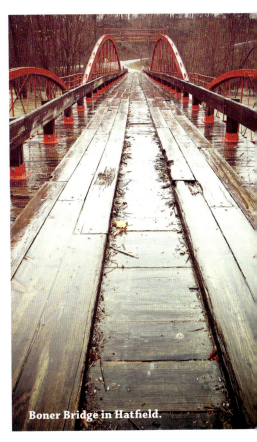

Boner Bridge in Hatfield.

73

Holton

Carolyn's Collectibles, Holton.

Platted in 1854, the same year that the Ohio and Mississippi Railroad began surveys in the area, most of the lots were owned by one man, Jesse Holman. That same year, folks encouraged Jesse Holman to name the town with his last name since the ties for the railroad came from his sawmill. He refused. They semihonored his wishes. They named their new town Holton, to match the first three letters in his last name.

A humble beginning, it remains small today, with fewer than one thousand residents calling Holton home. Join them the second Saturday during the summer for Music in the Park.

 shop

Carolyn's Collectibles possesses some of the most spectacular antique furniture—at reasonable prices. Vintage chairs, tables, and desks are in the back section of the shop. Up front, find what almost resemble collections. There aren't just two decorative plates, but a whole wall full. There aren't just a few vintage bottles, cookie jars, or a couple of thimbles, but dozens of them. Wonderfully unique!

NOTABLES

Pigeons in huge numbers came into the town in 1860, causing area woods to look as though a tornado had ripped through.

74

Huntingburg

L aid out in 1837, the area was a favorite hunting spot of Colonel Jacob Geiger, son of Tippecanoe War hero Captain Fred Geiger. As the town grew, so did the danger for fire. As is the case in many early histories, Huntingburg suffered a disastrous fire in 1889. Fire ripped through and destroyed seventeen buildings in the town. Rebuilt using brick, the downtown is a gorgeous and welcoming place today. Take the walking tour down historic Fourth Street to really get a look at these brick beauties.

Music always fills the downtown air. In December "Winter Wonderland" and "Carol of the Bells" play. Other months bring classic songs and even show tunes. Inviting and walkable, it's easy to fall in love with this superb Indiana town and winner of the 2014 Stellar Communities award.

Museum of Huntingburg.

☀ play

League Stadium is unlike any other baseball stadium. Built in 1894, the original League Stadium underwent quite a renovation process when it was used for the 1992 film *A League of Their Own,* starring Tom Hanks, Geena Davis, and Madonna. As the Home of the

Rockford Peaches, it received loads of airtime. After filming, the period light fixtures, retro advertising along the outfield, and bleachers weren't abandoned or discarded, but instead embraced as part of the town's heritage. It was used again in 1996 for the HBO movie *Soul of the Game,* and walking through the stadium is like stepping onto a big movie set. Time visits to line up with the Dubois County Bombers collegiate baseball team games at the stadium. An excellent park is right next door, so there's plenty of family bonding opportunity here.

The movie fun doesn't have to end. Browse the props from *A League of Their Own* at the Museum of Huntingburg. It's chock-full of town relics like the 1901 "Huntingburg Tour Car" manu-factured in the town and even the bed of the founder, Colonel Geiger, so expect the unexpected.

Old Town Hall was once a fire station and a jail but currently serves a different purpose. The main floor houses various com-munity groups, including the Chamber of Commerce, but up-stairs is where to find the real treasure. A second-floor ballroom with high ceilings, lovely windows, and even a stage is a multi-purpose rentable community space.

Serious movie buffs will want to drive past and ogle the Salem United Church of Christ. Yes, this was the site of a movie. The 1998 film *Hard Rain,* starring Morgan Freeman, Christian Slater, and Minnie Driver, was filmed right here. Located near the downtown, it is easy to find.

Take a load off at Cool Beans Java. Like any typical coffee shop, gourmet coffees and teas are available, but in an unexpected move, so too are spirits. Local food is frequently woven into a menu that features fresh breakfast pastry, wraps, and a savory lunch menu. It's modern yet inviting, clean and comfortable, and things really get hopping during special live music events and the occasional dinner menu.

Initially the Victory Theater in 1942, it became the Gaslight Restaurant and Pizza in 1970. Now known as Gaslight Pizza and

Grill, it harbors absolutely fantastic sandwiches. Opt for the Johnny Dart, a corned beef and pepper-jack cheese sandwich also available as a pizza, or the Sicilian, a bacon, ham, pepperoni, and sauerkraut sandwich piled high with mozzarella and swiss cheeses, topped with a tasty special sauce. Make sure to get the crisp and crunchy homemade chips. Have fun like the locals: the stage is still in use, hosting open-mic nights, special performances, and even movies.

🛍 shop

Scour the many vendor booths at Downtown Emporium. Vendors hold familiar antiques like toys, glassware, and dishes, even furniture and rag rugs. Large aisles make it easier to navigate than most shops of its ilk.

Too hot, too cold, or too rainy? Boredom is short-lived for anyone after entering Game Knight. This retail shop is devoted to games. These go way beyond the traditional money and dice-rolling games and enter innovative, clever territory. Knowledgeable

Greentree Furniture, Huntingburg.

staff match up interests to games. Card games, miniatures, and even comic books, there's plenty to see. Ample seating in the next room gives everyone a place to play—and space for epic gaming events.

Now in an 1880s built space, Grainry Antiques and Other Needful Things contains beautiful furniture. While there's more here than furniture, the ready-to-use vintage pieces really stand out. Featuring estate, homestead, and auction finds, this shop has loads of furniture still in storage that just won't fit inside. The selection is always rotating. Be sure to ask for help with a specific request—they just may have it.

Greentree Furniture is a corner shop that covers all the bases. There's vintage furniture here and plenty of it. The antique light fixtures and other items are beautiful. But that's only one side of this incredible shop. The other side boasts a women's clothing boutique with all the accessories and a ton of themed nooks of home decor.

Original local art, one-of-a-kind items, contemporary jewelry, handmade frames, rustic crosses, knit hats, and wall art are a few of the items tucked inside the Purple Plum. Serious shoppers will get lost in the spacious yet oh-so-classy retail space, divided into sections. Discover creative children's toys from fabulous brands, entertaining pieces, gifts, and accessories. There's so much to sift through and consider.

75

Leavenworth

Eighteen-year-old Connecticut-born Zebulon Leavenworth founded the town of Leavenworth in 1818–1819. By 1843 Leavenworth had expanded so much that it became the new county seat. This status lasted until 1896, when an armed group of men stormed the courthouse and fled with the records, rushing back to their nearby town of English (presently Indiana's smallest county seat). It would be the last county seat move in Indiana for more than one hundred years until Cannelton and Tell City would make the switch.

A Confederate spy for John Hunt Morgan, twenty-five-year-old Thomas Hines was sent up to Indiana from Kentucky in order to meet up with Southern sympathizers in the summer of 1863. Stealing Union uniforms and currency to aid in their charade as Union army deserters, the group of almost 100 men advanced to French Lick. Turned away, and with the Indiana Home Guards hot on their trail, they hired a Leavenworth resident to help them cross the river in order to escape back into their home state. But the Leavenworth local had them tricked. A Union supporter, the Leavenworth man quickly spread the word. Residents brought ammunition to Union troops, who were firing on the Confederates as they fled across the river. Three of the Southerners were killed, and many others were hauled in as prisoners of war, led into custody, and locked into the Methodist church in Leavenworth. Thomas Hines, however, succeeded in his escape.

The Leavenworth of 1863 was far different from the Leavenworth of the 1930s. It was in a different location. Rain fell and fell hard in 1937. To say that homes were destroyed is an understatement: in a town of 418 people, 400 were forced to evacuate. The entire town was a mess. Wise folks decided that the chances of a flood happening again in the future were far too likely, so the whole town moved to the top of the bluff, overlooking the river. At the town dedication in December 1938, state Works Progress Administration official John K. Jennings gave a stirring speech to the new town, remarking on the positive results from such a devastating beginning.

Up until the 1990s, it was the only rebuilt community in the state. Times are certainly far quieter for the town now. With a few hundred residents spanning both the ghost town of "Old Leavenworth" and the "new," they all gather together for a big fall festival. The Leavenworth Riverfest is a weekend full of family fun held the first weekend in September, with a parade, carnival rides, demonstrations, wood carving, and plenty more. Bring a chair and join the crowd.

stay

Four buildings, sixteen rooms, and six acres of land compose the Leavenworth Inn. Built in the 1800s, it was advertised in the 1900s as the "Place to Spend Your Vacation," with spring chickens, fine air, grape vineyards, and milk from Jersey cows. The basement still holds the original wine cellar. There's plenty to do for couples and families with its tennis courts, trails, shuffleboard, and even bikes to borrow, but space to sit around and do nothing too.

eat

Sharply decorated, this isn't a typical small-town pub. Situated above the river with breathtaking views off the spacious deck, Walter's Pub has incredible pizza. Located in the lower level of the Overlook Restaurant, Walter's Pub features flatbread pizza that can be topped with some pretty fun options. It's all amazing. Carry out when members of the group are under age twenty-one, or head upstairs for family-friendly dining.

Stephenson's General Store,
Leavenworth.

🛍 shop

Four generations of Stephensons ran Stephenson's General Store all the way up until 2008 before selling the business to the current nonrelated owners. The original (and gorgeous) wood counter and display cases are still here. So, too, are a variety of pictures from the big flood of 1937 and relics from the town's early days. The old ledger with its fancy writing and the button-making machine are a treat. Old-fashioned snacks, toys, and even gifts are available here. Part retail space and part café, expect simple, satisfying fare.

76

Lincoln City

Moving here in 1816 with his family, this unincorporated town is where young Abraham Lincoln spent his formative years. Laid out on the same area where once stood Abraham Lincoln's father's farm, Lincoln City was platted in 1872. An agricultural community, sloping hills, history, and unique attractions make it a scenic, worthwhile stop.

☀ play

The Lincoln Boyhood National Memorial features three attractions in one: it's part pioneer-era living-history farm, part museum, part nature hikes, and also the site of Lincoln's mother's and sister's graves. Step into the memorial center, admire the massive relief sculptures of Lincoln's life on the way in, and then watch the short orientation film narrated by a familiar voice. Don't miss the outline of the Lincoln family's third cabin or the seasonally open 1820s farm with knowledgeable period-dressed staff. Kids will enjoy the farm animals and trying their hand at basic pioneer tasks or games. Be sure to ask about the cured meat in the shed before leaving.

There are nature trails galore at Lincoln State Park, a 1,747-acre park boasting ten miles of paths. Catch shows in the outdoor amphitheater or pay a visit to the nature center or the Lincoln Living Historical Museum. Walk through the Colonel Jones Home, the merchant (and later Civil War officer) who was young Lincoln's employer.

NOTABLES

Jay Cutler (b. 1983), Denver Broncos and, later, Chicago Bears quarterback, attended Lincoln City's Heritage Hills High School, where he started as quarterback for three years. He is a record-breaking athlete with numerous awards and franchise records.

Abraham Lincoln (1809–1865) was the sixteenth president who brought about the emancipation of slaves. Six days after Robert E. Lee's surrender, Lincoln was assassinated by John Wilkes Booth during his favorite show, *Our American Cousin*. In-depth volumes could be written here regarding the life and times of Lincoln. In the interest of space, know that Abraham Lincoln spent his formative years, 1816–1830, in this part of Indiana.

Lincoln Living Historical Museum, Lincoln City.

77

Madison

John Paul founded New Albany, which he deemed "unhealthy," before founding Madison in 1809. He volunteered in the War of 1812, and then in 1813 he founded the second newspaper in the state, the *Western Eagle*. Designed to be the state capital, Madison possesses wide roads meant to draw attention to the lovely architecture.

Park the car and walk this one. Boasting more than 130 historically designated blocks, Madison feels almost like a step back in time. Known as the Madison Historic Landmark District, each block looks more beautiful than the next. But Madison is not just a pretty face. Packed full of shops, restaurants, galleries, and other things to see and do, this is one town that can easily become far more than a simple day trip.

Hammond Family Restaurant, Madison.

Since 1929 folks have streamed into the town for the annual Madison Regatta, otherwise known as the Lucas Oil Indiana Governor's Cup, an early July H1 Unlimited hydroplane race. It's a weekend of fun in water and on land.

☼ play

Located along the riverfront, the twenty-four-inch-thick stone walls of the Lanthier Winery are part of what makes this eighteenth-century building extraordinary. The Cellar Tasting Room is rumored to be an old fort. Maintaining that destination status, the winery carries more than a dozen wines, from dry to sweet, as well as special holiday editions.

Franco's Family Restaurant, Madison.

The Attic and Coffee Mill Café is well known for its gelato, coffee concoctions, and lunch offerings. But the homemade desserts, and especially the apple pie, are the real star of the show. Step in and shop for an assortment of nonfood gift items. It's easy to browse and snack inside this third-generation shop.

"Taste the Adventure" at Cocoa Safari Chocolates. Handmade chocolates are made in-store. There are even sugar-free chocolates available. Go for the orange buttercreams or one of the many chocolates from around the world.

It's not every restaurant that makes its own pastry and bread. Franco's Family Restaurant does things a little different. Opt for a breakfast sandwich on the freshly baked ciabatta bread.

Hinkle's Sandwich Shop, Madison.

Caricatures line the walls at Hammond Family Restaurant, a favorite breakfast spot. An artist has captured local folks with his fast (and hilarious) draw for years. The hard-workers breakfast is excellent. Not quite so ravenous? Go for any breakfast standard.

Hinkle's Sandwich Shop is famous for its mini burgers. Grab a seat at the counter—and don't forget the curly fries. Deciding on a milk shake is hard—there are a ton of flavors here. Make it easy: go for the dreamsicle or the banana-split shake.

Special occasion or not, Key West Shrimp House has been the local fine-dining destination since the 1950s. When stuck with a lengthy wait time, proceed to the lower level of this old 1800s button factory to take advantage of cushy seating and board games to pass the time. French-fried shrimp are their specialty.

Savor a snack at Madison Nut and Candy Company. Rows and barrels are full of open-stock nuts and candies. But the best seller is the homemade granola. Grab a bag and see why.

Red Pepper Deli and Café can't be missed—it's painted bright red and green. Housed in an old gas station, the sandwiches are scrumptious. Go for the Vampire Slayer, a garlic-filled sandwich, or the Hydro Plane panini.

The sister shop to the Red Pepper Deli listed above, the Red Pepperoni Pizzeria was the natural next step when pizzas kept flying off the menu. There are a lot of flavors not frequently found on a small-town pizza menu, like roasted artichoke or white pizza. Pair it with an Indiana beer or other microbrew and settle in.

🛍 shop

Gallery 115 is many things: coffee shop, art gallery, and gift shop. It is the site of three businesses: the Eric Phagan Art Gallery and Studio, the Gallery Café, and W of Madison Gifts. The building was a long-ago meeting place of the Boy Scouts back in the 1930s–1940s. Look at the second-floor meeting space to see an original Boy Scouts sticker still in the window.

Bubbles lead the way to All Good Things Soaps and Such, a handmade soap and more shop. Chemical free, these natural essential-oil soaps smell as nice as they make the skin feel. Scents run from the usual, like orange spice or roses, to the more obscure, like black licorice or charcoal and lava.

Bananas foster, honey cookies, or donut look-alikes, the items here might be human grade, but Blue Cerebus Dog Boutique is meant for pooches. This shop will certainly keep a dog rolling in contentment. Go out the back door for a doggie play area that lets pups let loose.

Seasonally open, Crawdaddy Music has absolutely every kind of musical instrument. Get in there and try before buying—and join the spontaneous jams. It's been going strong since 1987. Enjoy new, vintage, used, and even rare items.

Knitters, grab a set of knitting needles and head to Harriet's Knit Knook. Bright and well maintained, it is a knitter's paradise. Accessories and even crocheting supplies can also be had.

Little Golden Fox is an Etsy and Pinterest lover's dream come true. The antiques and shabby-chic items are adorable. There's always something new to see.

Madison Table Works handcrafts each of these gorgeous dining room sets. Working with the wood, they carefully create an heirloom piece. Browse the space for interesting items from a myriad of Indiana artisans like pottery, jewelry, and glass.

The days when this place was an 1850s butcher shop are obviously long gone. Fabric and notions are color coordinated inside Margie's Country Store. Home decor on the lower level is superbly arranged and lovely.

Everything a person would need to live in the nineteenth century can be found inside of Red Dog Arms. A specific antique shop, there are only eighteenth- and nineteenth-century objects here. Catch the owner hand-carving a rifle for a glimpse of masterful workmanship.

Kids won't believe their luck. Rock-a-Bye Lady is well stocked in name-brand toys and classic favorites. Finally, a shop where kids can be kids! Demo toys allow children to test drive before buying.

That Book Place not only carries rows and racks and shelves of books, but even possesses Indiana authors. Find old favorites or new classics right here. Look for their annual spring author fair to effortlessly discover new works in this awesome meet and greet.

Madison Table Works, Madison.

NOTABLES

Released in 2001, *Madison* shared the story of the 1971 hydroplane regatta. Jim Caviezel and Jake Lloyd were the lead characters in the film that was loosely based on a true story.

Some Came Running, a 1958 film starring Frank Sinatra, Dean Martin, and Shirley MacLaine, was shot in Madison. It received five Academy Award nominations.

Raised in Madison, Bryan Paul Bullington (b. 1980) graduated from Madison Consolidated High School and was named Mr. Baseball his senior year (1999). He played for the Pittsburgh Pirates (2005, 2007), Cleveland Indians (2008), Toronto Blue Jays (2009), Kansas City Royals (2010), Hiroshima Toyo Carp (2011–2014) (Nippon Professional Baseball), and the Orix Buffaloes (2015) (NPB).

Architect Francis Costigan (1810–1865) designed homes throughout Indianapolis and Madison. Madison buildings such as Lanier Mansion, the Charles Shrewsbury House, and his own home are on the National Register of Historic Places.

Five-time Academy Award nominee for best actress Irene Dunne (1898–1990) was raised in Madison. A star of stage and screen, she was nominated for the following films: *Cimarron* (1931), *Theodora Goes Wild* (1936), *The Awful Truth* (1937), *Love Affair* (1939), and *I Remember Mama* (1948).

Geologist and archaeologist Gerard Fowke (1855–1933) published more than fifty works, the majority of which dealt with Native American archaeology. He traveled the world studying prehistoric remains before spending his final years in Madison.

Science fiction and mystery writer Joseph "Joe" L. Hensley (1926–2007), sometimes known by the pen name Louis J. A. Adams, wrote more than twenty novels and collections and over one hundred short stories. Much of his work took place in Indiana. In fact, he used the towns of Madison and Bloomington as his model for the fictitious town of Bington, a frequent locale in his work. He was an attorney and circuit-court judge.

Artist William McKendree Snyder (1848–1930) spent his childhood in Madison, painting southern Indiana beech trees, a subject that helped earn him lasting recognition. He became one of the first artists to paint in Brown County.

The first brick mansion in the Northwest Territory, the 1818 home of Jeremiah Sullivan (1794–1870) is one of several properties handled by the nonprofit group Historic Madison. It is seasonally open for tours. Sullivan served in the state legislature and is responsible for the naming of Indianapolis. He served on the Indiana Supreme Court (1836–1846) and later as a judge in the criminal court of Jefferson County.

One of but a few navy officers turned infantry generals, Madison-born Jeremiah Cutler Sullivan (1830–1890) served in the Civil War.

A Madison resident all his life, Tommy Thevenow (1903–1957) was a shortstop in the Major Leagues. He played for the St. Louis Cardinals (1924–1928), Philadelphia Phillies (1929–1930), Pittsburgh Pirates (1931–1935), Cincinnati Reds (1936), Boston Bees (1937), and Pittsburgh Pirates (1938) until retiring from the game. After his ball-playing days were over, he ran a grocery store in Madison.

78

Marengo

Platted as Spring Town in 1839, the community's name was changed to Marengo due to the excitement of the Battle of Marengo. It was the 1800 skirmish when Napoleon Bonaparte defeated the Austrians in Marengo, Italy. Towns in Canada and the United States, like Spring Town, switched names to Marengo to honor the victory.

Marengo may be a town of fewer than one thousand people, but there's an unusual activity during the two-day Fourth of July celebration. Live music, food, fireworks show, and fun are found at typical Indiana festivals, but this one possesses one interesting difference: the Firecracker five-kilometer run and walk. This isn't a normal race. Beginning in downtown Marengo, it winds its way through the underground Marengo Warehouse and Distribution Center that features more than two miles of subterranean tunnels.

☀ play

Two children, Orris and Blanche Hiestand, discovered Marengo Cave on September 6, 1883. Blanche, a fifteen-year-old cook at the local school, had heard a few boys talking about a hole in the ground they had found. As soon as school was over, she enlisted the help of her younger brother; they grabbed some candles and became the first people to ever enter the cave. Since 1883 the public has toured Marengo Cave. Try one or try them both, the two cave tours at Marengo Cave differ in length and sites. The Crystal Palace Tour is forty minutes long and features helictites, flowstone, stalagmites, stalactites, cave popcorn, and draperies. It is a wonderful tour, thanks to informative guides and a gorgeous grand finale: Mirror Lake. Stunning and serene, it's truly a highlight. Ready for a longer trek? The Dripstone Tour begins with a short walk through the woods to get to the cave entrance. Wear clothing appropriate for the fifty-two-degree weather. This section of the cave has a story (or two) to tell. First, ogle at the tin cans stuck to the cave floor that mark the spot where the cave was closed due to land disputes years back. Then enjoy the story of the first and only robbery to ever occur in a cave. Folks thought it was part of the act until the robber fired his shotgun. Turning out the lights, he fled. Fortunately, the guides knew where the power supply was and,

Marengo Cave.

after waiting a moment or two, restored order. A disgruntled former employee, he was soon caught, and the 1980s cave robbery set into motion laws regarding such occurrences. There are a nice gift shop and gem mining out front. Feeling brave? Anyone in good health and possessing a fair bit of flexibility should try the Cave Simulator. It's no easy feat, and there is no turning back once inside. Yes, one man did get completely stuck, and the entire thing had to be taken apart, bit by bit, to get him out. It is not for the faint of heart.

NOTABLES

In 2008 *Fire from Below* was filmed in Marengo Cave.

Madison, a film starring Jim Caviezel and Jake Lloyd, was shot in downtown Marengo in 2001.

Marengo was once the site of a cannon factory.

The United States Department of Defense and the Centers for Disease Control lease space from underground storage facility Marengo Warehouse and Distribution Center. As per the contract, whatever lies inside of the storage space is confidential and unknown even to the warehouse owners.

79

Mauckport

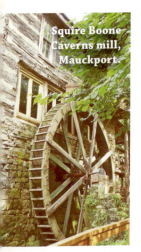
Squire Boone Caverns mill, Mauckport.

An area once frequently traveled by Daniel Boone and his brother Squire, the latter chose to settle it in 1806. Named by the Maucks, the first German family to put down roots here in 1811, Mauckport was originally termed "Maucks Port" for the ferry access it provided even in its early days. But by 1847, the residents of the blooming town were ready for a more modern name. Choosing "New Market," they filed a petition to legally switch the name. It lasted for all of four years until another town with the same name was discovered.

Incorporated in 1853, the town slowly grew. It wasn't until 1863 that the town had big excitement—it, too, was part of Morgan's Raid. Although the Home Guard retreated and fled to Corydon after the marauders returned their fire, the townsfolk had long since fled the town. The town reached its peak in 1900 when a series of setbacks hit. In 1900 ice destroyed the ships. In 1910 ice destroyed the wharf. The 1937 Ohio River flood took out a portion of the downtown, sealing its "small-town" status. Mauckport now supports a population of fewer than one hundred people. In spring the population swells as folks from the area celebrate the town during the "Mauckport Days" festival, full of events, booths, and a parade.

☀ play

Squire Boone Caverns was discovered by Daniel Boone and his brother Squire in 1790. A few years later, Squire Boone was back in the area, fleeing from angry Native Americans, when he remembered the cave and hid. Covering himself with branches and

leaves, he could hear the men above him, but they didn't find him. After that he felt like he'd found something really special. And he had. Squire Boone Caverns has streams, waterfalls, and formations. But none stands out so well as the Rock of Ages. At more than a million years old, the forty-foot floor-to-ceiling formation is incredible. It takes a seventy-three-step spiral staircase to get to the beginning of the tour way underground. Bring a jacket and wear appropriate footwear.

Squire Boone Caverns Zipline Adventure, Mauckport.

The courageous fly through the trees on six canopy ziplines at Squire Boone Caverns Zipline Adventure. Yelling through the treetops is encouraged. Even kids can get involved. A smaller version is available just for them. When finished, browse the gristmill rebuilt on Boone's original foundation—with his carved inscription intact.

NOTABLES

Squire Boone (1744–1815) settled in Mauckport with his wife, four sons, and their families. He wore many hats: explorer, gunsmith, hunter, minister, Revolutionary War hero, and statesman. Per his request, his final resting place is inside of the caverns named in his honor.

Mauckport-born Strother M. Stockslager (1842–1930) was a U.S. representative for Indiana from 1881 to 1885 and a lawyer. He was also the Department of Labor legal expert in 1918. During the Civil War, he fought for the Union, serving as a second lieutenant and captain of the Thirteenth Indiana Volunteer Cavalry (a division he had helped to gather).

Popular cookie company Oreo decided to "blanket the town" with mini Oreos—which resulted in exactly one mini Oreo sent to each household. Oreo later sent a full-size bag of minis to each home after the media backlash.

80

Milan

Milan, surprisingly pronounced "My-lun," was laid out in 1836 by three men: Isaac Hancock, Stephen Harding, and George Walker. The post office was established a year later in Harding's store, resulting in the town name of Harding's Store Community. Some speculate that wine-enthusiast settlers, mainly Germans, gave the town the proper name of Milan rather than the awkward Harding's Store Community in 1842.

As the railroads came in, the town shifted a little, settling itself in its present location. The discovery of mineral water led to the 1920 opening of the Miwogco Mineral Springs Hotel, or Milan Indiana Water, Oil, and Gas Company. Legend has it that the Milan hotel equaled the beauty of the French Lick Springs Hotel until a mysterious fire destroyed the building in 1928. With just under two thousand residents, it is currently one of the more populated towns in Ripley County.

More than a movie, the 1986 film *Hoosiers*, starring Gene Hackman, was loosely based on the 1954 Milan Indians. Tour the Milan 1954 Hoosiers Museum for all sorts of artifacts from the stunning basketball season as well as props from the *Hoosiers* movie. The collection is always changing, as fans and locals discover items in garages or attics and share them with the museum.

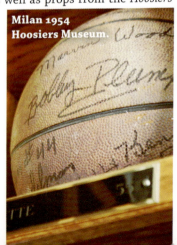

Milan 1954 Hoosiers Museum.

🍴 eat

Folks come from near and far for the (mostly) home-cooked

foods at Milan Reservation Restaurant. It's known for its crispy fried chicken, and locals can't get enough. During the summer, expect locally grown produce. No matter what the season, end with a piece of homemade chocolate cream pie.

🛍 shop

Shop kitty meows a loud hello at Milan Whistle Stop. Fantastic shabby-chic items like vintage windows and fireplace mantels are enticing. Candles, seasonal items, and home decor complete any look.

NOTABLES

Actor William Jordan (b. 1937) has appeared in numerous films and TV shows. He was also a member of the 1954 Milan High School championship basketball team.

Milan 1954
Hoosiers Museum.

The championship basketball game was just the beginning for Bobby Plump (b. 1936). He was "Mr. Basketball" in 1954, named by *Sports Illustrated* as one of the fifty greatest sports figures of the twentieth century, and played for the Phillips 66ers National Industrial Basketball League for three years. After a career in insurance and financial consulting, he opened Plump's Last Shot in the Broad Ripple area north of Indianapolis.

Milan
Whistle Stop.

81

Moorefield

James Alfrey platted Moorefield in 1834, naming it for the Moore family. An agricultural town from the get-go, it wasn't until the Civil War that the town would see a boost in its wealth due to its timothy hay. Timothy hay was a kind of grass that, when dried, made excellent animal feed. The end of the Civil War also marked the end of Moorefield's prosperity. It experienced a brief rebirth of growth in the 1900s, but by 1920 the town had become unincorporated.

Moorefield Market.

eat

Moorefield Market may be the only business left in town. It is also one of the only buildings left in town, but it manages to make this unincorporated town a "must see." General stores aren't exactly common—and this one cooks up fantastic sandwiches and homemade chips.

NOTABLES

During the 1940s, Moorefield business owners sponsored film screenings in a local field. Townspeople turned out in droves for the free movie events.

82

Nashville

Whispering Pines Alpaca Farm, Nashville.

Home of a historic artist colony, Nashville has long been a preferred locale for creative types. Founded in 1836 on land acquired from the Native Americans, Nashville began as Jacksonburg. In those early days, Brown County was slow in growing—some believe there were fewer than two hundred people in the entire county. But in just ten years, the population grew to more than two thousand people as the lumber industry took off. In the 1870s, artists began to arrive, captivated by the natural setting. The Brown County Artists' Colony, founded by Adolph Shulz, encouraged other painters to move to Nashville—or at least visit. Gaining traction with the addition of famed painter T. C. Steele to the area in 1907, the Brown County Art Colony became a recognized name.

Mostly wooded, there are no big farms here. It is said that parts of the area were so remote that even in the early 1900s, there were families still living like they did during the pioneer days. Gather at the National Maple Syrup Festival to get a glimpse of those earlier times, with scheduled activities, pioneer-garbed folks, and maple syrup made the old-fashioned way to celebrate this town's humble beginnings. It has truly cemented itself as a shopping and art destination, a place where small businesses reign supreme.

Decades of travelers have stayed in Abe Martin Lodge at Brown County State Park. Make a splash enjoying the new addition: an indoor water park. There are twelve thousand square feet of fun—but only for hotel guests.

Golfing ability isn't a factor for those wanting to stay at the Overlook Lodge at Salt Creek Golf Retreat. Independently owned spacious condos, the one- or two-bedroom units are fully equipped with everything guests need for a restful stay. The deck or patio overlooking the tidy golf course adds to the feeling of serenity.

play

Man or woman, there was just no escaping the 1879 Log Jail. Two layers of walls, extra thick, and a foot apart from each other, tiny barred windows, Dutch doors, and low doorways kept anyone from ever getting away. Peek inside both the lower men's level and the women's upstairs room. It is open for tours during special events.

At barely more than eight hundred residents, Nashville manages to be the only incorporated town in the county. It is also the county seat. Visit the Brown County Courthouse for simple 1874 style.

Nothing attracts kids like a fifty-foot water sluice. Panning for gems at Copperhead Creek Gem Mining is definitely the highlight of a kid's day. It's open as long as the water isn't frozen.

Ramp Creek Bridge is the easiest to find yet. Moved from its position over Ramp Creek in Putnam County (near Fincastle), it was relocated in 1932 to keep the two-lane bridge from demolition when the highway was upgraded. Located at the entrance to Brown County State Park, the 1838 Burr-arch bridge is not only the last of its kind, but also the oldest bridge in the state.

Outside of town, hand-feed alpaca at Whispering Pines Alpaca Farm. Gentle creatures, these fluffy-headed mammals are especially kind to special-needs children. Pop into the on-site shop for clothing made from alpaca.

Big Woods Pizza Company knows how to create an experience. Inventive pizzas feature fresh toppings. It's served with their own beer made nearby and paired with occasional live music events, taking supporting local to a new level. Quaff on!

The original Nashville candy shop, the Candy Dish makes its own handmade chocolates in-store as they have since 1977. No preservatives, waxes, or fillers, they use pure chocolate in their confections. Just taste the difference.

Get to work on the community puzzle while sipping a beverage at Common Ground. This welcoming coffee shop boasts a piano—and it is not just there for looks. Anyone searching for a pick-me-up will find it here.

Wear the Daily Grind Coffee Shop shirt anywhere, snap a pic, and they will add it to their wall of fame. Until then, sip coffee, teas, and other beverages in a coffee shop with atmosphere—since 1977. More than one hundred pounds of "by the pound" coffee are available.

Hobnob Corner Restaurant, Nashville.

There may be many rotating flavors of ice cream at seasonally open Fearrin's Ice Cream and Yogurt Depot, but the hot caramel pumpkin ice cream sundae is a must. There are a couple of tables inside as well as a drinking fountain. Homemade truffles and fresh-baked cookies are usually available just to mix things up a bit.

Breakfast is memorable at Hobnob Corner Restaurant. Notice the gorgeous cabinets full of stuff? Those are original items from the long-ago pharmacy that once operated here. If a maple and blueberry French toast special is available, get it. Otherwise, there are no wrong decisions here.

Miller's Ice Cream House churns out homemade ice cream as they have done since 1977. When autumn leaves change, business really gets busy—and they make more than one hundred gallons of ice cream each day. Pick persimmon, peanut butter, or Heath bar.

Lunch or dinner, Out of the Ordinary Restaurant is open for business. Live music events occasionally occur on the lower portion of the huge space. Order the OOTO (Out of the Ordinary) Nachos and the black-and-blue rib eye for a delightful ending to a small-town day.

Schwab's Fudge has kept fudge lovers happy since 1977. Fudge is made the old-fashioned way, using a copper pot and marble-slab table—and right before the eyes of visitors if the timing is right. Whiskey chocolate pecan fudge and the seasonal pumpkin are customer favorites.

Smell the tea at Sweeteas's Tea Shop. Patient staff guide visitors to a tea that fits. A high ceiling, exposed beams, and a fireplace add a comfortable ambience. Try a tea flight to sample five different kinds of tea without the commitment.

It's an Indiana University fan's dream made reality—That Sandwich Place is red and white from top to bottom. That's because this stick-to-the-ribs breakfast spot is devoted to former IU basketball coach Bobby Knight. When not gazing at the autographs, photos, newspaper articles, and signs, order anything that includes home fries.

There's no cuter place to dine than the Trolley, a converted trolley turned restaurant. Lemon or orange shake-ups, hickory-smoked pork BBQ sandwiches, and homemade sloppy joes are top picks. People watchers will especially love the outdoor-only dining.

 shop

Whether browsing dinosaur fossils or Ice Age alligator teeth, it will take some time to comb through the treasures at Brown County Rock and Fossil Shop. Glass cases and open bins hold rocks and fossils from around the world. Tip: a lighter geode contains more crystals than a heavier geode.

There's always room for more yarn. Clay Purl has all the knit and crocheting supplies needed for any project. Try something new: "Our Yarn" is created in Brown County.

An 1873 boardinghouse, the Ferguson House was created to provide rooms for artists. Legend has it that Mrs. Ferguson would not rent rooms to "women who wore knickers." Now it provides an eclectic selection of home decor, from iron objects to sports memorabilia to tableware.

Clay Purl, Nashville.

When Sharon's son, a freshman just entering college, was diagnosed with a debilitating brain tumor, tuberous sclerosis, she came up with the idea For Bare Feet to always provide him with a place to work. The mother of five children, she learned the business as she went. Heartbreakingly, Tim passed away, but for the schoolteacher turned entrepreneur, the family kept it going. Providing specialty socks to retail shops and even NBA teams, it only keeps growing.

It's All about Dogs—and that's no lie. Handmade outfits and hats for pampered pooches are crafted by the owner. Keep Fido well supplied with homemade treats and cute custom accessories.

All-natural soaps, bath bombs, sugar scrubs, and lotion bars are an indication of the products found at Johanna Lee Bathology. There are no chemicals, animal products, or preservatives used in her small-batch soap-making process.

Skillfully crafted, LaSha's really is "anything but ordinary." The owner has a way with metalwork, creating gorgeous pieces of jewelry from vintage coins or silver. Definitely one of Nashville's best shops, it is a must visit even for those with only a remote interest in jewelry.

Lawrence Family Glass Blowers, Nashville.

Learning the art of glass blowing from their father, twins John and Jim run the day-to-day operations of Lawrence Family Glass Blowers. Watch these Indiana artisans at work as they seem to effortlessly create an ornament, sun catcher, or figure from glass. There are two separate studios, so if there is no one in one, walk the short half-block distance to the other.

Overflowing with beautiful things to wear, Mulberry Cottage is a two-story boutique full of attractive clothing for women of all sizes. Ample scarves, dresses, skirts, blouses, and shoes are displayed with style on the second level. Downstairs, find amazing home decor and accessories.

"Gifts for home and happiness" is the motto at Madeline's French Country Shop. French country decor occupies the first floor of this amazing Victorian home turned business. Linens and pottery, candles and prints blend nicely with the stained glass and woodwork of this lovely shop.

Miss Moonpennies Emporium has a way with arrangement. Soaps and candles, baby wash and colored bottles, home decor, and essential items seamlessly blend together. Visit the adjacent building for a stash of seasonal items.

A beautiful Victorian built in 1886, the Olde Bartley House specializes in American-made home decor. Devoted to pretty things for the home, it is a joy to wander the rooms.

Spacious yet homey, Primitives and Pinecones focuses on country decor with an emphasis on repurposed and handmade.

There's a small selection of unique locally made teas and extracts like lavender and rose that are worth a try. Many beautiful seasonal items, linens, and artificial floral arrangements are also available.

Fans of primitives flock to Primitive Spirit. Everything here has that homespun country look for many a sewing project. Browse through fabrics, patterns, and more in cozy surroundings.

Reliable Vintage doesn't stock something because it is old. It stocks something because it is amazing—and in working condition. Find vintage wristwatches, records, cameras, wall art, and then some.

Leather coats for men and women are everywhere inside of Reynold's Leather and Gifts. More than just racks of coats, there are shelves of boots, too. Watch for spontaneous sales.

Care to pull a rabbit out of a hat? How about learning a new gag? Rich Hill's Magic and Fun Emporium knows magic—and loves to show off tricks to visitors. Kids get a kick out of figuring it out, but he'll show the trick only once, so be sure and pay close attention.

Fair trade can be found at September Elm. Coffee beans or serving ware, bags or clothing, these items are high quality. Eco-friendly and handcrafted, they are gifts to give and get.

Acid-etched mirrors and stone carvings are an interesting part of Through the Looking Glass. Located in Antique Alley, that artsy hive buzzing with the sounds of artisans at work, there are a lot of samples here. Order a custom stone carving or purchase one of the finished products from friendly folks.

Mulberry Cottage, Nashville.

It's not all shut tight in packages. Kids and adults can try out various toys for sale at Toy Chest. This third-generation toy store has everything from puppets to play food to books to dolls, keeping kids happy for more than forty years.

Women's clothing and accessories abound inside of Village Boutique. Now in a new location, it occupies an old bank building. Check out the sharp dressing room that's made out of the original massive bank safe.

Indiana-made musical instruments and accessories are easily found at Weed Patch Music Company. Workshops, loads of music chatter, and jam sessions let anyone join in the fun. The professional pieces here are true works of art.

Sample something a little different: a multitude of olive oils and balsamic vinegars. Grab a cup and give them a taste. The most popular flavors at Wild Olive are the Twenty-Five Star, an aged balsamic vinegar, or the strawberry balsamic vinegar, but the dark chocolate vinegar certainly hits the right notes too.

NOTABLES

Plein-air painted landscapes or portraits, Theodore Clement Steele (1847–1926) handled them both. He exhibited his work as part of the Chicago World's Fair in 1893, and many other national and international exhibitions followed. Moving to Nashville in 1907 sparked the relocation of other artists, igniting further growth of the Brown County Art Colony. His 211-acre property, called House of the Singing Winds, is now a part of the Brown County State Park and available for guided tours.

83

Osgood

The Ohio and Mississippi Railroad Company finished laying down line through Ripley County in 1854. By 1856 George W. Cochran purchased land between Napoleon and Versailles and began plotting a new town. With the town built for convenient access to the railroad, even the name made reference to the railroad. Osgood was named for A. L. Osgood, a chief engineer in charge of the surveying crew for the Ohio and Mississippi Railroad.

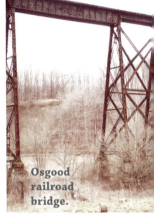

Osgood railroad bridge.

Osgood was also the site of the Cox Quarry, a limestone quarry that produced excellent hunks of limestone mainly for street curbing, in addition to the Row and Ashman Quarries. All of the work was done by hand. The quarries were big business in the early 1900s until the supply of limestone was exhausted.

☀ play

Jasper Sherman Bilby (1864–1949) designed the steel tower used for geodetic surveys. He wanted something that could be relocated and reduce costs. His revolutionary design ended up saving the government the equivalent of forty million dollars from 1927 to 1937. The Bilby Tower outer tower stands seventy-four feet tall, while the inner tower reaches sixty-four feet high. Moved to Osgood in 2013 from Couba Island in the Barataria Wildlife Preserve (forty miles south of New Orleans, Louisiana), the forgotten tower survived eighteen hurricanes since its construction back in 1972.

Drive past the Damm Theater for a laugh (or a show). More than first-run movies, it plays host to local theatrical productions. Believed to be Indiana's oldest family-owned theater, it once sat four hundred people—one-third the size of the town. During popular movie runs, it frequently did.

Now this is one amazing small-town museum. Thanks to a generous grant, the Osgood Historical Museum possesses a gorgeous space and, thanks to knowledgeable volunteers, people to talk more about the magnificent assortment of stuff. From cars to cameras, old quarry equipment and images to one-hundred-year-old graffiti, it's a fascinating place to spend an hour or two.

One-hundred-year-old graffiti at Osgood Historical Museum.

 eat

Osgood Grub Company, or "the Grub," as the locals call it, isn't hard to locate. Keep a lookout for the outdoor metal sculptures made by a man passing through in exchange for a few meals. Speaking of meals, the burgers and onion rings are a natural pair.

Osgood Grub Company.

NOTABLES

The 1939 Cowboys' triumph was the first (and only) time the high school team would win both the Ripley County tournament sectional as well as the sectional. The tallest player was barely over six feet tall, but they finished their season with eighteen wins and seven losses. In that time, the thirty points a game they scored was really something.

Locate the Freemen Opera House across the street from the Osgood Historical Museum. Long ago, the father of a young woman who enjoyed singing had it built to give her a space to perform. It is now used as a space for mixed martial arts and self-defense classes for teens through adults.

84

Paoli

Platted in 1816, Paoli is named for Pasquale Paoli Ash, the son of a North Carolina governor. It was laid out by Jonathan Lindley, the county agent, and it has been said that his own land became the site of the town. Paoli's large Quaker population during the mid-1800s helped runaway slaves continue on their journey up into Canada.

☀ play

Out of the ninety-two counties in Indiana, the Orange County Courthouse is one of the two courthouses not only counted among the oldest but in continuous use as well. The Greek Revival–style courthouse was built 1847–1850. Surviving two town fires and a tornado, it is a marvel. Even *Life* once featured the historic Orange County Courthouse within its pages. A cannon, presented to the county from the government as a gift in 1903, dates back to 1881 and serves as a Civil War tribute. A hefty memorial, it weighs in at 8,568 pounds.

Skiing or snow tubing? It's entirely possible to do both in Indiana with a visit to Paoli Peaks. If Mother Nature doesn't provide enough snow during the season, they will make it. Events like midnight skiing or early opening times mix it up a little.

The eighty-eight acres of the Pioneer Mothers Memorial Forest are all that remain of what was once widespread virgin central hardwood forest. This old-growth forest contains a mile-long walking trail through the forest, the type of which was lost in the 1800s due to settlers and industry. Family owned beginning in 1816, it stayed in family hands (uncut) until the death of the last family member 124 years later, when it became the protected area in use today.

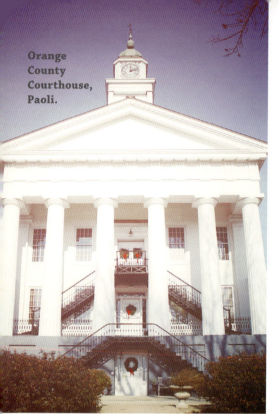

Orange County Courthouse, Paoli.

 eat

Lost River Market and Deli is all about local. Anything within a hundred-mile radius is fair game—and will probably find its way into their shop and kitchen. Gluten-free items are available. Eat in or carry out. Choose among soups and sandwiches or try to visit during Sunday brunch for the best of both worlds. It's all fresh and organic.

shop

Fort Half Moon Antiques is owned by an avid caver—and does he have stories to tell. Listen and browse his awesome antique-filled shop. There's a neat selection of local artifacts in there, too.

Absolutely fantastic gifts of all kinds are waiting to be discovered at Roslyn's Corner Gifts and Antiques. Need new candles or placemats? What about seasonal decor or toss pillows? That's all here, too. Browsing with kids is simple, since a local man made wooden toys for the kids to play with while the grown-ups shop.

85

Rockport

First settled in 1808, Rockport was originally named Hanging Rock for its two-hundred-foot rock formations along the Ohio River. Rockport became the county seat in 1818 and officially became Rockport . . . at least until the post office moved in with the name Rock Port in 1823. It would be roughly thirty years later before the spelling would change to become the single word, "Rockport," as it is known today.

☀ play

Everyone expects to see an Indiana apple orchard, but at Lakeview Orchard, they specialize in peaches. With something like a hundred acres of different varieties of peaches, it might seem more reminiscent of Georgia. Enjoy other fruits and locally canned goods inside the market.

The Lincoln Pioneer Village and Museum holds a multitude of interesting exhibits on the inside (including a cabinet thought to have been crafted in part by Abe Lincoln), but the outside holds quite the treasure. Fourteen cabins were completed as a Works Progress Administration project in 1937–1939 to represent Abraham Lincoln's childhood. It has such an authentic look about it that the cabins even served as the site for the filming of the 1955 Burt Lancaster film *The Kentuckian*.

"Cave" is a generous word for the gash that the first pioneer family used as shelter during their first winter in the area in 1808. The Ohio River Bluffs Cave housed James Lankford and his family. Travel farther down the area and look up to find the upper cave. A stone and metal stairway leads the way.

Peppers Ridge Winery captures that lodge feeling with its wood-covered walls. Loads of seating inside and out (and spanning outward from the building) ensure a spot for everyone. Frequent planned events provide an easy excuse for return visits.

The 1921 Spencer County Courthouse looks much like its Delphi, Indiana, cousin. Both were designed by noted architect Elmer E. Dunlap. Located in the seldom-used basement are a stage and even balcony seating from the building's time spent as a teachers conference space, which has been mostly untouched since its construction.

Spencer County Courthouse, Rockport.

¶ eat

Peaceful golf course views abound at the Rustic Country Club, previously branded as Lakewood Country Club. Open to the public, this restaurant has an incredible outdoor seating area. Multiple fire pits, six flat-screen televisions, and easy course access mark it as a relaxing pick for sports enthusiasts or families.

NOTABLES

Thomas Gamble Pitcher (1824–1895) was born in Rockport. His father, Judge John Pitcher, used to lend Abraham Lincoln his books to read. Pitcher grew up to become a Union general, the superintendent of the United States Military Academy (1866–1870), and the superintendent of the New York Soldiers and Sailors Home (1870–1877).

James C. Veatch (1819–1895) was a county auditor, Indiana state legislator, lawyer, and Union general of the Twenty-Fifth Regiment Indiana Infantry who lived out his days in Rockport.

86

Salem

In March 1814, the town of Salem was official. Named for Salem, North Carolina, the hometown of an influential family, the Lindleys, the town was decided upon as the county seat from the beginning. It is said that in those early days, Salem was measured out by use of a grapevine.

Salem was another town that suffered from John Hunt Morgan's raid. The group approached Salem on July 10, 1863, at nine in the morning. Morgan's guards covered the town and shops while the railroad depot, train cars, and bridges were burned. The flour mills were forced to pay taxes. When all was said and done, the troop took off with five hundred dollars stolen from the town, as well as pilfered items, by three that afternoon. Of the items they stole, Colonel Basil W. Duke, the brother-in-law of Morgan, stated, "They pillaged like boys robbing an orchard." One man was reported to have carried a birdcage with three canaries around with him for days.

Old settlers gathered together September 29, 1875, to share their stories of the early days of Salem. Amazingly enough, folks still gather together for two days of fun each year at the Old Settlers Festival. An open church and a main stage let anyone grab their instrument and join in. Period blacksmiths, gunsmiths, fur trappers, wood-carvers, soap makers, broom makers, and more are on hand to share their craft and stories of the town long ago. Local artisans and farmers center in the parking lot of the Stevens Museum to showcase their wares.

🛏 stay

Aptly named, the Destination Bed and Breakfast is truly a destination, planted out in the country. Drive over winding roads and hills to get to the scenic location and comfortable, classic furnishings. It's a home away from home, as the innkeepers treat everyone like family. Awaken to a scrumptious homemade breakfast and lively conversation. Children will enjoy seeing the animals on the property like a dog, cats, and horses. The antique shop next door is just a bonus.

☀ play

Originally built in 1808, Beck's Grist Mill handled settlers' needs until 1825, when a larger mill was built. It was rebuilt again in 1863–1864, adding on a second story, and continued its role until the 1950s, when it was shut down. Abandoned for fifty years, the mill has been renovated and is back in operation. Look for wonderful hiking trails of varying length that begin and end at the mill.

At the John Hay Center complex of buildings, 1840 is the magic number. It's the year that John Hay, the private secretary of Abraham Lincoln (with positions under four other presidents as well), was born, and it's also the time period presented in all of the different buildings. There's the Hay-Morrison House, where John Hay was born, which has been converted back to its 1840s look inside and out. There's an 1840s Pioneer Village, with a blacksmith, school, post office, and so much more. Special events find volunteers dressed and operating old-fashioned items just as they would have done many years ago. The Stevens Memorial Museum carries pieces and remnants of everything, from the old Salem Creamery to the courthouse to doll and insect displays. It's also the site of a well-appointed genealogy research center. The Depot Railroad Museum is also a part of this complex. Carrying a superior display of locally oriented railroad items from the Monon Railroad is just the beginning at the Depot Railroad Museum, which is fitting since the Monon Railroad began in Salem. There's even a worker's motorcar and the baggage wagon. Kids will like the HO-scale model railroad mimicking places in Washington County, some built from scratch using old photographs as a guide. The depot itself is a replica of the original, built with many grants and two years of help from the building-trades programs at the local high schools.

At fifty-eight miles through forty thousand acres, the Knobstone Trail is Indiana's longest hiking trail. Created from 1977 to 1990, this footpath is forested, rugged, and frequently used as training for the Appalachian Trail. Look for the old Native American "sign trees" along Trail 1, the Deam Lake Trailhead, and mile marker 21. The trail ends at Delaney Creek Park.

Downtown Salem.

Piper Flight Museum is something a bit out of the ordinary. Four out of five U.S. pilots in World War II received their original aviation training in Piper Cubs. By 1976 one out of every ten airplanes produced was a Piper. This museum honors the innovative design of the day. It holds a few Piper aircraft, a replica of the Wright Brothers' wind tunnel, a flight simulator, and advertising memorabilia relating to the small craft. There are a couple hundred books and dozens of films available for educational purposes, too.

Near the courthouse, but located across the street on a sidewalk, lies a monolith lion hand-carved by Collins James Morgan in 1884, who later worked on the courthouse during its construction in 1886.

What do Ted Horn, Parnelli Jones, A. J. Foyt, Bobby and Al Unser, Mario Andretti, Larry Dickson, Darrell Waltrip, and Jeff Gordon all have in common? They have all raced at the Salem Speedway, built in 1974. A half-mile thirty-three-degree banked and paved oval, it holds a variety of high-speed events nearing 140 miles per hour. The addition of a quarter-mile asphalt oval in the infield of the existing.555-mile track in 2010 adds to the fun.

Designed in the Richardsonian Romanesque style, the Washington County Courthouse was built in 1886. At the time,

Christie's on the Square, Salem.

CATS Trading Post, Salem.

the style was particularly urban, almost worldly, with its castle-like exterior of thick stone walls and round towers.

🍴 eat

Locals have long loved Christie's on the Square, a restaurant that even offers baking classes. Kids will love the scavenger hunt. Complete it and turn it back in before heading out of town for a small prize from the treasure chest. Adults will actually enjoy this one, too. As for dining, the yeast rolls are an old family recipe. If anyone falls in love with a particular menu item, they will even share the recipe. Try Christie's Hot Brown for something a little different.

🛍 shop

Brick Street Sampler is arranged so nicely. For more than twenty years, this longtime business has kept the area well decorated with its stock of art, furniture, and home decor. It's enormous.

Geodes for sale cover portions of the yard at CATS Trading Post, an acronym for collectibles, antiques, tools, and stuff. It is exactly that: a haven for items that catch the owner's fancy. Inside or out, it's a neat country shop.

Located next to the Destination Bed and Breakfast, Destination Antiques is a revamped barn filled with a mix of vintage and new goodies. There may be a horse and buggy out front—it's such a neat, eclectic business that even Old Order

Amish shop here. Locally made items or antiques, it's a nice blend.

It might be a sporting-goods store, but there are neat locally centered merchandise and women's clothing to be had at Lincks Clothing & Shoes. With items ranging from T-shirts to basketballs, it's an appropriate stopover for the sports enthusiast, too.

Past 'n' Present by Michelle is a downtown home turned wonderful country-themed shop. Find all the wood signs, candles, and potpourri to give any space that welcoming rustic feel. Grab a free cup of coffee and enjoy hassle-free browsing.

"Our medicine tastes better," declares the sign in front of Salem Apothecary. The full-service pharmacy includes a gift shop, called the Basket Case, as well as an old-fashioned soda fountain. Yes, they even serve lunch.

For more than a decade, Salem women have had a chic, locally owned apparel option thanks to Sisters, a beautiful boutique. Clothing, accessories, and even shoes are available. Sisters' spring and fall fashion shows are a fashion-forward social gathering.

T Antiques is a two-story shop with one spunky owner. Nothing slows her down. Once a department store, it now houses a slew of antiques. The wardrobes on the second floor are worth a view themselves—and were wanted by the people behind Miss America. Although the owner turned them down, as they are not for sale, it goes to show their uniqueness.

NOTABLES

Giant poplars were once common in and around Salem. The last mammoth tree was chopped down in the late 1870s. The stump alone measured eight feet across. That single tree was said to produce more than twelve thousand feet of lumber.

Salem Speedway was one of the first televised car-racing events broadcast by ESPN.

Once the wealthiest man in Indiana, Salem-born Washington C. DePauw (1822–1887) donated a substantial sum of money to Indiana Asbury University. Thankful for the funding, the school changed its name to DePauw University.

Indiana's first lieutenant governor, Christopher Harrison (1775–1863), acted as governor when Governor Jonathan Jennings headed to northern Indiana to negotiate with the Native Americans there. When Jennings returned, Harrison disagreed with Jennings's actions, arguing that Jennings had ignored the state constitution, and declined to give up his post. Setting up his own office, Harrison lost his battle to keep Jennings out of office. An angry Harrison resigned his post as governor. Jennings forgave Harrison, even appointing him as part of the committee that platted Indianapolis. Arriving at the wildness locale on time, and well before the rest of the committee, Harrison decided to begin platting the city. He was also a part of the team interested in building a canal near Clarksville, Indiana. Removing himself from politics and public service, he moved to Salem, becoming both an avid gardener and an artist before he moved back to Maryland a decade later. A downtown plaque points out the site of his home.

Considered the most prominent Salem resident, John Hay (1838–1905) was the private secretary to Abraham Lincoln and later the secretary of state to Presidents William McKinley and Theodore Roosevelt.

Long-ago Salem resident Walter Mobley lived to be almost one hundred years old. One of the early settlers, he remembered when George Washington frequently traveled past the town. Kids would clamber up the fences to watch the group go by. George Washington always had something nice to say to the assembled children.

Born in Salem, John Alfred Pickler (1844–1910) became a member of the U.S. House of Representatives for South Dakota.

Inventor of the Rodman gun, Thomas Jackson Rodman (1816–1871) created the most popular field artillery piece. Rodman was pursued by John Hunt Morgan's men during Morgan's raid through Indiana in an effort to get the gun into Southern hands. He eluded capture.

Lee Wiley Sinclair (1836–1916) built the largest mill in all of southern Indiana in Salem.

87

Santa Claus

With a name like Santa Claus, it's automatically assumed that the town probably has some great beginning story. It doesn't disappoint. Picture it: A group of mostly German settlers gathered together, again, trying to decide on a name to fit their town. It seemed as if all of the good names were taken. Their town was beginning to be known for its lack of a name—and after this 1852 Christmas Eve service in their little church, they weren't going to leave until they ditched their status of "nameless town." Suddenly, the doors blew open, and the sound of sleigh bells could be heard. The children perked up, yelling,

Santa Claus Museum.

"Santa Claus! It's Santa Claus!" The townspeople decided that Santa Claus was the right kind of name for their pleasant little town. In other versions of this story, the original town name, Santa Fe (pronounced "Fee"), was already in use, so the post office required the town to find a different name. They decided on Santa Claus, the post office changed it to Santaclaus, and it wasn't until 1928 that it went back to its original form.

It was generally a sleepy small town until a 1929 *Ripley's Believe It or Not* cartoon thrust the town into the spotlight. After that, the letters just kept coming. Santa Claus is the only town named of its kind. The post office vetoed all further requests for towns trying to name themselves Santa Claus based on the influx of holiday mail addressed to a certain guy in a bright-red suit. They couldn't keep up and decided that just one town with the name was enough. Santa Claus caught the attention of two rival developers, determined to build a holiday-themed attraction. Milt Harris created Santa's Candy Castle (which still stands today), while Carl Barrett asked for pennies from the children of the world to build a granite statue of Santa in his tourist attraction, Santa Claus Park. Barrett's supposed granite statue was a lie—cracks formed in the concrete years later. Still, both entrepreneurs battled out property disputes, taking their case to the Indiana Supreme Court and neglecting their original visions. Their parks would be the last the town would see until after World War II and the addition of Santa Claus Land, better known as the world's first theme park, Holiday World.

🛏 stay

Lake Rudolph Campground and RV Resort offers recreational vehicle rentals, tent camping, and Christmas cabins. With a cheery holiday theme, the cabins have a twinkling Christmas light–filled front porch (with a grill), fire pit, and space for the whole

Holiday World and Splashin' Safari, Santa Claus.

family to spread out a little. Organized campground activities and plenty of amenities keep everyone on the go.

Santa is easy to find at Santa's Lodge. There are all kinds of Santa visiting opportunities here during the season. Santa and Mrs. Claus's milk-and-cookies story time is one of the cutest.

☀ play

Holiday World and Splashin' Safari has free parking, sunscreen, and beverages—plus the number-one wooden roller coaster in the world. Families with little ones won't feel left out with a visit to Safari Sam's Splashland, a fabulous area with pool, multiple slides, and splash area in addition to the mild little kid-friendly rides that dot the park. Hint: Monsoon Lagoon has more than one hundred water elements (and a twelve-hundred-gallon tipping bucket) but is usually less crowded than Kima Bay.

Heartfelt letters from children, photos, town artifacts, and Santa Jim Yellig are detailed in the fabulous Santa Claus Museum. It is also the headquarters of Santa's Elves. See them at work during the holiday months as they respond to thousands of children's letters, from the hilarious to the tear-jerking. Before leaving, have children pen their own letter to Santa.

Carl Barrett's concrete Santa Claus statue has been restored. Perched at the top of a hill, the forty-ton, twenty-two-foot statue towers over the area.

 shop

Holly Tree Christmas and Seasonal Shop features uniquely decorated trees for inspiration. All the tree-trimming items are here along with many personalized ornaments. Browse gift items from watches to clothing.

Santa's Candy Castle became the nation's first attraction in 1935—and it was free. Toy sponsors provided items for kids to try out (and buy), providing the magic of Christmas morning during harder times. Today, there are books, classic candy, frozen hot chocolate, and Santa's North Pole Network, where, for a small fee, kids can find out if they are on the "Nice" list.

NOTABLES

Radio Shack featured Santa Claus in a 2008 commercial. However, the diner featured in the commercial was actually located in New Jersey.

Chicago Bears quarterback Jay Cutler (1983) was born in Santa Claus.

Another Santa Claus–born football player, Jon Goldsberry (1981), played for the Buffalo Bills and the Tampa Bay Buccaneers and was associated (briefly) with the Chicago Bears. He currently conducts a football camp near his hometown each summer.

Arad A. McCutchan (1912–1993) retired in Santa Claus after a successful collegiate basketball coaching career.

88

Scottsburg

Downtown Scottsburg.

Scottsburg began on donated land—and had an *h* at the end until 1892 and the installation of the post office. The three acres next to Centerville were meant to be the site of the new county seat—something that nearby Lexington, Indiana, wasn't completely on board with. Although Centerville was laid out in 1850 and Scottsburg didn't come along until 1871, it grew to envelop the older town. Those original boundaries were relatively within the streets of Kerton, North Main, and Owen. Scottsburg became the county seat in 1873 (after a few years of litigation), with a new courthouse and jail completed by 1874. But Lexington didn't give up. Scottsburg resorted to carrying away the courthouse documents and installing them in the new Scott County courthouse during the night. It has remained the county seat ever since. Built to look similar to the 1874 version, a 1997 addition tripled the size of the courthouse. Study the west wing for a look at the original.

Scottsburg also has a lovely collection of buildings downtown with really great features. Mayor William Graham had the foresight to prevent needless demolition of downtown buildings after becoming mayor in 1988. There are no unsightly parking lots in the quaint downtown. As he says, "If parking is the worst problem you have, you are doing something right." Park along the square to take advantage of small family businesses that run the range.

Celebrate the agricultural heritage of the town for the annual two-day July event MaterFest. Yes, this festival is all about the tomato, from the crowning of the MaterQueen and MaterKing pageant to a karaoke contest, movie night, MaterFest five-kilometer race, live music, food, and activities for the kids.

☀ play

Meander around the lakefront path at the William H. Graham Park at Lake Iola. Check out the old train car and remaining sliver of track from the interurban site, the first of its kind to use a 1,200-volt high-tension system. Kids will love the playground.

🍴 eat

Homemade pie is never done better than at the Coffee House and Café. The cream pies are just like Grandma used to make: mile high. Of course, the long list of coffee beverages is nothing short of tasty. Free Wi-Fi, breakfast or lunch menu, and cozy atmosphere create the best place for lingering.

Jeeves and Company is known for its burgers, roomy seating, and eclectic style. Don't forget to add on the homemade potato chips. Adult drinks are available at the new bar section of this local favorite.

🛍 shop

Clear out the trunk and bring in a trailer. Shabby-chic decorators will adore Rough Edges. Long windows in the front of the high-ceilinged shop light up countless treasures. Beautifully repurposed, sometimes painted, sometimes distressed, once ho-hum pieces are updated and anything but shabby. Book lovers should browse the back section of the shop. Other antiques are available here, but the redone furniture and decor really steal the show.

Two stories of mind-blowing antiques tempt at the Scottsburg Antique Mall. The furniture is incredible. Don't miss the vintage toys on the first level.

Scottsburg Antique Mall.

Ye Olde Homeplace Antiques and Collectibles contains a smattering of antiques and primitives. A long shop, there's plenty of space to hold an excellent assortment of furniture. Don't worry—smaller items like dishware, books, games, and other playthings have a place here, too.

NOTABLES

The 1904 Carnegie Library is still in use for its original purpose.

89

St. Meinrad

Meinrad
Archabbey.

The residents of this unincorporated town of six hundred people are mainly German and Catholic, reflecting the close association of the town and nearby St. Meinrad Archabbey. Founded in 1861, the town's location among the hills of southern Indiana makes it feel especially inviting.

☀ play

One son got most of the rest of the family on board, as he planted grapevines instead of corn. After a few years with little profit, Dad decided that they should start producing their own wine—or he'd plow down the vines. With award-winning wines behind them, they seem to have made the right decision. Monkey Hollow Winery is in a secluded, beautiful spot with a fabulous (and educational) tasting room. Be sure to ask for the story behind the Pasture Limit wine label, and don't miss out on trying the blueberry wine.

St. Meinrad Seminary and School of Theology is one of only two archabbeys in the United States—and one of eleven in the world. Laid out in the 1850s by two monks from the Einsiedeln Abbey in Switzerland, it occupies a startling amount of acreage and supports the third-largest population of monks in the United States. Visitors are always welcome.

90

Tell City

The Swiss Colonization Society was ready for a move. These German-speaking Swiss desired freedom—and what better place to find a spot for a town than Indiana. Originally called Helvetia, the town was soon renamed Tell City to honor the Swiss hero William Tell. It was a planned town from the start. Wide streets encouraged industry, while river access provided an important means of transportation.

Anyone purchasing lots in 1858 had to commit to constructing a home at a cost of at least $125. The Swiss Colonization Society even provided building materials, brick or frame. New citizens had three years to reimburse the society. When the lots were sold and the Swiss Colonization Society was no longer needed, it gave the rest of the land for schools and to the city before breaking up in 1879.

Tell City.

Every year, Tell City continues its celebration of the town with Schweizer (Swiss) Fest. Originally a sesquicentennial celebration, it proved so popular with local residents that they have thrown the festival every year since 1958. One of Indiana's oldest festivals, it features events like a talent show, horseshoe tournament, and, with a nod to its heritage, an archery contest.

☀ play

Engulfed by flames in the 1980s, the train depot mimics the long-lost original. It is the scene of a seasonal farmers market with more than delicious farm-fresh vegetables; baked goods often make an appearance as well. Step inside for the Perry County Convention and Visitors Bureau offices and loads of Tell City–themed gifts.

Tell City Pretzels.

The flood wall mural at Sunset Park was painted by residents.

Master baker Casper Gloor had a secret: his popular pretzel recipe. In 1858 as a part of the Swiss Colonization Society, he settled in Tell City and opened up Tell City Pretzels. Passing on from one person to the next as the business changed hands, it only briefly experienced a closing before reopening in 2009. Visit during cooler morning hours for a chance to jump in the assembly line and hand-twist pretzels. Honey mustard, original, or lightly salted, the pretzels are incredible.

Originally a 1916 Carnegie Library (with a 1966 addition), the Tell City Historical Society and Museum is huge. Having more than thirty-five hundred square feet of exhibit space lets the museum display a really nice range of town artifacts. Genealogy lovers will make good use of the special research area just for them.

¶¶ eat

No one does root beer floats better than Frostop. Grab ice cream or a cherry milk shake from this town landmark. With a lot of outdoor seating, it maintains its original vintage cool.

🛍 shop

Hair salons aren't generally considered a destination for travelers, yet Domestic Goddess Salon and Boutique places a nice emphasis on "boutique." New Tell City–themed items like dish towels and throw pillows are a useful memento to bring home.

Find local art as well as scads of bags, jewelry, and even toys.

Stained glass, vintage items, and historic town photos are abundant at Finley's Antiques and Custom Framing. Cannelton pottery, Perry County photos, and one-of-a-kinds occupy the gleaming downtown shop. The inventory is always changing.

Specializing in Tell City Chair Company furniture (1865–2011), William Tell Antiques & Collectibles houses showroom pieces. Sometimes topped with area pottery or local artifacts, it's a nice blend of furniture and antiques.

NOTABLES

ESPN analyst and former professional basketball player for the New South Wales Australia team (1994–1995) and the Kentucky Marauders of the Women's Basketball Association (1996), Krista Blunk got her start playing three sports at Tell City High School and then at the University of Evansville. She was named to the Indiana Basketball Hall of Fame 2014 Silver Anniversary Team.

The last coach to make the leap from high school coaching to college coaching, John Ray Eddy (1911–1986) coached first in Tell City for five seasons, acquiring three Indiana high school sectional titles, before switching to the high school in Madison, Indiana. There they would win ten sectionals, six regionals, three semistates, and the 1950 state championship. Moving to the college level, he coached for Purdue University with a win record that ranks him third all-time at the school.

Another Tell City high school basketball player, Thomas M. "Tommy" Kron (1943–2007) played pro ball with the St. Louis Hawks (1966–1967), Seattle SuperSonics (1967–1969), and the Kentucky Colonels team of the American Basketball Association (1969–1970).

James Robert Polk (1915–1988) was a men's basketball head coach for Trinity University, Vanderbilt University, and Rice University, later becoming assistant athletic director at the University of Alabama–Birmingham, from which he retired in 1977. Six of his players were NBA draft picks.

91

Versailles

Accounts differ for how Versailles, the long-ago home of the mound builder Native Americans and a few other tribes, got its name. The likely story is that Frenchman John DePauw, for whom DePauw University is named, was part of the group that voted for Versailles becoming the county seat and that he named the town for French Versailles in 1818. How its pronunciation was changed is unclear.

🛏 stay

Let the glow of the neon sign guide the weary traveler to family-owned Moon-Lite Motel. Reflecting 1950s style on the outside, it's a welcoming throwback. Expect simple, clean, no-fuss furnishings thanks to recent renovations.

☼ play

The Busching Covered Bridge extends 170 feet over Laughery Creek. Built by Thomas A. Hardman, a man praised for rebuilding area bridges destroyed by John Hunt Morgan and his men during Morgan's Raid in 1863, the Howe truss bridge, altered in 1885, now welcomes visitors to Versailles State Park. It is said that the wood used in the making of the one-lane bridge came from the site of the Versailles Baptist Church.

The Greek Revival Ripley County Courthouse, built in 1861, is nice to view on the

Moon-Lite Motel, Versailles.

outside, but time a visit to coincide with government hours to view the carved tree containing the names of important area people and landmarks just inside.

Tyson Temple United Methodist Church, Versailles.

Tyson Auditorium is another Art Deco building that was future forward. When construction was completed in the 1950s, there were more seats inside of Tyson Auditorium than there were people living in the town. Even the Milan Indians used the space after outgrowing their own. Listed on the Indiana Landmarks Endangered List in 2011, it was turned into apartments that same year.

Named for James "Uncle Jim" Tyson, the cofounder of Walgreens, the Tyson Temple United Methodist Church, built in 1937, is dedicated to his mother. Built without the sound of hammers or the use of nails, it used local items in its construction in addition to its terra-cotta from Italy and the gold or silver leaf from Germany. Look up—the stars are the same as they appeared in the sky on the night his mother died. Still in use today, it is a prime example of Art Deco architecture.

🍴 eat

Grab a seat by the door at Crossroads Restaurant. It's famous for blueberry pancakes, but the french toast is a tasty alternative. There's tons of room for a crowd.

Offering paninis and other homemade goodies, G. H. Coffee Company is a welcoming coffeehouse. In addition to typical coffee drinks using coffee roasted in-house, the gelato and Italian sodas are a delicious complement. Gluten-free and vegetarian selections are available. Every small town needs a place like G. H. Coffee Company.

Country Creations has expanded over the years. Carrying fresh produce during warmer months, they also have loads of interesting canned goods under their private label from flaming red beets to hot pickled asparagus. Baked goods, a deli, and general market items are available from the Amish-owned shop.

Loads of items are helter-skelter outside, providing a clue to the type of content inside of Good Stuff for Sale. There's no telling what will be discovered on these rows of shelves or in boxes and baskets. Buy, sell, or swap.

Flours and sugar, baking chips or extracts, Pat's Bulk Food has a diverse, well-stocked selection. Kids will love the bags of bulk candy. Locals appreciate area honey, refrigerators of chilled items, and spices in addition to savory or sweet seasonal munchies. Grill lovers should buy a container of applewood smoked salt before leaving.

NOTABLES

Saloons sprang up before churches did when Versailles was first formed.

Versailles jeweler Alfred H. Beer was known for his zany marketing schemes. In October 1899, he launched the first Versailles Pumpkin Show. There were five prizes that ranged from a gravy ladle to a violin to a gold watch. It wasn't until 1907 that the town got involved—and it's been growing ever since.

Cofounder of Walgreens James H. Tyson (1856–1941) had several structures built in the town of his childhood and included Versailles in a generous endowment.

Addresses

NORTHERN INDIANA

Bremen

play

Bremen Historical Museum
111 North Main Street

Bremen Train Depot
810 Douglas Road
574.546.4340

Jane's Park
512 South East Street
574.546.3390

eat

Netter's Restaurant
1106 West Plymouth Street
574.546.4225

shop

Bremen Hobbies and Art
308 North Bowen Avenue
574.546.3807

Loft Art Studio
4122 State Road 331 South
574.248.0453

Brookston

eat

Klein Brot Haus
106 East Third Street
765.563.3788

shop

Twinrocker Handmade Paper
100 East Third Street
765.563.3119

Two Cookin' Sisters
210 North Prairie Street
765.563.7377

Chesterton

stay

Riley's Railhouse Bed and Breakfast
123 North Fourth Street
219.395.9999

play

Westchester Township History Museum
at Brown Mansion
700 West Porter Avenue
219. 983.9715

eat

Dog Days Ice Cream Parlor
119 South Calumet Road
219.661.7890

Lucrezia Café
428 South Calumet Road
219.926.5829

Octave Grill
137 South Calumet Road
219.395.8494

Peggy Sue's Diner
117 South Calumet Road
219.926.8524

Popolano's Italian Restaurant
225 South Calumet Road
219.926.5552

Red Cup Café
115 Broadway Avenue
219.929.1804

Tonya's Patisserie
321 Broadway Avenue
219.929.1415

shop

Chesterton Bicycle Station
116 South Fourth Street
219.926.1112

Ella's Bella
119 Broadway Avenue, Suite 1
219.929.1047

Holly Jackson Art Studio and Gallery
103 South Second Street
219.926.8290

Indian Summer Boutique
131 South Calumet Road
219.983.9994

Katie's Antiques
219 South Calumet Road
219.926.5559

O'Gara and Wilson Antiquarian
Booksellers
223 Broadway Avenue
219.728.1326

Russ and Barb's Antiques
222 West Lincoln Avenue
219.926.4937

Yesterday's Treasures Antique Mall
700 Broadway Avenue
219.926.2268

Converse

play

Eastern Woodcarvers Association
101 South Jefferson Street
765.395.3023

Oak Hill Winery
111 East Marion Street
Indiana State Route 18
765.395.3632

eat

Big Dipper
104 South Jefferson Street
765.395.1331

Jefferson Street Barbecue
101 North Jefferson Street
765.395.5117

shop

Antiques, Collectibles, and Gifts
401 North Jefferson
765.633.3049

Cahoots Soap Company
107 North Jefferson Street
765.517.1902

Itty Bitty Acres
315 North Jefferson Street
765.395.3632

DeMotte

eat

Bub's BBQ
120 Eighth Avenue Northeast, Suite 3
219.987.2909

Jim's Café
616 Fifteenth Street
219.987.7995

Sandy Pines Sports Grill
10527 Bunker Drive
219.987.3674

shop

Another Season Floral
605 North Halleck Street
219.987.2511

Movie Madness
800 South Halleck Street
219.987.4041

Sell-It-Again Shop and DeMotte
Mercantile
821 South Halleck Street
291.987.5735

Denver

play

Doud Orchards
8971 North State Road 19
765.985.3937

Francesville

eat

Five Loaves Bakery and Café
106 South Bill Street
219.567.2600

Patio Drive-In
234 North U.S. Highway 421
219.567.2268

shop

Gene Speicher Pottery
4828 South U.S. 421
219.567.9584

Furnessville

play

Furnessville Cemetery
275 East 1500 North

shop

Schoolhouse Shop and Antiques
278 East County Road 1500 North
219.926.1551

Kniman

play

Kniman Christmas House #
9099 North 500 West

Kniman Christmas House #2
4849 West 1075 North

eat

Kniman Tap
4766 West 900 North
219.956.3008

Kouts

play

Dunn's Bridge
N 41°13'11", W 86°58'09"

eat

Country Folks Pizza
401 Main Street
219.766.3877

George's Koffee Kup
105 South Main Street
219.766.2414

Piggies 'n Cream
104 Railroad Street
219.766.0263

La Fontaine

play

Metocinyah's Village
N 40°39.474', W 85°45.141'

Miami Indian Cemetery and Indian
Village School
2820 North 600 West

Mississinewa Battlefield
N 40°37.797', W 85°44.107'

Lowell

stay

Thyme for Bed
12567 West 185th Avenue
219.696.6307

play

Buckley Homestead
3606 Belshaw Road
219.696.0769

Freedom Park
17105 Cline Street
219.696.1570

eat

Athens Grill
116 Mill Street
219.696.4700

Lowell Pizza House
108 West Commercial Avenue
219.696.5600

McVey's Restaurant
312 East Commercial Avenue
219.696.7784

Mi Ranchito
149 West Commercial Avenue
219.696.2270

shop

Aunt Nae's
302 East Commercial Avenue
219.690.1180

Dragonfly Antiques and Accessories
402 East Commercial Avenue
219.690.1901

Earle's Home and Garden
135 West Commercial Avenue
219.696.8364

Felicia's Antiques
324 East Commercial Avenue
219.696.1221

Sickinger's Jewelry
314 East Commercial Avenue
219.696.7616

Spike's Railhead
422 East Commercial Avenue
219.488.7251

Spring Run Farm
2110 West 169th Avenue
219.696.9357

Tish's Antiques
201 East Commercial Avenue
219.690.1666

Monon

play

Monon Connection Museum
10012 U.S. 421
219.253.4101

eat

Papa Angelo's Café
210 North Market Street
219.253.7272

Reme's Monon Family Restaurant
104 East Fourth Street
219.253.8550

Whistle Stop Restaurant
10012 U.S. 421
219.253.4101

Monticello

play

White County Historical Museum
101 South Bluff Street
574.583.3998

Whyte Horse Winery
1510 South Airport Road
574.583.2345

eat

Abe's Pizza
234 North Main Street
574.583.9600

John's Bakery and Café
1017 North Sixth Street
574.583.3325

Kinser's Bakery
215 North Main Street
574.583.9740

shop

Garden Station
702 West Broadway Street
574.583.5532

Used Book Store Exchange
2661 East 24 West
574.870.0542

Morocco

play

Efroymson Restoration at Kankakee
Sands
Kankakee Sands Project Office: 3294
North U.S. 41
219.285.2184

Scott-Lucas House
514 South Main Street

Nappanee

stay

Homespun Country Inn
Bed and Breakfast
302 North Main Street
574.773.2034

Victorian Guest House
Bed and Breakfast
302 East Market Street
574.773.4383

play

Amish Acres Historic Farm and Heritage
Resort Round Barn Theater
1600 West Market Street
574.773.4188

Nappanee Welcome Center
302 West Market Street
574.773.7812

eat

Amish Acres Threshers Dinner
1234 West Market Street
574.773.2011

Veni's Sweet Shop
101 West Market Street
574.773.4242

shop

Coppes Commons
401 East Market Street
574.773.0002

North Judson

play

Hoosier Valley Railroad Museum
507 Mulberry Street
574.896.3950

eat

Fingerhut Bakery
119 Lane Street
888.540.6573

Route 10 Bar and Grill
613 West Talmer Avenue
574.896.5555

Wooden Nickel Restaurant
117 Main Street
574.896.5215

shop

Pioneer Florist and Country Store
224 Lane Street
574.896.5421

North Liberty

stay

Bluebird House Bed and Breakfast
107 East Market Street
574.656.8093

play

Potato Creek State Park
25601 State Road 4
574.656.8186

eat

Yum Yum Shoppe
139 North Main Street
574.656.3245

shop

Dogwood Designs
108 North Main Street
574.656.3999

Peru

play

Miami County Museum
51 North Broadway Street
765.473.9183

Seven Pillars
80 West Sixth Street
765.472.4162

eat

East End Double Dip
451 East Main Street
765.472.3436

McClure's Orchard
5054 U.S. 31
765.985.9000

Siding
8 West Tenth Street
765.473.4041

Southside Scoops
302 South Broadway Street
765.472.4041

shop

Annie's Attic
57 North Broadway Street
765.473.4400

Farris Wheel Antiques and Collectibles
630 West Main Street
765.472.3684

Lillian's Prom and Fashion Boutique
19 East Main Street
765.472.1614

Peru Music Center
15 East Main Street
765.473.6608

Porter

play

Joseph Bailley Home
Highway 20 and Mineral Springs Road

eat

Santiago's Mexican Restaurant
124 Lincoln Street
219.926.6518

shop

Bigg's Violin Shop
106 Lincoln Street
219.926.1033

Remington

play

Carpenter Creek Cellars
11144 Jordan Road
219.866.4334

Water Tower
Intersection of East Michigan Street and
North Ohio Street

eat

Homestead Buttery and Bakery
36 South Ohio Street
219.261.2138

shop

Mini Measures Antiques and Collectibles
4 South Ohio Street
219.261.3665

Rensselaer

play

Carnegie Center
301 North Van Rensselaer Street

Embers Venue
230 West Washington Street
219.869.9537

Jasper County Courthouse
115 West Washington Street

Jasper County Historical Society and
Museum
479 North Van Rensselaer Street (what
locals call Five Points)
219.866.7767 or 219.866.7825

Mathew's Tree Farm and Pumpkin Patch
224 East 900 South
219.866.3388

Sayler Makeever Cemetery or Old
Settlers Cemetery
750 West and 460 South

eat

Ayda's Mexican Cuisine
305 North College Avenue Street
219.866.5370
Busy Bee
331 West Washington Street
219.866.3233

Martin's Restaurant
101 East Elm Street
219.866.5283

Schmidy's Pizza Palace
1451 North McKinley Avenue
219.866.4001

Willow Switch
215 West Washington Street
219.866.7106

shop

Greene's Exit 215 Antique Mall
3300 West Clark Street
219.866.5140

Long's Gifts and From the Needle's Point
125 North Front Street
219.866.5353

Steffen's Jewelry
217 West Washington Street
219.866.8781

Unique Finds
116 West Washington Street
219.866.1888

Roann

play

Roann Carnegie Library
240 North Chippewa Street
765.833.5231

Roann Covered Bridge
County Road 700 West

Stockdale Mill
North 40 54.85'--West 85 56.61'

eat

Lynn's Restaurant
170 North Chippewa Street
765.833.5191

shop

Barn Antiques and Collectibles
200 North Chippewa Street
765.833.6542

Log Cabin Antiques
165 North Chippewa Street
260.571.3135

Mom and Pop's Jazzy Junk
175 North Chippewa Street
765.833.2233

Roselawn

eat

J&J's Pizza Shack
11920 West State Road 10
219.345.5511

Jordy and Jax BBQ
10072 North 600 East
219.270.8071

Sycamore Drive-In
11806 West State Road 10
219.345.5656

Star City

play

Jones Robotic Dairy
6814 East 700 South
574.595.7887

eat

Oak Grove Restaurant
5401 South U.S. Highway 35
574.595.7126

Wabash

stay

Charley Creek Inn
111 West Market Street
260.563.0111

play

Eagles Theater
106 West Market Street
260.563.3272

Wabash County Courthouse
Intersection of West Hill Street at North
Wabash Street

Wabash County Historical Museum
36 East Market Street
260.563.9070

eat

Aztecaz Mexican Grill
256 South Miami Street
260.569.0519

Market Street Grill
90 West Market Street
260.563.7779

Modoc's Market
205 South Miami Street
260.569.1281

shop

Artistica Gallery and Woods Framing
70 West Market Street
260.563.1915

Crow's Nest Antique Mall
12 West Market Street
260.563.1228

Dorothy Ilene Gallery
78 West Canal Street
260.579.6130

Ellen's A Dress to Impress
36 West Canal Street
260.571.7572

Jack in the Box
122 Hale Drive
260.563.5609

Precious Gems and Metals
3 East Canal Street
260.563.4780

Reading Room Books
264 South Wabash Street
260.563.6421

Thriftalicious
75 West Market Street
260.225.3505 or 260.225.7108

Wakarusa

play

Wakarusa Quilt Garden
116 Elkhart Street

eat

Cook's Pizza
101 South Elkhart Avenue
574.862.4425

shop

Mom and Me Floral Boutique
103 South Elkhart Street
574.862.4888

Wakarusa Dime Store
103 East Waterford Street
574.862.4690

Wakarusa Pro Hardware
108 South Elkhart Street
574.862.2775

Yoder Brothers Mercantile
114 South Elkhart Street
574.862.2179

Walkerton

play

Heritage House Museum
413 Michigan Street
574.586.2852

Hester's Log Cabins
71880 State Road 23
574.586.2105

eat

Corner Cup Café
600 Roosevelt Road
574.586.3010

shop

New Kitchen Store
330 Liberty Street
574.586.2745

Wheatfield

play

JT's Shrimp Farm
4836 West 1450 North
219.987.3809

eat

Marcella's Pizzeria
3854 West State Road 10
219.956.0525

Schnick's Good Eats
16 North Bierma Street
219.956.4883

Williamsport

play

Williamsport Falls
N 40.286140°, W 87.292630°

Wolcott

play

Anson Wolcott House
403 North Fourth Street
219.279.2951

eat

Bell's Pizza
100 South Range Street
219.279.4090

Wolcott Theater Café
201 North Range Street
219.279.2233

shop

Timeless Treasures
101 South Range Street
219.279.2148

CENTRAL INDIANA

Arcadia

play

Arcadia Arts and Heritage Depot
107 West South Street
317.946.6792

Hedgehog Music Showcase
101 West Main Street
317.984.3560

shop

Hartley's Interiors and Antiques
103 East Main Street
317.984.3424

Tabby Tree Weaver
107 East Main Street
317.984.5475

Battle Ground

play

Tippecanoe Battlefield and Museum
200 Battleground Avenue
765.567.2147

eat

Eye Opener Café
103 Main Street
765.430.2495

shop

Shoup House Antiques
100 North Winans Street
765.567.4132

Cambridge City

stay

Lehman House
130 West Main Street
765.580.1098

play

Cambridge City Public Library
600 West Main Street
765.478.3335

Huddleston Farmhouse
838 National Road
765.478.3172

eat

Lumpy's Café
20 South Foote Street
765.478.6510

Hilltop Drive-In
705 West Main Street
765.478.5880

No. 9 Grill
27 West Main Street
765.334.8315

shop

Amish Cheese Shop
2001 North State Road 1
765.478.5847

Building 125
125 West Main Street
765.478.5000

Doublehead Trading Company
137 West Main Street
765.478.3800

Dusty Rusty Stuff (Formerly Known as
This 'n That Antiques)
7 West Main Street
765.478.9300

Hole in the Wall Antiques
131 West Main Street
765.478.6363

Log House Antiques
124 West Main Street
765.334.8268

National Trail Antique Mall
39 West Main Street
765.478.9070

Vinton House Antiques
20 West Main Street
765.478.9371

Centerville

play

Doddridge Chapel and Cemetery
9465 Chapel Road

eat

Americana Pizza
215 East Main Street
765.855.2601

Cinnamon Spice Bakery
6884 West U.S. Highway 40
765.855.3344

Stone Hearth Café
2131 North Centerville Road
765.855.2233

shop

Centerville Antique Mall
200 Union Street
765.855.5551

Enchanted Sleigh
410 East Main Street
765.855.2567

Mockingbird Antiques
107 South Morton Avenue
765.855.1570

Scott Shafer's Stoneware Pottery Studio
610 North Morton Avenue
765.855.2409

Warm Glow Candle Company Outlet
Store
2131 North Centerville Road
765.855.2000

White River Architectural Salvage and
Antiques
100 West Main Street
765.855.1908

Cicero

play
Morse Reservoir
N 40°06'30", W 86°02'22"
317.984.3475

eat
10 West
10 West Jackson Street
317.606.8542

Alexander's on the Water
369 West Jackson Street
317.984.8173

Cicero Coffee Company
150 South Peru Street
317.984.2739

Erika's Place
40 West Jackson Street
317.984.9303

Lazy Frogg
409 West Jackson Street
317.843.9100

shop
Upscale Junk and Antiques
23478 U.S. Highway 31
317.758.5515

Covington

play
Circle Trail Bridge
N 40°08'56", W 87°23'41"
Fountain County Clerk's Building
516 Fourth Street

765.793.4432

Fountain County Courthouse
301 Fourth Street

Inspired by Nature Sand Bar
Indoor Beach
318 Fourth Street
765.814.2030

eat
Beef House
16501 North State Road 63
765.793.3947

Snoddy's Mill
1104 Liberty Street
765.793.2600

Sundae Shop
216 Fourth Street
765.793.4981

shop
Covington Antique Company
6431 West U.S. Highway 136
765.793.3881

Glorie Bee Antiques
314 Liberty Street
765.793.0688

Holly's Scent-Sations
1501 Ninth Street
765.585.2176

Hue
212 Fourth Street
765.585.8257

Jake's Farm
326 Liberty Street
765.793.2298

Cutler

play
Adams Mill
500 South 75 East
765.268.2530

Danville

stay
Marmalade Sky Bed-and-Breakfast
337 North Washington Street
317.718.0598

play

Beasley's Orchard
2304 East Main Street
317.745.4876

Hendricks County Courthouse
355 South Washington Street

Twin Bridges
N 39°45'15.0", W 86°30'15.0"

eat

Beehive
55 East Main Street #D
317.718.8470

Bread Basket Café and Bakery
46 South Tennessee Street
317.718.4800

Confection Delights
57 South Washington Street
317.718.7060

Frank's Place
33 South Washington Street
317.718.1146

Mayberry Café
78 West Main Street
317.745.4067

shop

Carla's Creations and Gifts
59 West Marion Street
317.745.4200

Gallery on the Square
51 South Washington Street
317.386.3111

Jane's on the Square
65 West Marion Street
317.745.0222

Outta the Shed
71 South Washington Street
317.518.4249

Raders Fabrics
56 North Washington Street
317.745.6023

Seize the Night Designs
51 West Marion Street
317.563.3190

Dayton

eat

Buck Creek Pizza
2988 Dayton Road
765.296.7950

Delphi

play

Canal Interpretive Center and Museum
3198 North 700 West
765.564.6572

Carroll County Courthouse
101 West Main Street

Delphi Opera House
109 South Washington Street
765.564.4300

Noble Bikes and Concessions
1030 North Washington Street
765.427.3320

Wabash and Erie Canal Park
1030 North Washington Street
765.564.2870

eat

Andy's Place
213 South Market Street
765.564.2733

Sandwich Shop
112 East Main Street
765.564.6252

Stone House Restaurant and Bakery
124 East Main Street
765.564.4663

shop

Bill's Rock Shop
113 South Washington Street
765.564.3073

Fairmount

play

Fairmount Historical Museum
203 East Washington Street
765.948.4555

Park Cemetery
8008 South 150 East
765.948.4040

shop

D&M Variety Shop
124 South Main Street
765.948.6173

Hi-Fi Stereo Shop
111 South Main Street
765.948.4533

James Dean Gallery and Rebel Rebel
425 North Main Street
765.948.3326

Farmland

play

McVey Memorial Forest
7399 North State Road 1

eat

Chocolate Moose
101 North Main Street
765.468.7731

shop

Bright Ideas Stained Glass
112 North Main Street
765.468.8411

Farmland General Store
113 North Main Street
765.468.6472

Fortville

stay

Ivy House Bed and Breakfast
304 North Merrill Street
317.485.4800

play

Piney Acres Christmas Tree Farm and
Pumpkin Patch
1115 East 1000 North
317.326.1700

Studio 309
309 Noel Avenue
317.362.4536

eat

Indulge Ice Cream Parlor and Café
10 South Main Street
317.660.4460

Java Junction
226 South Main Street
317.485.0085

R-Smokehouse
222 South Main Street
317.747.4905

shop

Best of What's Around
230 South Main Street
317.747.4920

Gypsy Chicks Boutique
106 South Main Street
317.747.4916

Palette & Paper
515 East Broadway
317.747.4906

Simply More
218 South Main Street
317.698.2632

Stable Tack Shop
18 South Main Street
317.747.4979

Studio
35 South Main Street

Fountain

play

Portland Arch Nature Preserve
North Portland Arch Road

Portland Arch Cemetery, Bear Cemetery,
or Portland Cemetery
N 40°12'54"8, W 87°20'00"6

Fountain City

play

Levi Coffin House
115 West Main Street
765.847.2432

Willow Grove Cemetery
U.S. 27 South

Gas City

eat

Payne's Custard and Café
4925 Kaybee Drive
765.998.0668

shop

Balloons, Flowers, and Gifts
102 West Main Street
765.674.3103

Dragonfly Cottage
125 West Main Street
765.506.2556

Hotheads Pepper Store
425 West Main Street
765.499.9676

Mama Pearson's Soaporium
109 North First Street
765.251.6616

Mick's Flea Market
212 East Main Street
765.677.0281

Rescued Treasures
210 East Main Street
765.674.1997

Greencastle

stay

3 Fat Labs Bed and Breakfast
2009 South County Road 400 West
765.653.0308

play

Oakalla Covered Bridge
N 39°37'35", W 86°55'01"

Putnam County Courthouse
1 Courthouse Square

eat

Almost Home Restaurant
17 West Franklin Street
765.653.5788

Casa Grande Mexican Restaurant
1360 Indianapolis Road
765.653.2309

shop

Eitel's Florist
17 South Vine Street
765.653.3171

Isabella Marie's Antiques and Things
614 South Bloomington Street
765.653.0370

Greens Fork

play

Clay Township Historical Society
Museum
19 East Pearl Street
765.886.5166

Hagerstown

play

Hagerstown Airport
999 South Washington Street
765.489.7926

eat

Abbott's Candy
48 East Walnut Street
765.489.4442

Bowman Bakery
48 South Perry Street
765.489.5644

shop

Hagerstown Arts Place
96 ¹/₂ East Main Street
765.489.4005

Main Street Antiques
96 East Main Street
765.489.5792

Payne's Music and Recording Studio
99 East Main Street
765.541.0263

Kirklin

play

Kid Domino Museum
102 South Main Street

Kirklin Park
N 40°11'39", W 86°21'50"

eat

Booker's Bar and Grill
109 North Main Street
765.279.5133

Empire Pizzeria
106 South Main Street
765.279.8220

shop

3 Stray Cats Vintage
111 South Main Street
765.426.0794

Black Crow
105 North Main Street

Clementine's Antiques and Accents
101 North Main Street
765.427.1222

K&G Time Traveler's Antique Mall
108 East Madison Street
317.697.8604

Old Bank Antiques
109 South Main Street
765.279.8311

White Lion Antiques
113 South Main Street
765.279.5777

Wikerdoodles
104 East Madison Street
765.415.9478

Knightstown

play

Hoosier Gym
355 North Washington Street
765.345.2100

eat

Knightstown Diner
12 East Main Street
765.445.2328

shop

Bittersweet Memories
121 East Main Street
765.345.7480

Glass Cupboard Antiques
115 East Main Street
765.345.7572

Maplewood

eat

Polly's Freeze
5242 IN-62
812.945.6911

Martinsville

play

Art Sanctuary
190 North Sycamore Street
765.342.8422

Art Work by Elizabeth
96 East Morgan Street

Sterling Butterfly
190 East Morgan Street
317.459.3581

Three Pints Brewing
610 West Mitchell Avenue
765.476.6118

eat

Café 166 Smokehouse and Deli
166 East Morgan Street
765.315.0067

Martinsville Candy Kitchen
46 North Main Street
765.342.6390

Mimi's Fatcakes
20 North Main Street
317.893.9142

shop

Art Gallery and Framing
75 East Washington Street
765.342.0153

Berries & Ivy Country Store
28 North Main Street
765.342.7722

Sheep Street Fibers
6535 State Road 252
812.597.5648

Matthews

play

Cumberland Covered Bridge
11160 South 990 East

Morgantown

eat

Bernie's Barbecue
679 East State Road 135
812.597.5921

shop

Antique Cooperation
129 West Washington Street
812.597.4530

Graham's Bee Works
125 West Washington Street
812.597.2000

Jeepers Dollhouse Miniatures
69 West Washington Street
812.597.4346

Mulberry

eat

Southfork Restaurant and Pub
105 South Glick Street
765.296.2096

North Salem

eat

Perillo's Pizzeria
5 South Broadway Street
765.676.4171

shop

Garden Gate Gifts and Flowers
107 West Pearl Street
765.676.5039

North Salem Antiques and Sundries
15 West Pearl Street
765.676.5527

Perkinsville

eat

Bonge's Tavern
9830 West 280 North
765.734.1625

Romney

shop

Romney Toy Shop
11501 U.S. Highway 231 South
765.538.2887

Rossville

play

Skiles Orchard and Farm Market
9811 North County Road 600 West
765.379.2339

eat

Dan the Man's Taco Stand
22 West Main Street
765.379.3600

Flour Mill Bakery, Bulk Foods, and
Cheese
5450 West Main Street

Lions Den
24 West Main Street
765.543.5953

Sweet Spot Bakery and Café
57 North Plank Street
765.379.2332

Treece's Restaurant and Lounge
26 West Main Street
765.379.3550

shop

Rossville Quilts
356 West Main Street
765.379.2900

Swayzee

shop

Swayzee Antique Mall
115 North Washington Street
765.922.7903

Upland

stay

LaRita's Lodge Bed and Breakfast
9315 South 950 East
765.998.1002

eat

Ivanhoe's Ice Cream and
Sandwich Shoppe
979 South Main Street
765.998.7261

Winchester

play

Randolph County Courthouse
100 South Main Street

eat

Bogie's Soft Ice Cream
75 Sunny Knoll Drive
765.584.1328

El Carreton Mexican Restaurant
910 East Greenville Pike
765.584.3124

House of Flavors Café and Coffee Bar
625 West Washington Street
765.584.7153

shop

Countryside Antiques and Collectibles
1969 East Washington Street

Meeks Consignment and Antique Store
118 South Meridian Street

SOUTHERN INDIANA

Batesville

stay

Mary Helen's Bed and Breakfast
13296 North Coonhunters Road
812.934.3468

play

Batesville Historical Society Museum
15 West George Street
812.932.0999

Ertel Cellars Winery
3794 East County Road 1100 North
812.933.1500

Gibson Theatre
107 North Main Street
812.934.3404

eat

Lil' Charlie's Restaurant and Brewery
504 East Pearl Street
812.934.6392

Pizza Haus
104 East Boehringer Street
812.934.4004

Schmidt Bakery
125 Village Square
812.934.4501

shop
Bookshelf
101 North Walnut Street
812.934.5800

Gooseberry Flower and Gift Shop
209 North Walnut Street
812.934.4500

Grinning Goblin Comic Books and
Games
200 Cross County Plaza
812.932.0014

RomWeber Marketplace
7 South Eastern Avenue
812.932.2606

Turquoise Hen
213 North Walnut Street
812.577.2561

Weberding's Carving Shop
1230 State Road 46 East
812.934.3710

Bean Blossom

play
Bean Blossom Covered Bridge
N 39°15'39", W 86°15'19"

Bill Monroe Bluegrass Hall of Fame &
Country Star Museum
5163 State Road 135 North
812.988.6422

shop
Plum Creek Antiques
5163 State Road 135 North

Cannelton

stay
Blue Heron Bed and Breakfast
812.547.7518

play
Blue Heron Winery
5330 Blue Heron Lane
812.547.7518

Cannelton Cotton Mill
310 Washington Street

Cannelton Locks and Dam
N 37°53'59", W 86°42'21"

Celtic Cross
5330 Blue Heron Lane

Flood Wall Mural
N 37°54'560", W 86°44'772"

Froehlichs Outfitter and Guide Horse
Rides
8388 Deer Creek Road
812.836.2117 and 812.608.2170

Hoosier National Forest
River Forest Road
866.302.4173

Lafayette Springs
N 37°54'624", W 86°41'430"

Myers Grade School (Free School)
615 Taylor Street

Perry County "Old Courthouse" Museum
125 South Seventh Street
812.548.6781

Shubael Little Pioneer Village
7590 East State Road 66
812.836.4344

eat
Rocky Point Waterfront Grille
7398 East State Road 66
812.547.2210

Wall's Drive-In
East Highway 66
812.547.8501

Corydon

stay
Kintner House Inn
101 South Capitol Avenue
812.738.2020

play
Battle Park
100 South Highway 135

Corydon State Historic Site
126 East Walnut Street
812.738.4890

Golf Shores Fun Center
2510 Landmark Way Northeast
812.738.0802

Indiana Caverns
1267 Green Acres Drive Southwest
812.734.1200

Leora Brown School
400 Summit Street
812.738.3376

O'Bannon Woods State Park
7234 Old Forest Road Southwest
812.738.8232

Scout Mountain Winery
2145 Scout Mountain Road Northwest
812.738.7196

Turtle Run Winery
940 Saint Peters Church Road Northeast
812.952.2650

eat

Alberto's Italian Restaurant
2137 Edsel Lane Northwest
812.738.4900

Emery's Premium Ice Cream
112 West Walnut Street
812.738.6047

Frederick's Café
400 North Capitol Avenue
812.738.3733

shop

Bookworm Used Bookstore
110 East Walnut Street
812.738.3720

Collections of the Home Place
210 North Elm Street
812.738.1480

Conrad Music Service
220 North Elm Street
812.738.2111

Harrison County Arts and the Artisan
Center
117 East Chestnut Street
812.738.2123

Old Town Store Antiques
110 South Mulberry Street
812.267.4101

Red Barn Antique Mall
215 West Highway 62
812.738.6000

Red, Wine, and Blush
117 West Walnut Street
812.738.4792

White Cloud Window Stained Glass and
Supplies
231 East Chestnut Street
812.596.0393

Zimmerman Glass Factory
301 Valley Road
812.738.2206

French Lick

stay

French Lick Springs Resort
8670 West State Road 56
812.936.9300

play

Big Splash Adventure Indoor Waterpark
8505 Indiana 56
877.936.3866

Shotz Laser Tag and Mini Golf
8529 West State Road 56
812.936.2386

eat

French Lick Winery and the Vintage Café
8145 West Sinclair Street
812.936.2293

Friendship

play

Friendship Bridge
N 38°58'26", W 85°09'33"

Greensburg

stay

Nana's Bed and Breakfast
3126 East Base Road
812.663.6607

play

Art on the Square
114 East Washington Street
812.663.8600

Decatur County Courthouse
150 Courthouse Square

Last Supper Museum
311 West Walnut Street
812.662.9756

eat

Carriage on the Square Smokehouse
117 North Broadway Street
812.222.2727

Cecil's Pork 'n More
119 South Michigan Avenue
812.222.0505

Dawg House Diner
116 East Washington Street
812.222.2100

Funky Monkey Café
(Inside of It's Your Dime)
121 East Main Street
812.663.0040

Highpoint Orchard
3321 North Old Highway 421
812.663.4534

Mayasari Indonesian Grill
213 North Broadway Street
812.222.6292

Storie's Restaurant
109 East Main Street
812.663.9948

shop

Denim and Honey
217 North Broadway Street
812.222.2009

It's Your Dime
121 East Main Street
812.663.0040

Little Frogs and Fairies
105 North Broadway Street
217.898.1494

Magnolia Mercantile
128 North Franklin Street
812.222.6246

Old Picket Fence
115 East Main Street
812.222.0246

Pickers Paradise
129 North Broadway Street
812.663.0021

Tree City Stitches
125 East Main Street
812.222.0920

Hatfield

play

Boner Bridge
Junction of Red Bush Road and Boner
Road
N 37°56'32", W 87°15'07"

Holton

shop

Carolyn's Collectibles
22 North Old Michigan Road
812.689.5180

Huntingburg

play

League Stadium
203 South Cherry Street

Museum of Huntingburg
508 East Fourth Street
812.683.2211

Old Town Hall
(Huntingburg Event Center)
327 East Fourth Street
812.683.2221

Salem United Church of Christ
202 East Fourth Street

eat

Cool Beans Java
410 East Fourth Street
812.683.5851

Gaslight Pizza and Grill
328 East Fourth Street
812.683.3669

shop

Downtown Emporium
407 East Fourth Street
812.683.0123

Game Knight
411 East Fourth Street
812.661.1844

Grainry Antiques and Other Needful
Things
415 East Fourth Street
812.683.0234

Greentree Furniture
330 East Fourth Street
812.683.2000

Purple Plum
417 East Fourth Street
812.683.4649

Leavenworth

stay

Leavenworth Inn
930 West State Road 62
812.739.2120

eat

Walter's Pub
1153 State Road 62
812.739.4264

shop

Stephenson's General Store
6 8 West State Road 62
812.739.4242

Lincoln City

play

Lincoln Boyhood National Memorial
3027 East South Street
812.937.4541

Lincoln State Park
15476 North County Road 300 East
812.937.4710

Madison

play

Lanthier Winery
123 Mill Street
812.273.2409

eat

Attic and Coffee Mill Café
631 West Main Street
812.265.5781

Cocoa Safari Chocolates
118 West Main Street
812.273.8800

Franco's Family Restaurant
119 East Main Street
812.265.5626

Hammond Family Restaurant
221 East Main Street
812.265.3237

Hinkle's Sandwich Shop
204 West Main Street
812.265.3919

Key West Shrimp House
117 Ferry Street
812.265.2831

Madison Nut and Candy Company
207 East Main Street
812.265.0050

Red Pepper Deli and Café
902 West Main Street
812.265.3354

Red Pepperoni Pizzeria
842 West Main Street
812.274.0111

shop

All Good Things Soaps and Such
318 West Main Street
812.801.4700

Blue Cerebus Dog Boutique
113 East Main Street
812.265.5219

Crawdaddy Music
130 East Main Street
812.265.6087

Gallery 115
115 East Main Street
812.274.4371

Harriet's Knit Knook
103 East Main Street
812.274.2040

Little Golden Fox
402 Broadway Street
812.274.1080

Madison Table Works
325 East Main Street
812.273.5050

Margie's Country Store
721 West Main Street
812.265.4429

Red Dog Arms
322 West Main Street
812.701.1468

Rock-a-Bye Lady
113 West Main Street
812.265.2990

That Book Place
337 Clifty Drive
812.574.4113

Marengo

play

Marengo Cave
400 East State Road 64
888.702.2837

Mauckport

play

Squire Boone Caverns
100 Squire Boone Road Southwest
812.732.1200

Milan

play

Milan 1954 Hoosiers Museum
201 West Carr Street
812.654.2772

eat

Milan Reservation Restaurant
1001 South Warpath Drive
812.654.2224

shop

Milan Whistle Stop
201 North Main Street
812.654.3764

Moorefield

eat

Moorefield Market
8189 Highway 129
812.427.3970

Nashville

stay

Abe Martin Lodge
Brown County State Park
812.988.4418

Overlook Lodge at Salt Creek Golf
Retreat
2359 State Road 46 East
812.988.7888

play

1879 Log Jail
Old School Way

Brown County Courthouse
20 East Main Street

Copperhead Creek Gem Mine
57 North Van Buren Street
812.988.2422

Ramp Creek Bridge
N 39°11'44", W 86°12'59"

Whispering Pines Alpaca Farm
Call for Address
812.988.7419

eat

Big Woods Pizza Company
44 North Van Buren Street
812.988.6000

Candy Dish
61 West Main Street
812.988.7606

Common Ground
66 North Van Buren Street
812.988.6449

Daily Grind Coffee Shop
114 South Van Buren Street
812.988.4808

Fearrin's Ice Cream and Yogurt Depot
95 South Van Buren Street
812.988.7677

Hobnob Corner Restaurant
17 West Main Street
812.988.4114

Miller's Ice Cream House
61 West Main Street
812.988.0815

Out of the Ordinary Restaurant
61 South Van Buren Street
812.988.6166

Schwab's Fudge
102 South Van Buren Street
812.988.6723

Sweeteas's Tea Shop
225 South Van Buren Street, Suite C
812.988.6515

That Sandwich Place
15 South Van Buren Street
812.988.2355

Trolley
11 East Gould Street
812.988.4273

shop

Brown County Rock and Fossil Shop
57 North Van Buren Street
812.988.2422

Clay Purl
58 East Main Street, Suite 3
812.988.0336

Ferguson House
78 West Franklin Street
812.988.7388

For Bare Feet
75 South Jefferson Street
812.988.2067

It's All about Dogs
81 South Jefferson Street
812.988.4228

Johanna Lee Bathology
58 West Main Street
812.988.6898

LaSha's
60 North Van Buren Street
812.988.0522

Lawrence Family Glass Blowers
36 East Franklin Street
812.988.2600

Mulberry Cottage
46 West Main Street
812.988.9803

Madeline's French Country Shop
100 South Van Buren Street
812.988.6301

Miss Moonpennies Emporium
44 West Franklin Street
812.988.6510

Olde Bartley House
96 South Van Buren Street
812.988.4047

Primitives and Pinecones
76 East Main Street
812.929.0977

Primitive Spirit
82 East Washington Street
812.988.8200

Reliable Vintage
49 East Main Street
812.988.1199

Reynold's Leather and Gifts
40 North Van Buren Street
812.988.0147

Rich Hill's Magic and Fun Emporium
75 South Jefferson Street
812.720.7029

September Elm
84 South Van Buren Street
812.988.4010

Through the Looking Glass
75 South Jefferson Street
812.988.1724

Toy Chest
125 South Van Buren Street
812.988.2817

Village Boutique
76 East Main Street
812.988.7950

Weed Patch Music Company
58 East Main Street
812.988.1180

Wild Olive
37 West Main Street
812.988.9453

Osgood

play

Bilby Tower
1855 West County Road 300 North

Damm Theater
117 North Buckeye Street
812.689.3266

Osgood Historical Museum
128 South Buckeye Street
812.689.1876

eat

Osgood Grub Company
406 North Buckeye Street
812.689.4362

Paoli

play

Orange County Courthouse
1 East Court Street

Paoli Peaks
2798 West County Road 25 South
812.723.4696

Pioneer Mothers Memorial Forest
N 38°32'22", W 86°27'06"

eat

Lost River Market and Deli
26 Library Street
812.723.3735

shop

Fort Half Moon Antiques
368 North Court Street
812.653.2577

Roslyn's Corner Gifts and Antiques
306 North Court Street
812.723.3576

Rockport

play

Lakeview Orchard
2315 North Orchard Road
812.649.2753

Lincoln Pioneer Village and Museum
928 Fairground Drive
812.649.9147

Ohio River Bluffs Cave
Follow Main Street as it winds around
and turns into South First Street by the
Ohio River.

Peppers Ridge Winery
4304 North County Road 200 West
812.649.9463

Spencer County Courthouse
200 Main Street

eat

Rustic Country Club
1375 South State Road 35
812.649.9258

Salem

stay

Destination Bed and Breakfast
206 North Harristown Road
812.896.1369

play

Beck's Grist Mill
4433 South Beck's Mill Road
812.883.5147

Depot Railroad Museum
206 South College Avenue
812.883.1884

John Hay Center
307 East Market Street
812.883.6495

Knobstone Trail
Delaney Park Loop
State Road 135

Piper Flight Museum
Salem Municipal Airport
State Road 56
812.472.3749

Salem Speedway
2729 West State Road 56
812.883.6504

Washington County Courthouse
99 Public Square

eat

Christie's on the Square
34 Public Square
812.883.9757

shop

Brick Street Sampler
36 Public Square
812.883.1473

CATS Trading Post
3703 Highway 56 East
812.844.0165

Destination Antiques
206 North Harristown Road
812.896.1369

Lincks Clothing & Shoes
15 Public Square
812.883.4154

Past <APOS>n' Present by Michelle
211 North Main Street
812.883.9600

Salem Apothecary
3 Public Square
812.883.4500

Sisters
35 Public Square
812.883.1776

T Antiques
48 Public Square
812.883.3005

Santa Claus

stay

Lake Rudolph Campground
and RV Resort
78 North Holiday Boulevard
812.937.4458

Santa's Lodge
91 West Christmas Boulevard
812.937.1902

play

Holiday World and Splashin' Safari
452 East Christmas Boulevard
877.463.2645

Santa Claus Museum
69 North State Road 245
812.544.2434

shop

Holly Tree Christmas and Seasonal Shop
8 North Kringle Place
812.937.4600

Santa's Candy Castle
15499 North State Road 245
812.544.3900

Scottsburg

play

William H. Graham Park at Lake Iola
N 38°41'49", W 85°46'29"

eat

Coffee House and Café
36 East McClain Avenue
812.752.3000

Jeeves and Company
64 South Main Street
812.752.6559

shop

Rough Edges
10 East McClain Avenue
812.752.2160

Scottsburg Antique Mall
4 South Main Street
812.752.4645

Ye Olde Homeplace Antiques
and Collectibles
40 South Main Street
812.414.2189

St. Meinrad

play

Monkey Hollow Winery
11534 East County Road 1740 North
812.357.2272

St. Meinrad Seminary and School of
Theology
200 Hill Drive
812.357.6611

Tell City

play

Perry County Convention and Visitors
Bureau
601 Main Street, Suite A
812.547.7933

Sunset Park
Seventh and Washington Streets

Tell City Pretzels
1315 Washington Street
812.548.4499

Tell City Historical Society and Museum
548 Ninth Street
812.772.2020

eat

Frostop
947 Main Street
Tell City, IN 47586
812.547.8510

shop

Domestic Goddess Salon and Boutique
745 Main Street
812.547.2575

Finley's Antiques and Custom Framing
739 Main Street
812.547.3255

William Tell Antiques & Collectibles
302 Ninth Street
812.548.0640

Versailles

stay

Moon-Lite Motel
520 South Adams Street, U.S. 421 South
812.689.6004

play

Busching Covered Bridge
Versailles State Park
1387 East U.S. Highway 50
812.689.6424

Ripley County Courthouse
115 North Main Street

Tyson Auditorium
100 South High Street

Tyson Temple United Methodist Church
324 West Tyson Street
812.689.6976

eat

Crossroads Restaurant
615 West U.S. Highway 50
812.689.3000

G. H. Coffee Company
1177 North Washington Street
812.689.4900

shop

Country Creations
6851 South U.S. 421
812.689.4243

Good Stuff for Sale
26 North U.S. Highway 421
812.689.1787

Pat's Bulk Food
4492 South U.S. Highway 421
812.689.6582

Index